Re-schooling So

Educational Change and Development Series

Series Editors: Andy Hargreaves, Ontario Institute for Studies in
Education, Canada and
Ivor F Goodson, Warner Graduate School, University
of Rochester, USA and Centre for Applied Research
in Education, University of East Anglia, Norwich, UK

Re-schooling Society
David Hartley

The Gender Politics of Educational Change
Amanda Datnow

The Rules of School Reform
Max Angus

Educational Change and Development Series

Re-schooling Society

David Hartley

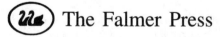 The Falmer Press

(A member of the Taylor & Francis Group)
London • Washington, D.C.

UK   The Falmer Press, 1 Gunpowder Square, London, EC4A 3DE
USA   The Falmer Press, Taylor & Francis Inc., 1900 Frost Road, Suite 101, Bristol, PA 19007

First published in 1997

A catalogue record for this book is available from the British Library

Library of Congress Cataloging-in-Publication Data are available on request

ISBN 0 7507 0623 6 cased
ISBN 0 7507 0624 4 paper

Jacket design by Caroline Archer

Typeset in 10/12pt Times by
Graphicraft Typesetters Ltd., Hong Kong.

Printed in Great Britain by Biddles Ltd, Guildford and King's Lynn on paper which has a specified pH value on final paper manufacture of not less than 7.5 and is therefore 'acid free'.

Every effort has been made to contact copyright holders for their permission to reprint material in this book. The publishers would be grateful to hear from any copyright holder who is not here acknowledged and will undertake to rectify any errors or omissions in future editions of this book.

Contents

Contents

Acknowledgments

Many people are due my thanks, especially: Ed Wendrich and Angela Roger, both of whom read and commented upon the manuscript; members of the Education Research Seminar at the University of Dundee, in particular John Drummond and Paul Standish; and participants at the Scottish Council for Research in Education seminars on postmodernism and action research.

I should also like to thank the editors and publishers of the *British Journal of Educational Studies* for permission to quote extracts from my article 'Mixed messages in education policy: Sign of the times?', **42**, 3, pp. 230–44, published in 1994. The same thanks are extended to the editor and publishers of *Studies in Higher Education* for permission to quote extracts from 'Teaching and Learning in an Expanding Higher Education System (the MacFarlane Report): a technical fix?', **20**, 2, pp. 147–58, published in 1995.

Acknowledgements

FOR ELIZABETH HARTLEY

Chapter 1

Re-schooling Society: An Introduction

There is an old saying: 'My momma told me life's just like a box of chocolates — you just never know what you're gonna git'. Here speaks the voice of the fateful and the faithful, prone to the vagaries of destiny. But to those born into the optimism of the post-war industrial democracies, the hand of fate could be steadied. Disease, destitution, ignorance and idleness could all be reduced. For in the offing was a civilized world of welfare states: they were to be safe and stable; they were to be run rationally and bureaucratically; they were to be scientific and secular; and they were to be liberal in their polity.

But it had not always been so. This modern and civilized world had emerged from the murk of the Dark Ages, into the Renaissance, to Enlightenment and beyond. This implies that we have been on a march, a way forward, a progression. Indeed, it seems that of late the path to peace and prosperity has been cleared considerably. In Europe, communism has almost been laid to rest. The threat of global war has retreated, enabling us now to reap the peace dividend. It is indeed a comforting thought.

Yet there are doubts. The 'feel-good-factor' ratings reveal something rather less than optimism, especially among the middle classes, many of whom believe that their children will not be as well-off as they themselves now are. And their concerns are not only financial: violence, drugs, AIDS and a sense of personal, family and social disintegration all loom large, both in Britain and in the United States. Himmelfarb (1995, p. 224) refers to all this as the 'de-moralization of society'. She cites the fact that teenage illegitimacy rates in the USA tripled between 1960 and 1991, with the rate of increase in Britain even more rapid. Much more serious are similar patterns for the incidence of violent crime. There is, she argues, a reluctance to be judgmental of others' behaviour lest we be thought illiberal. We opt for relativism, unlike the Victorians, who did the opposite. And it is not just the so-called underclass who may become 'de-moralized': this 'same pathology' (p. 245) begins to afflict affluent areas, where teenage addictions and levels of illegitimacy are also rising.

Economic growth in the early 1990s has not produced a corresponding growth in jobs. Competition from Asia increases. For example, in 1975 Japan had 9.8 per cent of world MVA (manufacturing value added), a figure which by 1990 rose to 13.7 per cent; western Europe's corresponding figures fell from 34.5 per cent to 28.5 per cent. North America's share of the distribution of MVA during that period remained at just under 23 per cent (United Nations Industrial Development

Organisation, 1992, p. 26). Attempts to deal with the fiscal overload of the welfare state are producing a widening gap between the 'haves' and the 'have-nots' as social benefits are pruned. In *The Jobless Future* Aronowitz and DiFazio (1994, p. 3) are not optimistic about the capacity of global capitalism and high technology to generate jobs. It is not workers which the economy needs; it is consumers.

Take an example. In January, 1995 at the General Motors Oshawa car plant in Ontario, some 15,000 hopefuls reportedly queued in the winter cold in response to the company's call for applications for a number of *unspecified* jobs. And the increasing dearth of jobs is not confined to those which require low levels of skill. Middle management layers have also been eliminated as companies 'down-size'. Moreover, there is continuing disquiet about the power of politicians to do much about it all.

Perhaps we are beginning to witness what the French sociologist Alain Minc (1993) refers to as 'Le Nouveau Moyen Age' (The New Middle Ages), or what Stjepan Mestrovic (1993) calls the 'Barbarian Temperament', or what Andrew McMurry (1996) refers to as the 'slow apocalypse'. In other words, is there a case to be made that the so-called civilized world has reached the limits of civility and of social (not scientific) progress? We may not be on the brink of global war, but is the 'enemy', so to say, closer to home?

So these are turbulent times. It is tempting to say that this sense of disorder is somehow mystically connected to a *fin de siècle*, a new millennium. Slogans such as 'Education 2000' and 'Goals 2000' alert us to the 'new age' which is upon us. And they imply an urgency, a need to act, now, before it's all too late. To the new millennialism may be added other ritualistic clarion calls, both to nationalism and to religious fundamentalism. In times of uncertainty and ambivalence, it seems that we seek the security of the collective, and we ritualize our belonging to it, thereby excluding the outsider. Uncertainty can be coped with in other ways: for example, by shopping sprees or by consulting psychoanalysts, and their like. None of this explains the uncertainties of the age; and nor, as stated, does the explanation inhere in the fact that the millennium is nigh — we cannot say that it is all because of '2000'.

These 'new times' attract new terms. When I began to think about this book I was drawn to the terms 'postmodernism' and 'postmodernity', but I came to feel increasingly uneasy about them, for two reasons: first, because there is very considerable conceptual elasticity in the way they are used; and second, because the prefix post implies an *ante* state of affairs which has long gone, implying a clean historical break, a view not taken here. Bernstein (1991) defines the issue thus:

> Even when this confusion is acknowledged there has been a strong tempta-
> tion to go on using them, to slide into a quasi-essentialism where we talk as
> if there are a set of determinate features that mark off the'modern' from
> the 'postmodern'. [. . .] My own conviction is that we have reached a stage
> of discussion where these labels (and their cognates) obscure more than
> they clarify — that it is better to drop these terms from our 'vocabulary',

and to try to sort out the relevant issues without reifying these labels.
(Bernstein, 1991, p. 200)

Nevertheless, the usage of these terms is now so widespread that I have not discarded them, for to do so would be cumbersome when referring to the many publications which use them.

It is necessary to make another important caveat. Whilst it may be convenient, for analytical purposes, to talk about different periods of time — be they decades, centuries or millennia — it is worth bearing in mind that whilst these terms are chronological constructs they are nevertheless cultural constructs. So, for example, the '60s is not unto itself a self-contained, discrete cultural period, with neither antecedent nor aftermath. The slate is not clean at the beginning of a new 'time', and nor is it wiped clean at the end of it. Cultural forms anticipate and succeed a given time. All this may seem obvious enough, but as we shall be dealing here with the prefixes 'pre-' (as in 'pre-modern') and 'post-' (as in 'post-modern'), the temptation to infer complete cultural breaks is an easy one to succumb to if these considerations are not borne in mind. Furthermore, there are usually — within a 'time' — conflicts and contradictions which are all subsumed under its integrating terminology, so as to distinguish between it and other 'times'.

Education is always set within the realms of the cultural (which includes also the intellectual), the economic and the political; it is never 'above' them, always *of* them. If we are to try to make sense of the changes taking place in education then we must clearly regard it not as an institution unto itself but as one to be seen in relation to these realms. We live in a time when the cultural code and the economic code are increasingly out of kilter. We face mixed messages and paradox (Hartley, 1994; Hargreaves, 1995a). In some countries — England, for example — the government has been highly directive in its dealings with teachers, riding roughshod over what it disparagingly refers to as the 'educational establishment'. Official policy papers on education are usually riddled with terms to do with competition, efficiency, effectiveness and enterprise. But in addition — and here lies the confusion — appeals to ownership and empowerment insinuate themselves into this terminology. How is it that strong central control can sit easily with local and personal empowerment?

The efficiency-related discourse in these policy documents is driven by an *economic* imperative (doing more with less), but the 'ownership' rhetoric draws upon consumerist *culture*. Similarly, the confidence with which central government defines official knowledge — the curriculum — flies in the face of deep epistemological uncertainties now emerging within academe about truth and certainty. This confusion is worth re-stating. O'Neill (1988) puts it this way:

In short, late capitalism may prove unable to integrate its postmodern culture with its technological base. This is because the efficiency values of the latter are difficult to reconcile with a culture of narcissism and a politics of egalitarianism. (O'Neill, 1988, p. 493)

This is a very succinct statement of our present dilemma: the need for technical efficiency — with all of its down-sizing, quality control and monitoring — is at odds with our self-centred, me-too, and often narcissistic tendencies. How can this producer ethic sit easily with the consumer 'ethic'? Education is influenced by this paradox. In trying to remove it, government has sought to reconcile these economic and cultural trends in a highly manipulative way, framing its policies in terms of an eloquent discourse of duplicity.

This can be put another way. Increasingly, technical considerations outweigh moral considerations. The means are taken to be the ends, in constant need of refinement, for efficiency. Individualism is related to this: that is, *competitive individualism*, so the argument runs, will maximize quality, productivity and efficiency in a relationship among pupils, teachers and schools which approximates to the workings of a market. But individualism can be of a different kind: one to do with how we reflect on, understand, construct and reveal ourselves — *self-centred* and *narcissistic individualism*. These two individualisms — the competitive and the self-centred — are implicit in much official discourse about curriculum, pedagogy, assessment and management. In other words, government has meshed two codes — or frameworks for thinking — about education: the *economic* (stressing cool reason and technical efficiency); the *cultural* (stressing selfhood, emotions and empowerment). The former invites the qualification 'effective'; the latter, 'affective'. There is also a third notion of individualism which stands beyond much of the official discourse on education, namely the *individual as a democratic actor*.

The articulation between the two official codes is achieved as follows. The emphasis on selfhood and empowerment resonates very much with a consumerist 'ethic', and with the tenet of democratic freedom, thereby appealing to the cultural vernacular. But this appeal is framed in such a way that it is not so much functional for the self as it is for the economy. An emerging service sector and a shift towards flatter hierarchies in the work-place will require of employees a new disposition to work and a new repertoire of social skills. These skills include working in teams, multi-tasking and self-supervision. So, this new self-centred approach as we see it in education is intended to be functional or instrumental for the economy, enabling the pupil or teacher to reconstruct their subjectivity anew, after 'reflection'.

It may turn out that co-opting the culture for instrumental and economic purposes will be effective. In the longer term, however, this therapeutic and empowering rhetoric may come to be regarded as overly psychologistic, admitting only reflection of the self rather than of the social structures in which the self is set. Cynicism may set in. Already stress-levels in education are high, and they are not easily lessened by appeals to reflection and empowerment. The manipulation of the kind now being made by government may soon reach the limits of its power to legitimate policy. This issue is explored more fully in the final chapter.

This is not a 'how to' book. It does not purport to offer suggestions for coping with the ambivalences and uncertainties which are rife in our schools and colleges. Others have already made a good start on this endeavour, and they will be referred to. Rather, using a mainly sociological approach, I look beneath the surface of education, and try to bring together the cultural, economic and intellectual movements which have, or may have, consequences for education. Some of these consequences are already with us; others are the subject of speculation. Although this does not set out to be a prescriptive and practical book it nevertheless relates to practice, and is written with the intention of informing it. There is some appeal in the remark, 'OK. That's fine in practice, but how does it work out in theory?'

The meaning of 'school' in the title, *Re-schooling Society*, is meant to include all levels of education, including universities. So the analysis is not confined to any one level — that is, to the primary, the secondary or the tertiary; nor to any one country, though references to Britain and to the United States are most common. Moreover, at the risk of taking historical liberties, the analysis is prefaced by an overly brief conceptual consideration of the mind-sets of the medieval and the modern, both of which serve as a necessary basis for a fuller consideration of the changes now upon us in what has been referred to as the age of postmodernity.

Specifically, the chronology of the book is as follows. In Chapter 2, the path towards postmodernity is charted by considering some interpretations of the pre-modern and modern world-views. Chapter 3 provides a fuller consideration of the *economic* (post-Fordism), the *cultural* (postmodernism) and the *intellectual* (post-modernist theory) shifts which are occurring in the closing decades of the twentieth century, the so-called age of postmodernity. Chapter 4 gives some brief sociological interpretations of postmodernity. In these three chapters, little explicit mention is made of 'education'. This is deliberate, for these chapters construct the necessary theoretical framework for thinking about the educational changes which are occurring. That is to say, before we can consider the *re-schooling* we must deal with the *society* in which schooling is set. As I consider this re-schooling, I refer to these three chapters which logically comprise the first part of the book.

The broad purpose of the following chapters is to address the question: given these economic, cultural and intellectual shifts, what consequences do they have, and might they have, for curriculum, for pedagogy, for assessment and for the management of education, respectively? In dealing with each of these aspects of education, I preface the discussion with a brief consideration of how it was expressed during most of the age of modernity, up to about 1975.

To give a flavour of the approach, take curriculum. First, I shall refer to the form and content of curriculum during the greater part of this century. Thereafter, in relation to the 1980s and 1990s, the following questions are put: is curriculum being shaped by economic forces which seek to render it more technical and instrumental; is the flux and flow of postmodernist culture having an effect; are the epistemological battles being fought by some postmodernists and feminists against the rationalists winning the day; are new subjects being introduced into the curriculum — and if so, why, and for whom? Are governments so concerned by this moral uncertainty that they seek to impose a kind of cultural fix — a national curriculum — in order to re-focus the somewhat centrifugal cultural trends in play?

I go on to deal with pedagogy, assessment and management. For each, I refer to its expression in the age of modernity, and thereafter consider how the economic, cultural, intellectual and political changes which are now in train have, or may come to have, a bearing on it. Let it be stressed here that these 'changes' are shot through with contradictions and ambivalences. I argue that governments' attempts to reconcile these contradictions and ambivalences often result in a somewhat tortuous discourse. As the analysis unfolds, it should become clear that the dilemma or paradox to which I referred earlier is expressed in all of these aspects of education. That is to say, the contradictory pressures wrought by the cultural and the economic influences on education may be difficult either to legitimate or to contain if current policy runs its course.

Chapter 2

The Path to the Postmodern

The Medieval World-view

We begin first with a qualification. The sub-heading '*The* medieval world-view' implies a coherence and homogeneity which was absent. Eco (1985) defines two periods within the Middle Ages: the first, ranging from the fall of the Roman Empire to the year 1000AD; the second, to the Renaissance and the rise of humanism. The former period was one of 'crisis, decay, violent shifts of populations and the clash of cultures' (p. 490); the latter revealed increasing levels of civility. In general, the social structure of the Middle Ages comprised three functional ideal types: the *oratores* (the monks, who prayed); the *bellatores* (the knights, who fought); and the *laboratores* (the peasants, who worked) (Le Goff, 1990). Orme (1973, p. 12) defines the social structure of England in the Middle Ages as comprising three estates: the clergy; the military (including kings, nobles, gentry and all those, such as lawyers, who supported them); and merchants, craftsmen and artisans. This social structure was God-given, unchangeable. But, even so, there were variations, both spatial and temporal.

Life and limb were constantly on the line in the early medieval period. The peasantry, bound to their lord in a very unequal relationship, led rather predictable lives, but only in their social relationships, officially confined largely to their villages. Even so, the avoidance of war and the search for work caused many a peasant to roam the realm. Illiterate, they left little written record of their lives, and we must resort to the sometimes coloured reports written (in Latin) by their ecclesiastical 'betters', who were wont to allude to the peasantry's filth, poor clothing, minimal diet, and 'a sort of bestiality' (Cherubini, 1990, pp. 132–3). Vestiges of the pre-Christian pagan era remained: rites, magic and animistic rituals were not uncommon, and were practised in order to assure the health and good fortune of the peasantry. The church itself was compelled tactically to appeal to the 'myth, epic, pagan ritual and magic' in the cultural tradition of the people (Gurevitch, 1988, p. 2).

This pre-modern world — before the establishment of what Norbert Elias has called 'courtly society' in the reign of Louis XIV of France — was a dark and dangerous place, relatively speaking. It was a 'warrior society', the threat of violence never far away. Both the person and property were vulnerable to robbers, day and night. Plague and pestilence added to life's precariousness. In the absence of safe drinking water, the people resorted to alcoholic drinks, imbibing them at levels we would regard as very dangerous. The state had yet to pacify and police large areas of the realm (Luchaire, 1912, p. 8). Added to the suspicion of others was a constant fear of that dreadful destiny, the Day of Judgment, and the possibility of eternal damnation.

Some of us today would have found it all rather unsavoury. Indeed, life then was bereft of that repertoire of crucial competences of modern life: manners. Picture this, a scene reported as late as 1609:

> [...] those whom we sometimes see lying like swine with their snouts in the soup, not once lifting their heads and turning their eyes, still less their hands, from the food, puffing out both cheeks as if they were blowing a trumpet or trying to fan a fire, not eating but gorging themselves, dirtying their arms almost to the elbows and then reducing their serviettes to a state that would make a kitchen rag look clean. (della Casa, 1609, transcribed in Elias, 1978 [1939], p. 90)

On the other hand, in the cities of the late Middle Ages, life could be different: it was changeable, crowded and (among the well-to-do) increasingly 'urbane' and 'civilized'. Unlike the peasantry, the lives of city-dwellers were more fragmented: that is, the integration between their home and work was weakened; and their families were less cohesive, and very much more cramped in their living quarters. Life was somewhat 'measured', by the clock. Even so, accounts of city-life in the later Middle Ages differ. Rossiaud cites one report of London by Richard of Devizes at the end of the twelfth century. Its central (and rather homophobic and patriarchal) message was: '[...] If you do not want to dwell with evildoers, do not live in London', for it was there that you would reportedly have been in the doubtful company of 'actors, jesters, smooth-skinned lads, Moors, flatterers, pretty boys, effeminates, pederasts, singing and dancing girls, quacks, belly-dancers, sorceresses, extortioners, nightwanderers, magicians, mimes, beggars, buffoons' (Rossiaud, 1990, p. 139). In contrast, a contemporary account by William Fitzstephen waxes lyrical about the citizens — note the word *citizen*, a term associated with civility (as opposed to rusticity) which entered the language more generally after 1550 — being 'everywhere regarded as illustrious and renowned beyond those of all other cities for the elegance of their fine manners, raiment and table'. Probably both accounts were sustainable; the former of the poor, the latter of the rich.

So the Middle Ages were not culturally or politically harmonious. In its initial phase, it had drawn on the preceding classical Roman period which for two to three centuries had persisted, only to break down, thereby casting the Middle Ages into the turmoil to which Luchaire has referred (Smith, 1992). Gradually, for some, law and order returned, and the development of courtly and urban society enabled the emergence of civilized behaviour: that is, behaviour in which the affects are self-regulated so as to accord with what counts as good manners. But civilized behaviour was more the exception than the rule, confined to the wealthy. For the rest, the suppression of affects — or self-repression — was little in evidence; for them, survival came before civility. Embarrassment was a notion yet to gain currency, for there was little sense of shame. Practices which today we would regard as strictly private were then openly engaged in. Little cultural distinction was made between children and adults; and children were aware of, and often party to, nearly all aspects of adult life. Adulthood held no mystery for children, and the notion of childhood innocence would have seemed ridiculous.

This, therefore, was no age of reason. The irrational was paramount — the spirit prevailed over the mind, the heart over the head. In this, women were seen as more so than men, and many were accused of being servants of the devil, witches. The mass persecution of women as witches during the Renaissance and even in the early stage of the Enlightenment attests to this (Gurevitch, 1988, p. 86). Explanations of everyday events did not often turn on the laws of science. A thunderstorm would not have been explained as the result of a set of meteorological conditions, but perhaps as the wrath of God. The print medium had yet to be widely adopted. Only the great illuminated texts circulated, but they were few, and were written by clerics in the *lingua franca* of the age, Latin. Later, as trade expanded, French and English might be used, though rarely, and then among merchants. Those who were educated to be literate were held in high esteem. For the rest, folklore, story-tellings and rituals bound the present to the past. People acted out of habit. A good memory attracted much status. Colours were important, for they were highly symbolic — yellow, for example, symbolized deceit; green prompted hesitation. Dreams during the late medieval period were the subject of much fascination and analysis (Le Goff, 1990, pp. 32–3). Numbers, too, had their symbolic meanings — there was a particular dread of the year 1000AD. Not surprisingly, astrology and superstition were common. Evil spirits, like storms, were to be warded off by the ringing of church bells, and by the ghoulish gargoyles which embellished the external masonry of the churches. Relics were sought, miracles expected, magic condoned. Punishment was prompt, public and (by modern standards) brutal. Retribution, not rehabilitation, was the order of the day: '[. . .] it was a society in which cruelty and physical violence were not considered unusual or inhumane' (Gurevitch, 1988, p. 29).

For the peasantry, time was cyclical, turning with the sun, the season and the tide. There were few clocks, only church bells; and the importance of punctuality would have been alien to them. Time simply 'passed' — there would have been no concept of 'wasting time'. Tidiness and neatness in spatial arrangements held no compulsion for them. In the late Middle Ages, in the cities, activities and behaviour were to become more measured, not only by the clock, but also by the self, acting in response to the emerging code of civility towards others. And there were some signs, too, of social mobility. But in the main, obedience was quite literally regarded as a virtue. Even so — again in the late medieval cities, and to a lesser extent in the countryside — the peasants did revolt, as in England in 1381.

The architectural monuments of the age were the great cathedrals, built over centuries, with some — like Beauvais in France — never to be completed. Imagine the sense of awe which the lowly peasant must have felt on entering these buildings. They were indeed enchanting places, suffused with a sense of lofty space, with the smell of incense, with the sounds of heavenly music, with powerful paintings pointing the way to Heaven; or to Hell. Within these earthly representations of Heaven would be found a totally coherent way of making sense of life — a physical structure which represented both a social and a psychological structure, itself hierarchical, immutable, ordained by God, but mediated by men. Indeed, these magnificent churches had been as significant then as the great railway stations were to become in the age of entrepreneurial capitalism. Both were the icons of their respective times, binding people together.

Both Elias and Bakhtin provide two authoritative impressions of the mind-set of the Middle Ages. First Elias,

> Much of what appears contradictory to us — the intensity of their piety, the violence of their fear of hell, their guilt feelings, their penitence, the immense outbursts of joy and gaiety, the sudden flaring and the uncontrollable force of their hatred and belligerence — all these, like the rapid changes of mood, are in reality symptoms of the same social and personality structure. The instincts, the emotions, were vented more freely, more openly than later. (Elias, 1978 [1939], p. 200)

And Bakhtin,

> One can say (with certain reservations, of course) that medieval man lived as it were two lives: one — *official*, monolithically serious and gloomy, subordinated to a strict hierarchical order, full of fear, dogmatism, veneration and piety, and another — *carnival* — vulgar, free, full of ambivalent laughter, blasphemies, profanations of everything sacred, lowerings and obscenities, familiar contact with everybody and everything. (Bakhtin, 1963, quoted in Gurevitch, 1988, p. 178; my emphasis)

But perhaps most important for what follows historically is that so great was the intensity of their relationship with nature that they were unable to distance themselves from it (Gurevitch, 1988, p. 96).

The Modern World-view

In the modern age, distance becomes no object, both geographically and intellectually. It became this very ability both to master nature and to stand 'above' it which was to become so central to the condition of modernity. Even so, despite this confident assertion, there is a good deal of uncertainty about the definition of 'modern'. Again, therefore, '*The* modern world-view' is an oversimplification. Consider the following:

> When, and how, what we call 'the modern' emerged is an inchoate question. (Bell, 1990a, p. 43)

> Indeed one of the remarkable features of contributions to debates on this issue (modernity) is the extent to which key terms and ideas have evaded clarification. (Smart, 1990, p. 16; with brackets added)

Modernity, after all, has always been a highly relativist term. It emerged in the fifth century when newly Christianized Romans wished to distinguish their religiosity from two forms of barbarians, the heathens of antiquity and the unregenerate Jews. In medieval times, modernity was reinvented as a term implying cultivation and learning, which allowed contemporary intellectuals to identify backwards. With the Enlightenment, modernity became identified with rationality, science, and forward progress, a semantically arbitrary relationship that seems to have held steady to this day. (Alexander, 1995, p. 66)

Although the age of modernity anticipates the Enlightenment, nevertheless the modern mind-set is succinctly put by Kant: 'The motto of enlightenment is therefore: *Aude Sapere*! (Dare to know, Dare to be wise) Have courage to use your *own* understanding!' (Kant, 1991 [1784], p. 54; brackets added).

It is appropriate to stress here that this quest for Kant's 'maturity' (that is, to 'dare to know') is one that sees women's reasoning subsumed by men's. It is related to a wider point:

Despite its aspirations to timeless truth, the History of Philosophy reflects the characteristic preoccupations of the kinds of people who have had access to the activity. [. . .] But there is one thing that they [philosophers] have had in common throughout the history of the activity: they have been predominantly male; and the absence of women from the philosophical tradition has meant that the conceptualisation of Reason has been done exclusively by men. (Lloyd, 1984, p. 108; brackets added)

For Kant, 'the entire fair sex' were 'immature', which is to say that they lacked the ability 'to use one's own understanding without the guidance of another' (Kant, 1991, p. 54). Only a few — all men — would be the 'guardians' of the 'immature'. Education was to be a masculine preserve. Even Rousseau's *Emile*, a book which had, and still has, profound influence in Europe was extremely reactionary when it came to the education of girls. In the editorial introduction to *Emile*, Jimack (1989, p. xviii) regards Rousseau as 'retrograde' on the subject of a girl's education, it being 'entirely subordinated to the needs of man'. To be sure, Rousseau regarded the minds of men and women as complementary, but different, as nature had intended (Lloyd, 1984, p. 74). Rousseau (1989) in Book V of *Emile* (devoted to the education of Sophie) does not mince his words, 'A perfect man and a perfect woman should no more be alike in mind than in face, and perfection admits of neither less nor more' (p. 322). He goes on, 'A woman's reason is practical, and therefore she soon arrives at a given conclusion, but she fails to discover it for herself' (p. 340). So, whilst the Enlightenment set in train an age of reason, it was not women's reason. Women were said to be different — for which read deficient — in matters of reason. If men were reasonable, women were emotional, not naturally given to science and to theorizing. And it was Rousseau who gave currency to the view that children were no mere proto-adults; they were not deficient. Children were children. They were not only biologically different but also culturally different from adults. Childhood as a cultural category begins to emerge (Wardle, 1974).

But let us say that the 'modern' constitutes something of a new mode of thought — a new interpretive framework, or matrix, for making sense of the world. It is to lay to rest the comfort of religious and metaphysical certainties, and to awaken critical reasoning. It is a refusal to allow others to make sense of the world for us. And this 'world' is both the inner world as well as the world 'out there'. The world was to be understood, not accepted. It was to be changed, for the better. Debate, not dogma, would prevail. Progress to the desired end would ensue. In that sense it was a teleological view. Destiny was to be supplanted by decision-making. No longer would it suffice simply to give assertions — arguments, with evidence, had to be set out. In the pre-modern medieval period, there was little notion of the individual. The 'individual' was simply a part of the wider order of things. Questioning one's position was not an option. A person was above all a social being, not a solitary one. In the modern period, the autonomous individual, not society, becomes central.

The modern age assigns considerable power to the prefix 're-': it does so in the belief that the world can be made anew. It is not an immutable, God-given structure. It is a human construct, changeable. Whereas the medieval period had been a warrior society, the modern period was to set itself the task of conquering nature. Whereas hitherto the will and the irrational ran amok, now all would succumb to scientific reason. Paradoxically, the increasingly secular world was to have 'faith' in science. The holistic world-view of the medieval period was no longer sustainable. The disciplines spawned by the Enlightenment gave the lie to this unitary order. These disciplines purported to uncover the laws which governed the physical, the social and the psychological worlds. The truth lay waiting to be discovered. Those who held to an essentialist interpretation of the world — one wrapped up in the certitudes and canons of the Church — found themselves increasingly out of step. The chanting of canons had no place in the new citadels of science. Science was to spawn dissent and disbelief in the consciousness of certitude that for so long had held sway. All the same, just as vestiges of the pre-Christian Roman period remained during the Middle Ages, so too do vestiges of the medieval lurk within the modern period. Indeed — as I noted in Chapter 1 — we may well be seeing the emergence of a 'new' middle ages. Put in ideal-typical terms, we may say that in the medieval world there was a unity, everlasting. In the age of modernity, according to Daniel Bell, there are three realms: economy, polity and culture. Whilst in the early modern period they formed something of a unity, of late this uniformity is in question, for reasons which will become apparent. Consider each of these realms in turn, starting with the economy.

Capitalism was — and remains — the dominant mode of production throughout modernity. Weber distinguished between two types of capitalist: the 'entrepreneurs' and the 'rentiers'. The 'entrepreneurs' were a typical example of what Weber called a 'privileged income class' — 'merchants, ship owners, industrialists', for example (Weber, 1978 [1922], p. 9). But the entrepreneurs were more than mere merchants. They did not simply meet a demand for goods and services: they created the demand, and they met it. Their motive was accumulation, profit. They were prone to take risks with the lives and limbs of others in the pursuit of profit for themselves. Neither sombre nor sedate, they ranged the globe in their endeavours. They were not men 'of substance', but men whose 'calculation' was felt somewhat irrationally. They colonized and they controlled, at first coercively, then bureaucratically, thereafter co-opting the indigenous elites, schooling their offspring in the metropolis, all with an eye to the succession and longterm profit. A quite different breed were the 'rentiers', whom Weber regarded as a typical 'privileged property class', and their rents could be derived from the likes of land, mines, shipping and from the giving of credit. These were men of strict sobriety, vision, thrift and prudence, born to the bourgeoisie of Calvinist heritage. These were men of cool head and cold calculation, far removed from the enchanted minds of medieval man. They entered into contracts, not relationships: their word was their bond, but if trust were breached, then so was the law, which was then invoked to make the contract binding. Not much was left to chance with this 'rentier' class.

Capitalism required a certain type of liberty: liberty to engage in the scientific endeavour in order to develop the new products that would continually generate business. And liberty allowed the entrepreneur free rein in the free market. In the classic economic liberalism of Ricardo and Smith, there was no truck with economic regulation, but there was much emphasis on the moral regulation of workers, many of them children. There was exploitation, of children especially, for they were cheap and more easily chastened than their elders. Nature *and* children were being tamed, in the name of economic liberalism. The welfare state was a long way off. Charity was meant to provide what the family could not. Of course, it was not all plain sailing for the capitalists, especially when the glaring inequalities became too obvious to ignore. Nevertheless, there were powerful intellectual (and therefore cultural) supports for what was happening. The Darwinian thesis of the survival of the fittest was invoked to justify the hierarchical order: after all, had not the wealthy and the privileged simply evolved from better 'stock'? Take, for example, the noted eugenicist, Francis Galton, Fellow of the Royal Society, prominent scientist, and a relative of Darwin: .

> I propose to show in this book that a man's natural abilities are derived by inheritance, under exactly the same limitations as are the form and physical features of the organic whole. Consequently, it is easy, notwithstanding these limitations, to obtain by careful selection a permanent breed of dogs or horses gifted with peculiar powers of running, or of doing anything else, so it would be quite practicable to produce a highly-gifted race of men by judicious marriages during several consecutive generations. (Galton, 1869, p. 1)

But the justification to exploit did not rest only on natural selection. It had something of the seal of divine approval. The Calvinist ethic — for some the Protestant ethic, for others simply the work ethic — required that one had to demonstrate before God that one was worthy of membership of God's Elect, and it was through the accumulation of wealth that this was to be shown.

In the medieval world the division of labour had not been great. It tended to turn on gender: most women could do most women's jobs, the same applying to men. This is what Durkheim referred to as a society bound together 'mechanically'. But the quest for efficiency under capitalism was to transform not only the owner-ship of the means of production (into social classes) but also the way in which production itself was technically (and therefore socially) structured. For the most part, factory owners tended to devolve the day-to-day managerial tasks to engin-eers, who came to generate a technocratic prescription for the social arrangement of the workplace. Workers were treated as if they were things, to be pressed and manipulated in the interests of efficiency.

The history of management theory is replete with accounts of the fine-tuning of time and space. Time no longer was allowed to 'pass', as it had on the seas and in the fields during the Middle Ages. In the modern age, time gradually comes to be 'spent' — it has value — and it was measured, ever more accurately, and ever more publicly. Time came to be regarded as a linear progression. The notion of punctuality enters the common consciousness. It was represented not only visually by the clock face, but could also be heard by the factory hooter or bell. Clocks could be turned back by the owners in order to lengthen the working day. Indeed, the working day began early and ended late. It 'shifted': that is, shift-work developed, enabled by the invention of artificial lighting. The relationship between time and task was recognized in the early years of this century in America. So begins 'piece work'. Space, too, became highly regulated. Whereas before both work and domestic life had been conducted in the same place, in the industrial urbanized society they became separated. More than this, the world outside of the factory was walled from view. The windows were placed far above head-height, admitting only sufficient for the workers to tend to their task. The outside world was kept at bay whilst hands were kept on the job. And if the sights of nature were restricted, so too were its sounds, insulated by the walls, drowned by the machinery. Within the factory, spaces were clearly demarcated, for efficiency, but also for status — the supervisor was often located above the workshop floor, sometimes with a small porthole window to allow his eyes to range over his charges. Here was a closed world, hierarchical, artificial, carefully structured, examined, specified, noisy.

These procedures had ramifications for education. As early as 1797, Dr Andrew Bell had published a small pamphlet containing the outline of his new monitorial system of instruction: *An Experiment in Education, made at the Male Asylum of Madras*. In a report of the trustees of the charity-aided school of St Mary, Whitechapel in London on 7 April, 1807, the 'chief advantages' of his plan were listed thus:

I   It completely fixes and secures the attention of every scholar: the indolent are stimulated; the vicious reclaimed; and it nearly annihilates bad behaviour of every sort;

II   The children make regular progress in their learning, which is daily noted and registered; no lesson being passed over till it be correctly studied;

III   It saves the expense of additional instructors; the eye of one intelligent master or mistress alone, being required to see that their agents, the senior boys and girls, do their duty in teaching their juniors.

IV   It not only possesses excellent mechanical advantages in communicating instruction generally, but it is particularly adapted to instil into, and fix practically in the mind, the principles of our holy Religion; whilst it materially secures the moral conduct of the children, both in and out of school; and,

V   By economizing time, hitherto so lamentably wasted in Charity-Schools conducted on the old plan; it affords ample and very inviting opportunity to add to the ordinary establishment, a School of Industry. (quoted in Bell, 1807, pp. 19–20)

Industrial production could be made yet more efficient. And it was, by an engineer turned management guru: F.W. Taylor. His book, *The Principles of Scientific Management*, brought to management theory the fruits of empirical research. Tasks were observed, and were broken down into their component stages. The time taken to perform a set task was noted. Best practice was defined. These ideas were taken further by Henry Ford in his Detroit car assembly plants during the 1920s. The elegance and efficiency of the car assembly-line was that control over the 'line' workers could be regulated technically by setting the speed at which the assembly-line moved. The rate for the job was determined by the number of times the worker performed his standardized task. Again, as with Taylor, it was assumed that workers would comply out of a sense of calculated self-interest — higher performance, higher pay — rather than out of some intrinsic self-motivation. But they did not. Strikes were called, and were broken. In addition, not only were the owners vulnerable to disruptive strike action and sabotage of the assembly line, but they were equally vulnerable to the vagaries of a market of mass consumption. Consumers' tastes could change quickly, and therefore they also needed to be 'engineered': mass consumption as well as mass production (Sloan, 1964).

It is worth noting in passing that Taylorism was not confined in itself to capitalist labour management. Its hierarchical and centralized structures, and its large-scale ventures, were no less attractive to Lenin in the Soviet Union than to Henry Ford in Detroit, Michigan. For example, Albert Kahn, chief architect of Ford factories in Detroit, built some 520 industrial complexes in the USSR between 1929 and 1932. Nor, one suspects, did the shipping of animals and the mechanization of death in the Chicago slaughterhouses entirely escape the attention of the architects of the Holocaust which was to come. The writ of Taylorism and Fordism ran throughout industrialized society, both capitalist and socialist. And just as capitalists had a 'mass' (production) mentality, so too did labour organize itself into powerful trade unions, themselves the epitome of bureaucratic structures; and beyond them, in Britain at least, were the formal political parties upon which the unions bestowed legitimacy and funds. In post-New Deal America, and in the post-war Keynesian solution to economic growth in Britain, the trade-off between labour and capital was formalized in a regulatory state which socialized the costs of the economic infrastructure — health, social security, transportation, communications and education. All of these elements revealed the same modes of regulation and control as the production process itself. A structural isomorphism suffused the system.

Daniel Bell's second realm of modernity, the polity, was founded on liberalism. That is to say, on individual rights. As implied earlier, more than anything else, it is the concept of the individual which sets apart the modern from the medieval. Rights protect the individual. They are inalienable, framed constitutionally, as in the United States of America. *E pluribus, unum*; and *liberté, egalité, fraternité* were the maxims of the American and French republics, respectively. Citizens exercise their rights, but only if they do not contradict the public good. That is the trade-off between the private and the public. Implicit within the modern endeavour is emancipation — social progress, as well as technological progress. Modernity took the long view. Even so, there is an uneasy relationship between liberal democracy and capitalism, for capitalism *must* produce inequality, not equality.

So, in their earlier formulations, rights protected the individual. They were set down in a constitution (at least in some countries). With these rights came responsibilities — the responsibility to place the common good over the private interest. This is fast changing. What is occurring now is that private passions and interests are being defined in terms of rights (Seligman, 1990, pp. 230–31). Rights are even extended to the non-human, a kind of anthropomorphization process. Connected with all these new causes are an abundance of interest groups, coming and going with the issue of the day. They are sophisticated in the use of modern communications technology, not only to shower the media with press releases, but also to organize themselves.

> Rights are no longer framed in terms of citizens' or civil rights, but of human rights. [. . .] Indeed (for example) the ecology movement can be seen as imbuing natural phenomena, the oceans, whales, trees, etc., with 'rights'. [. . .] For it is not that kitty-cats become citizens — but rather that the realm of shared public space, within which the citizen is constituted, has itself disappeared. (*Ibid.*, brackets added)

Universal rights also assume that there is an essence to the self, a transcendental ego, an integral self. But if — as postmodernists aver — the self is a *construct*, not an essence, then the notion of universal rights is logically difficult to sustain (Blake, 1996, p. 5).

Culture is the third realm of modernity defined by Bell. How was the age of modernity symbolized? What was the prevailing consciousness, or way of seeing? What were the 'givens', the commonsense? How was the objective world defined? If, as Jencks (1986, p. 47) suggests, the culture of the pre-modern period had been 'aristocratic', with a highly integrated world-view, then the dominant culture of the modern age was 'bourgeois'. Here begins the age of reason, of disciplines, of positivism. Consider, for example, the crucial idea of the *Panopticon*, first written about in 1791 by Jeremy Bentham. Incarceration, he suggested, need no longer be coercive. It could be civilized, so to say. If, by civility, is meant that individuals suppress or regulate their own emotions and impulses, then 'civilized' prisoners would be those who would come to regulate themselves, without constant supervision and coercive reminders to comply. The elegance of Bentham's *Panopticon* was that its architectural structure was such that inmates would not know if they were either being overheard or overseen. Thus the prisoners had to assume that supervision was indeed continuous. And the supervisor, too, could be placed under the same mode of control. The panoptical principle was efficient and effective, and it could be applied equally to schools, factories and prisons; especially to the factory.

The metaphor of the machine was central to modernist thought. And in modernism we lost our sense of enchantment, to use Weber's term, for we became locked in the clean, cold cage of bureaucratic rationality. Much was structured with this in mind, especially modernist architecture. Rising above the detritus of the streets, the high-rise buildings promised efficiency, light and uniform predictability. Streets, especially in America, were set out in grid-pattern; and numbered, not named, in sequence, so that it would be difficult to get lost. The great public buildings, especially the railway stations and main post offices, were monuments of light, space and progress, often emulating the neo-classical splendour of confident progress.

The cultural values of deferred gratification underlined the Protestant work ethic, or the central value system, as Parsons was to call it. Here was a world of orderly acquiescence which, although it became increasingly secularized, was nevertheless bound together through a work ethic disseminated in the schools. Even so, as we have noted, modernism had its dark side. Sequestering us in cities, it separated us from the rhythms of nature, its flora and fauna. The range of our sense experience was reduced by the rhyme and reason of instrumental rationality.

What is of central importance is that Daniel Bell's three realms — *economy* (capitalism), *polity* (liberalism) and *culture* (the Protestant work ethic, bureaucratic thinking) — were all of a piece. There were no rifts between them. They have been subjected to a number of descriptions based upon the static metaphor of the machine, or upon the biological metaphor of an organism; and, related to the biological metaphor, an evolutionary metaphor which allows for notions of natural development and progress to emerge. The impression generated by these metaphors is of a society in good order, whose 'parts' function interdependently, smoothly, consensually; a society where 'dysfunctions' can be compensated for in other parts of the system, thereby accomplishing an evolutionary homeostatic balance. Just as the medieval, pre-modern world had an internal coherence, so did the modern, and our brief reference to Andrew Bell's monitorial system illustrates the emerging correspondence between school and factory. But the modern world is showing signs of disintegration. No longer are the three realms defined by Daniel Bell of a piece.

Chapter 3

Post(?)Modernity

Has the age of modernity ended? Are the changes in modernity to which Daniel Bell has referred of such moment that it would seem inappropriate to continue to use the very term modernity to describe what is now before us? These questions presuppose that the 'end' is recognizable. Put another way, what would be the empirical evidence which would constitute the end of modernity? Is a clean break possible? And if it were to be argued that there has indeed been a break with modernity, then how might it be explained? The position to be taken here is that no such clean break has occurred (and in that sense any usage of the term postmodern should perhaps be written as post(?)modern, or, as Alexander puts it, 'neo-modern'). Laclau (1988, p. 65) argues that postmodernity does not mean a mere rejection of modernity, but rather 'a different modulation of its themes and categories, a greater proliferation of its language games'. And yet we may sense that something is different. It seems so, and it is difficult not to agree with Alexander (1995):

> In this recent period we have witnessed perhaps the most dramatic set of spatially and temporally contingent social transformations in the history of the world. [. . .] we are witnessing the death of a major alternative not only in social thought but in society itself. (Alexander, 1995, pp. 64–5)

There is no alternative, it seems. The path to development has clearly been shown by capitalism. But these are early days. It remains to be seen if, for example, market economics can simply be grafted on to the cultures of Eastern Europe. On this, it is worth noting that the communists made the mistake of believing that socialism could be simply imposed on a culture not then ready for it. Capitalism may yet make the same mistake.

Notwithstanding this, vestiges of modernity remain, as Alexander asserts. There may even be something in the view that there are signs of the pre-modern now coming to the fore: New Age cults; astrology; alternative medicine; home-schooling; fundamentalist revival; the search for a spiritual dimension; the increasing number of places where there can be no assurance of personal safety. I referred earlier to the work of Eco (1985) and Minc (1993) who both consider the possibility that we are entering a 'new' Middle Ages. For example, Eco draws a comparison between the decline of the 'Great Pax (military, civil, social and cultural)' of the Roman Empire and what he calls the 'crisis of the Pax Americana' (p. 491). Today, private security firms mushroom. Public, private and corporate buildings deploy a panoply of defensive devices. There is ecological decline. 'Neonomadism': the tourist routes of today are the counterpart of the pilgrim routes then; and air travel now is tinged with a sense of uncertainty as security checks of passengers and their baggage imply inherent danger.

So something seems to be afoot, even if it is no more than the impending millennium; and there is no shortage of 'new times' slogans (Hall and Jacques, 1989; Kenway *et al.*, 1994), defined in terms of the new post-Fordist global capitalism and as the relative demise of both class-based struggle and the manufacturing sector (Boyne and Rattansi, 1990, p. 19). Few education reports will catch the eye unless phrases like '2000' or the 'Twenty-First Century' figure in their titles. A New World Order is said to be nigh. Is it the case that there is a neat coincidence between the new millennium and the profound changes to which Alexander referred; or are these economic, cultural and political configurations of great moment, rending asunder much that has been revered since the Enlightenment?

But: to postmoder*nity*; to postmoder*nism*; and to postmoder*nists*. Let us consider these in turn, for analytical purposes, but bear in mind that they are logically related. By 'postmodernity' is meant an age or epoch which both overlaps with, and goes beyond, what we have come to regard as the post-Enlightenment modern age. Included within it are the social and economic forms of that epoch. It is therefore a chronological term, a periodizing concept, but the temporal dividing line is not easily agreed upon, though there is some cluster of consensus defining its beginning in the 1960s and 1970s. First to be considered is the economic expression of postmodernity — variously referred to as post-Fordism or disorganized capitalism. This leads to an analysis of the *cultural expression* of postmodernity, referred to here as *postmodernism*. This will be followed by a necessarily brief consideration of *postmodernists*: that is to say, some of the theorists such as Lyotard, Derrida and Foucault who have brought to bear a mainly philosophical gaze on the state of knowledge in postmodernity. These cultural and economic expressions of the postmodern comprise what Biesta (1995, p. 163) calls the *condition* of the postmodern age. That done, attention will be turned in Chapter 4 to what he calls the *positions* — the mainly sociological perspectives which can be taken on this condition.

Post-Fordism: The Emerging Economic Expression of Capitalism

It is nowadays a common assertion — though far from empirically verified — that the era of mass production has had its day. By 'mass production' we mean '[. . .] long runs of standardized products made on dedicated special purpose equipment by Taylorized semi-skilled workers. Mass production in this sense is often used interchangeably with the concept of 'Fordism' [. . .]' (Williams *et al.*, 1992, p. 518). This concept of 'Fordism' has gone largely unexamined, resting on the following principles, some of which are contained in the previous quotation. These are: first, standardized products which allow for standardized production methods, which in turn allow for economies of scale; second, purpose-built machinery which will be dedicated to the task of producing the said standardized products; third, the application of Taylorist management theory whereby tasks are broken down into their component sub-tasks, thereby allowing for the close monitoring of time-on-task and overall through-put; and fourth, the moving assembly line, which regulates the flow of sequentially-ordered tasks. All this presupposes the following: a stable consumer market; a stable product with well-understood raw materials and technologies; large stock-piles of materials; a rigidly bureaucratic organizational form, strongly hierarchical, highly routinized, with written manuals for every facet of production; and, finally, an adherence to Keynesian economics whereby the state would intervene in order to regulate supply and demand. None of these principles and practices turned on the ownership of the means of production: they were as agreeable to the Soviets in the 1920s as they were to their American capitalist counterparts.

In practice it did not always work according to plan. Taylor's assumptions were based on a *homo economicus* view of the worker. But the compliance of workers did not simply turn on their wages. The turnover rate of workers was initially high. Williams *et al.* (1992, p. 533) reported that in 1913 at Ford's Highland Park factory in Detroit the rate had reached a 'phenomenal 70 per cent'. At first, all that disaffected workers could do was to withdraw their labour and resign. All the same, Ford realized that these rates were excessive. In an attempt to 'sell' the regime of Fordism to the workers, he increased wages to five dollars a day, comparatively a very high wage. The turnover rate fell. Working for Ford became relatively attractive, but his workers were required to be clean, prudent, abstemious and non-smokers — and docile. Even so, Watkins makes the important point that mass production along Fordist lines was not the rule for most businesses, most of them too small to employ the economies of scale which Fordism provided (Watkins, 1994, pp. 4–7).

In the late 1960s, the weight of these grand structures became too much to tolerate. The 'mass' of modernity began to look too burdensome, and it began to be undermined. The certainties and stabilities of mass production and consumption seemed dated, dysfunctional. Long-adhered to patterns of consumption and compliance began to fragment. Moreover, the resistance of organized trade unions became more marked, allegedly diminishing levels of profitability and investment. And to all this was added the OPEC oil embargo which resulted in a near-fourfold increase in the price of oil in the early 1970s. An industrial recession ensued (Murray, 1992). Meanwhile, it began to emerge that in Japan, especially in the Toyota company, new kinds of production process were in train. The efficiency gains were reportedly considerable and they would soon strike at the heart of the competitiveness of American and European business. At the same time, other economies in Asia — Taiwan, Korea and Malaysia — began to stir. Like the West, they had a well-educated workforce and access to capital. Unlike the West, tax rates were low in the absence of a welfare state, and they were not burdened by a weakening work ethic and trade union movement.

The 'answer' is now well known. The market was deregulated by a neoliberal government advised by New Right think-tanks. Organized labour was undermined. The social wage was cut. The private was set to prevail over the public. The consumer was primed to prod the provider into service. Whereas before the consumer had taken what was on offer from the supplier, now the supplier was to provide what the consumer demanded. Even so, what the consumer desired was not necessarily to be left entirely to the consumer. The consumer's desires could be designed to fit the material and cultural products of the advertisers, who themselves were retained by producers. In all of this, market research became an essential procedure. The consuming public was to be very finely categorized, and thereafter targeted. Colour, space, sounds and texture could all be coordinated to generate integrated habits of consumption which are particular to each social category in the market (Sloan, 1964).

Consider post-Fordism a little further. Jean-Francois Lyotard in his seminal book *The Postmodern Condition* has pointed up the central importance of information technology and computerization in post-Fordist economies:

> [. . .] it is fair to say that for the last forty years the 'leading' sciences and technologies have had to do with language: phonology and theories of linguistics, problems of communication and cybernetics [. . .], problems of translation and the search for areas of compatibility among computer languages, problems of information storage and data banks, telematics and the perfection of intelligent terminals, paradoxology. (Lyotard, 1984, p. 45)

Computerization will not only have profound consequences for what counts as knowledge, but this knowledge will itself constitute a commercial product — it will become mercantilized, in Lyotard's terms — to be transmitted not necessarily physically, but electronically, in digital form, along information highways. Moreover, information which can be rendered digital will become not only a product unto itself — for example, a video or a databank — but it will also constitute a crucial source of information on consumers' spending patterns. And the consumers will be unaware of how the various data-banks are being 'mined' for information about them.

In manufacturing, the trend throughout the development of capitalism has been to reduce unit labour costs. The moving car assembly line was the forerunner of the computer-controlled industrial robots of today. The percentage of workers employed in manufacturing continues to decline as technology-driven 'down-sizing' proceeds apace. Of late, there has been considerable pessimism about the flight of multi-national corporations to the low-wage, non-unionized and compliant pools of labour in the Pacific-rim economies. But even here the logic of competition will still run, and this will drive even these economies to pursue the use of robotic technologies in manufacturing. Performativity is the principle: the technical means will always supersede the moral purpose of the defined ends. The response in the United States and Europe has been to realize that nation states can no longer act on behalf of their own manufacturing organizations. The liberalization of world trade makes national government interventions to protect their domestic economies from international competition increasingly inappropriate. And even if they wanted to, it would be very difficult. As Lyotard foresaw, the transnational corporations can move capital and production almost at will across the globe, forever in search of a better rate of return.

But it is in the realm of work organization that post-Fordist techniques have gained ground; and not just in manufacturing, but also — as I shall argue later in Chapter 8 — in the agencies of the welfare state. Put generally, post-Fordism is said to accord with flexible specialization. Hirst and Zeitlin (1991, p. 2) define it as [...] 'the manufacture of a wide and changing array of customized products using flexible, general-purpose machinery and skilled, adaptable workers.' They make three further important points.

- First, mass production is not inherently inferior, because this kind of evaluation has to be made in relation to the market environment of the organization. That is to say, a stable product in a stable environment would be more efficiently produced by using mass-production techniques; on the other hand, a fast-changing market might be better served by a flexible specialization mode, one able to cope with the demand for customized products.
- Second, they suspect that firms choose neither one form nor the other, preferring to keep their options open (6).
- Third, they suggest that it is somewhat tempting to link post-Fordist work processes with postmodernist culture (which is considered in the next section), thereby presenting an interpretation of society which is fluid not fixed, which is individualistic not collectivistic, which is consumerist and service-oriented rather than focused on production, which emphasizes style not substance, and which is marked by interest-driven politics rather than mass movements (11).

On this third point, they make the telling point that Italy, Germany and Japan are hardly models of 'post-modernist social and cultural fluidity', yet each one, Japan especially, has adopted forms of flexible specialization. This 'post-modernist social and cultural fluidity' is now analysed.

Postmodernism: The Cultural Expression of Postmodernity

The American sociologist, Daniel Bell, has argued that capitalism has evolved from entrepreneurial capitalism (to about 1850), to monopoly capitalism (to about 1960), and beyond to the current capitalism of transnational corporations operating in global (not local, or national) markets. This development has seen an emerging and profound cultural contradiction: the work ethic which hitherto had enabled the process of production has now been superseded by a consumerist 'ethic', an ethic which capitalism, in order to generate mass consumer needs, has had to foster. It is as if, now, the only thing that we all agree upon is that we should each be different, and that our individual differences are but manifested by the symbolization of the self, be it in the form of clothing, cars or whatever 'taste'. In this creeping development of 'odious individualism', Bell refers to man as 'solus' not 'socius'.

This, he asserts, has emerged in a market-driven society which spawned strong notions of individual choice and individual responsibility. Thus ensues a 'corruption' of the social order: unemployment and the destruction of the environment (Bell, 1990b, p. 74).

In this century, according to Bell, we have seen the decline of the Puritan temper and the Protestant ethic which had permitted capitalism to develop. Capitalism is said to have consumed the very moral legacy which had served to build it up. Nevertheless, the recent re-assertion of the work ethic (for those in work) by employers has been strongly felt, but it is also associated with an emerging 'fat cats' hedonism for some managerial groups. Deferred gratification has increasingly given way to immediate narcissism and hedonism, or at least to a 'calculating hedonism' (Featherstone, 1991, p. 59). The advertisers promise everything, and the credit card enables some of us to get it, now. In sum, postmodernist culture raises very serious questions about the capacity of society to cohere. In one sense, postmodernism is not a culture at all. Bauman (1988, p. 798) is very blunt about this: '[. . .] the concept of postmodern culture is a contradiction in terms, an oxymoron. [. . .] Postmodernity, in other words, is a post-cultural condition'. Why? Because there is no authority left which is prepared, or able, to arbitrate, to evaluate. Equally, if we define a culture as a shared way of seeing the world, then postmodernism as a culture does not easily meet that criterion, except in the sense that individuals may share only the idea of wishing to be different, and to express it through a 'bought' identity, one adorned with the labels which name the producers of the products. To consume, however, presupposes that we have the money to do so. Those who have it can rest easily in the belief that those who lack it have chosen not to have it. 'In postmodern practice, liberty boils down to consumer choice. [. . .] With bated breath, residents of the theft-proof, fortified homes glue themselves to their TV screens for the spectacle of brutality that is the mark of the brutalized' (Bauman, 1991, p. 259). The dispossessed become mere spectacles, the objects of aesthetic, not ethical, deliberation by the 'contented' middle class (Harvey, 1989, p. 328; Galbraith, 1992). Even so, the middle class may not now be as contented as they used to be, caught between the pull of market forces and humanism, or between work and unemployment.

Few join in the collective rituals of the church; many worship, privately, in the new citadels of consumption, the shopping malls. For example, in Canada the West Edmonton Mall touts itself as the eighth wonder of the world, boasting the world's largest shopping edifice, with 800 shops and services; with GalaxyLand, the world's largest indoor amusement park; with World Waterpark, the world's largest wave pool; and so on. The Fantasyland Hotel with 'themed' rooms completes the attraction. In such settings the object of worship is the self. It is an age of niche marketing, not mass marketing. It is an age of spectacle, where superficiality runs deep. It is an age of consumer choice, of private providers, of diversity, of flexibility, of flux, of uncertainty; perhaps even of confusion, not to say panic. Indeed, according to Bell, bourgeois culture 'has collapsed and the demonic cavorts everywhere, for there are few taboos' (Bell, 1990b, p. 69). The consumption is both of the material and of the visual. We quite literally 'buy into' ideas and experiences which are sold, for profit, as life-styles. As illusions, or simulacra, these life-style 'products' can enable us to 'be', but only for a while, until we 'need' a new set of illusions to help us to make sense of it all. Public discourse is trivialized. The Watergate investigative journalist Carl Bernstein refers to America as a 'talk-show nation', in which public discourse is reduced to 'ranting and raving and posturing', an 'idiot' culture (Bernstein, 1992, p. 19). Since 1992 in the United States privately funded 'talk radio' stations have been accused of impassioned right-wing diatribes (Dunn, 1996). There is said to be an 'amusement', theme-park culture of commodified spectacles and simulated realities which promise gratification, but which instead produce panic (Langman, 1991, p. 166). America is said to be a society in which heroes are mass-produced, one even having been elected president (Langman, 1991, p. 183). Theme-park culture is writ large.

Baudrillard's (1988) *America* reinforces the superficiality of the sign — of the simulation — in America:

> America is the original version of modernity. We (the Europeans) are the dubbed or subtitled version. America ducks the question of origins; it cultivates no origin or mythical authenticity; it has no past and no founding truth. Having known no primitive accumulation of time, it lives in a perpetual present. Having seen no slow, centuries-long accumulation of a principle of truth, it lives in perpetual simulation, in a perpetual present of signs. (Baudrillard, 1988, p. 76; brackets added)

Increasingly, experience is lived vicariously. Image and reality blur. The age of 'virtual reality' is said to be in the offing, as is the 'cyberspace', itself held together by the fibre-optical technology which is rapidly being 'cabled' along new electronic highways. Meanwhile, the traditional work ethic, the ethic required for production, is said to be increasingly set aside in favour of the consumer ethic. So marked has been this cultural change that it has come to be regarded as the cultural expression of the postmodern condition, and is referred to sometimes as postmodernism.

The postmodern world-view, argues Bauman (1988, p. 799), 'entails the dissipation of objectivity'. Contemporary art is beyond theory and validation. The 'overall impression', he suggests (p. 793), is 'of disorientation and chaos'. Anything goes. There is no quest to represent reality accurately. Especially is this the case in advertising. There is little attempt to inform about the product — merely to associate it with some emotion, with sexuality, with power, with status — with whatever will prompt us to part with our money. British readers may be aware of Channel 4's *Big Breakfast Show*, a pseudo-structured shambles of what has been termed 'toastmodernism', a kind of unrehearsed adult *Sesame Street* with people and puppets. It can be contrasted to its rather more sedate and serious BBC counterpart which seeks to inform rather than to entertain.

Take another example. Architecture can range from neo-classical revivalism to external lifts, open pipe-work and reflective glass. Materials are mixed: the natural with the artificial, or the artificial which is made to look natural. Or there can be a blatant mix of styles, a celebration of confusion, as in the AT&T building, where Chippendale sits atop Le Corbusier. Gone are the museums whereby there is a rigid classification of objects into dedicated spaces. The Groningen museum in The Netherlands celebrates disorientation — it is not easy to find your way out, or to know where you are, an experience felt also in the Bonaventure Hotel in Los Angeles. It is all a far cry from the modern purity of Le Corbusier's grand designs where there was a stark clarity about the match between structure and function. In postmodern culture, there is said to be no morality. Science, too, is said to be losing its way, bereft of its unity, left only with a constellation of what Lyotard calls 'language games', none of which holds sway. Meanwhile the scientists strike back in the new 'science wars' (Sokal, 1996a, 1996b).

It seems that the weight of opinion is to say that these configurations are indeed of great moment. Gellner summarizes these emerging cultural expressions of postmodernity thus: 'Postmodernism would seem to be rather clearly in favour of relativism, in as far as it is capable of clarity, and hostile to the idea of unique, exclusive, objective, external or transcendent truth. Truth is elusive, polymorphous, inward, subjective [. . .]' (Gellner, 1992, p. 24). Gellner is dealing here with the cultural expression or, as Harvey (1989) calls it, the condition of, this age of postmodernity. Postmodernism is prone to fragmentation, to ambiguities, to an irreverence to any canon, or to what Lyotard calls overarching 'metanarratives'. It lapses into perspectivism, into pessimism and absurdity, into the deconstruction of so-called totalizing discourses which have hitherto trapped us in a kind of immaculate perception of the world. It is playful, celebrating the image. The representation is detached from the object which it purports to represent. It is always slipping its anchor, drifting, without making progress. All is contingent, provisional, beyond benchmarks. If, after all, we concede that *all* claims to truth are situationally contingent, then the modern project of understanding the world objectively, causally and essentially is surely doomed. Let it not be said that this contemporary culture is entirely postmodernist. Far from it. Old ways — modern and pre-modern — co-exist with consumerism; rather, it is to say that postmodernism is increasingly a feature of contemporary culture (Lash and Urry, 1987).

Postmodernism and Postmodernists

There is an argument which suggests that *postmodernism* — the subject of the previous section — may have a strong affinity with some recent ideas put forward by so-called *postmodernists*. In order to locate their ideas it is necessary to re-state briefly the Enlightenment view. What, so to say, is to be illuminated? What ceases to be in darkness? In Kant's view, it was possible — and indeed crucial — for there to be universal principles of rational communication. The important consideration here is the term *universal*: that is to say, these principles do not waver; they are not contingent upon circumstance. They are objective. So, by educating people to think rationally, reflexively and critically we serve to diminish the likelihood of their falling to predatory ideas. They will be able to look beneath the surface and discover the hidden truth, thereby emancipating themselves from the prospect of perpetual ignorance and imposition. Thus it was that the Enlightenment was to mark the dawn of progress, of development. By discovering the laws which govern the world we could thereby change it, for the better, for everyone. Certainty would replace uncertainty and the fear of the unknown.

But it has not quite turned out that way. What has occurred is that scientific rationality has taken hold, so that it increasingly is being applied to realms for which it is not appropriate. It has gone beyond its remit. Thus, matters to do with, say, morality and politics are increasingly being cast in instrumental or technical terms. Questions of value are turned into questions of efficiency. 'Why' questions are bracketed out in favour of 'how to' questions.

A number of postmodernist thinkers have raised very serious doubts about the modern project. In order to deal with them, we need to set out clearly Habermas's case that the modern project should not — indeed, logically, need not — be abandoned. That done, we can proceed with Lyotard. And we might note, too, that both Habermas and Lyotard are not so much concerned with the sociology of post-modernity, but rather with *the status of knowledge* in that era. Put another way, they are not in search of a theory of postmodern society, but rather they concern themselves with a critical examination of the modern tendency for all aspects of our lives to come under rational control. They question the modern view that the world is waiting to be somehow discovered, its essence rendered explicit. They are doubtful that Truth is within our grasp. They question the view which privileges only the rational mode of understanding, and which sets aside intuition and feeling. They do not see the world unfolding, according to a pre-ordained plan. Here are introduced three such sceptics: Jean-Francois Lyotard; Michel Foucault; and Jacques Derrida.

In *The Postmodern Condition*, Lyotard (1984) sets out to undermine profoundly our faith in the scientific world-view:

> Social pragmatics does not have the 'simplicity' of scientific pragmatics. It is a monster formed by the interweaving of various networks of the heteromorphous classes of utterances (denotative, prescriptive, performative, technical, evaluative, etc.). There is no reason to think that it would be possible to determine metaprescriptives common to all those language games [. . .]. (Lyotard, 1984, p. 65; brackets in original)

If his arguments hold sway, then the modern age will have lost its coherent view of how the world holds together. Just as religion in the pre-modern age had provided an integrating world-view, so, in the modern age, had scientific rationalism served the same purpose. Religion and science were both, respectively, grand narratives which constituted overarching symbolic universes. But no longer, for what the postmodern condition reveals is that science cannot be legitimated. The postmodern age is one of 'delegitimation', when the 'grand narrative has lost its credibility [. . .]' (Lyotard, 1984, p. 37).

Why has this happened? What, for Lyotard, constitutes legitimation? There are, he says, two major versions of the narrative of legitimation. One is more philosophical, the other more political. Take the first case: the philosophical narrative of the legitimation of knowledge — scientific knowledge must meet its own criteria of truth. So, in this case, legitimation does not turn on its use-value, or on its importance as a means to an end, but according to the rules of authenticity within its own 'language game'. In the second case — the *political* — legitimation turns on the use-value of science in the public realm, and how it serves notions of justice and freedom. But science is caught between the two: between *knowing* (the philosophical narrative) and *willing* (the political narrative):

> [. . .] it is a conflict between a language game made of denotations answerable only to the criterion of truth, and a language game governing ethical, social and political practice that necessarily involves decisions and obligations, in other words, utterances expected to be just rather than true *and which in the final analysis lie outside the realm of scientific knowledge.* (Lyotard, 1984, pp. 32–3; my emphasis)

Here, therefore, is a crucial distinction: that between *is* and *ought*, between description and prescription (Best and Kellner, 1991, p. 161). Scientific rationality cannot reconcile them: it may be able to establish the facts, but not what is to be done with them. It is the distinction between fact and value. For science, says Lyotard, the game is up. The grand narrative — the all-encompassing metaprescription — has collapsed, and we are left with many language games, many diverse and fractured narratives each with their own modes of legitimation.

As for Habermas's quest to arrive at universal principles of rational justification in order to allow for an ideal speech situation, Lyotard firmly closes the door:

> This double observation (the heterogeneity of the rules and the search for dissent) [Lyotard's position] destroys a belief that still underlies Habermas's research, namely that humanity as a collective (universal) subject seeks its common emancipation through the regularization of the 'moves' permitted in all language games and that the legitimacy of any statement resides in its contributing to the emancipation. (Lyotard, 1984, p. 66; brackets[ ] added; other brackets in original)

Lyotard does not purport to offer a social theory of modernity or of the postmodern condition. Lyotard's cause is mainly philosophical, not sociological. Indeed, logically, given his rejection of grand theory, he cannot offer a sociological theory of postmodern society. So, for Lyotard, the quest for certainty is a lost cause. Whereas Habermas seeks consensus, Lyotard sees dissensus. Whereas Habermas has not given up on the emancipatory possibilities of modernity, Lyotard has his doubts. Both Habermas and Lyotard, however, have moved towards philosophy, away from social theory. Both have relatively little to say about power in society, unlike their one-time contemporary, the late Michel Foucault.

Foucault was no advocate of overarching, systemic canons of thought. For him, knowledge was but a construction, perspectival, relative. But, equally, knowledge was power; and if the age of reason had done anything, then it had refined the modes of regulation in society. This power is not obviously exerted. It has no discernible author. A given 'regime of truth' may have all of the appearance of a transcendental set of universal meanings — a structure, we may say. But this truth is provisional, contingent. The disciplines which the Enlightenment had spawned are such regimes of truth. They have constituted us, framed us, defined us. We defer to the experts in this and that discipline. Their vocabulary defines us. They allow us to think this, but not that; how to say it this way, but not that way. Social work, education and management all draw on the disciplinary discourses of psychology, sociology and philosophy. We are the subjects of these academic disciplines. We are disciplined by the disciplines and their 'regimes of truth'. We are not merely the derivative of our social class location, anymore than we are controlled only by the law and moral codes. For Foucault, '[. . .] knowledge is indissoluble from regimes of power' (Best and Kellner, 1991, p. 50). This mode of regulation — this disciplinary power — marks off modernity from the medieval:

> Traditionally, power was what was seen, what was shown, and what was manifested and, paradoxically, found the principle of its force in the movement by which it deployed that force. [. . .] Disciplinary power, on the other hand, is *exercised through its invisibility*; at the same time it imposes on those whom it subjects a principle of compulsory visibility. In discipline, it is the subjects who have to be seen. [. . .] And the examination is the technique by which power, instead of emitting the signs of its potency, instead of imposing its mark on its subjects, holds them in a mechanism of objectification. In this space of domination, disciplinary power manifests its potency, essentially, by arranging objects. (Foucault, quoted in Rabinow, 1991, p. 199; my emphasis)

This is not to argue that all is lost — that we are as much the prisoners of Foucault's disciplines as of Weber's iron cage of bureaucratic rationality. It is not to endorse Berman's (1983) rather acidic comment:

> [. . .] we realize that there is no freedom in Foucault's world, because his language forms a seamless web, a cage far more airtight than anything Weber ever dreamed of, into which no life can break. The mystery is why so many of today's intellectuals seem to want to choke in there with him. (Berman, 1983, p. 34)

This is to misrepresent Foucault: it is to assume that power is both omnipresent and omniscient. Foucault argued for the former, not the latter. There are always gaps opening when discourses have run their course. In these spaces resistance can take hold. The cries of the marginalized can still be heard in the wilderness. Power is never total. Even so, Foucault may have understated the place of coercion in the wake of unsuccessful disciplinary-discourse power (Best and Kellner, 1991, pp. 55–71); and has also insufficiently attended to the notion of power-as-resistance from below (Touraine, 1995, p. 170).

Derrida raises even further epistemological doubts. Meanings, he argues, differ in space and are deferred over time. There is no end to interpretation. There is no transcendental meaning, no first principle which is itself irreducible. There is just a process — deconstruction — an ongoing deferral of meaning, an infinite regression towards the meaning. Presumably, by this logic, Derrida's deconstructionism itself holds no immaculate perception either. It rails against authority, playfully, endlessly, admitting no privileged meanings, or even the possibility of them. It frees the reader; it frees the text; it disrupts what were once thought to be timeless traditions, underlining their fragility. So we could go on, and on, defining and redefining text, only to arrive at a meaning, but then to despair as that very meaning dissipated into yet more interpretations. I stated in the opening sentence of this section that the culture of *postmodernism* may have a strong affinity with some *postmodernist* epistemological critiques. The affinity may now be more clear, and is well put by Wexler (1995):

> [...] postmodernism (that is, the epistemological critique to which we have been referring) fulfills Horkheimer and Adorno's warning about the incorporation of thinking into the logic of advertising — which is the lowbrow analogue to highbrow postmodern anti-representational forms of representation. (Wexler, 1995; p. 76, brackets added)

This chapter has turned on the possibility that the age of modernity — its economy, culture and ideas — is either in terminal decline or is undergoing such a profound transformation that it ceases to be recognizable as what it once was. If the view is taken that modernity has ceased to be, then logically it is reasonable to say that we are in a *post*-modern age. If so, then the term postmodern is decidedly unhelpful, for it is but a temporal construct (*after* the modern) rather than a construct which encapsulates in its meaning what the new order indeed is. The question mark in the title of this chapter *post(?)modernity* suggests that it may be premature to sound the death knell of modernity. A compelling reason for holding on to the notion of modernity as an organizing concept is that capitalism continues to be the dominant mode of production, and for some end-of-history pundits it shall remain so. And even in architecture — which is often said to have spawned the very term 'postmodern' — the modern form has not been eradicated: it has been mixed, added to and re-formed with other architectural styles. What we see emerging in post-Fordist work regimes, in the fast and fickle flow of postmodern culture, and in the attempt to undermine the rational mode of thought may all arguably be no more than the re-formation of modernity. But these profound shifts — however we might wish to label them — give cause for concern about the very capacity of society to cohere, and indeed at a broader level about the very survival of the planet. This is therefore a matter which prompts a sociological perspective, the subject of the next chapter.

Chapter 4

Sociological Theories of the Postmodern

How can the culture of postmodernism and some strands of postmodernist theory be interpreted? In particular, what are the consequences for social cohesion of a culture which celebrates individualism, a culture which appears fractured, devoid of moral absolutes, ephemeral, uncertain? And what part does education play in the production of social cohesion? Needless to say, sociologists of various theoretical approaches — all of them, we should say, rooted in the disciplinary structures of the Enlightenment — have analysed the implications of this question of social order. None more so than those whose intellectual heritage draws on Durkheimian functionalist theory.

Neo-Durkheimian Theory and Postmodernism

The neo-conservative social theorist Daniel Bell regards rampant consumerism as a disintegrating tendency in society, and he seeks integrating rituals — he suggests those based on religion — which draw upon the forms of solidarity typical of the pre-modern age. In suggesting this solution, Bell comes up with a solution (a religious revival) which Durkheim expressly saw as dated, preferring the inculcation of civic morals (Archer, 1993, p. 101). If Weber saw modernity as the age of disenchantment, Bell might wish to see it re-enchanted, at least to some extent. But perhaps the most prolific neo-Durkheimian social theorist of postmodernity is Stjepan Mestrovic. 'The important point', he argues, 'is that modernity produces its own nemesis. In seeking to establish order and eliminate sentiment, modernity paradoxically produces disorder, fragmentation, and heightened passions — in a word, the anti-modern (or the genuinely postmodern)' (Mestrovic, 1994, p. 137). The social constraints are slipping. Civility is ebbing away in the wake of niche narcissisism. Fashion disintegrates into an ever-changing and inchoate mish-mash of 'styles'. This is designer difference, chaotic certainty. Gone is what Archer (1993, p. 98) calls the moral vantage point, and what Mestrovic calls 'healthy individualism'. The moral code is cracking; and, paradoxically, in this age of ultra-relativism, absolutely everything comes and goes. Before us is only a 'Nietzschean abyss' — cynicism and nihilism (Seligman, 1990, p. 122). Differences are but differences — no more, no less. Inequalities are mere differences, beyond the judgment of an ethical standard, for there is none.

This is by no means a recently observed phenomenon. David Riesman *et al.*'s *The Lonely Crowd*, published in 1950, set the trend for a number of analyses which alerted their readers to the growing numbers of unattached individuals, adrift, bereft of a sense of belonging. There is *The Homeless Mind* (Berger *et al.*, 1973), a victim of technocratic consciousness, wrapping up feelings in the certainties of applied science, rationalizing the irrational. And of late there has been J.K. Galbraith's (1992) *The Culture of Contentment* — perhaps written with Los Angeles in mind — where the privileged sequester themselves and their property in the opted-out security zones of suburbia, leaving those in the inner cities to 'choose' the poverty which is viewed from afar by the 'contented'. Personal security becomes a growth industry. People are guarded in themselves and of themselves. In his depiction of Los Angeles as the postmodern city, Davis (1995, p. 355) does not baulk at calling it the city which 'bristles with malice', where the wealthy threaten would-be in-truders with 'ARMED RESPONSE' signs. And even where the consumers shop, all is secured on their behalf: 'In (the district of) Watts, developer Alexander Haagen has pioneered the totally secure shopping mall, a latter-day Panopticon, a prison of consumerism surrounded by iron-stake fences and motion detectors, overseen by a police substation in a central tower'. The privatization of public spaces proceeds apace. There are few places to sit, a dearth of public toilets. Sprinkler systems randomly shower parks and other places where the dispossessed might take refuge.

Times have changed. Lyndon Johnson had conducted War on Poverty in the 1960s, but now it is more like war on the poor. Elias (1978 [1939]) was surely correct when he stated in *The Civilising Process* that the 'battlefield' increasingly resides within us, as we seek to suppress our affects rather than give vent to them in an unbridled, uncivilized manner. But not only is the 'battlefield' within us, it is now arguably also 'out there' too, especially in the inner cities. Even elsewhere, the eye of the security camera is never far away — watching.

Modernity, in its quest for certainty, has paradoxically come to produce ever more uncertainty, of many forms. There is a sense of decay: of modern cities, of race relations, of the family, of relations between the sexes, of religion, and in morality (Mestrovic, 1993, p. ix). In a similar vein is Alain Minc's (1993) *Le Nouveau Moyen Age*. The market produces the marginalized, the excluded, the homeless, all living beyond the arm of the state, ruled only by the ways of the urban clans and tribes — the local 'macromafias' (p. 89). Even so, we have heard all of this before in various guises from the 'fathers' of sociology. And Mestrovic draws appropriately on the *fin de siècle* philosopher Arthur Schopenhauer, who argued that there is no necessary relationship between reason and morality; or, for that matter, between poverty and immorality. Although the modern age has not been without its benefits — the spread of democracy, the growth of literacy and some technical derivatives of science, to name but three — nevertheless it also bears witness to two world wars, to the concentration camp, Vietnam, Bosnia, the Gulag and the Gulf War. And the appliance of science need not wreak havoc in large set-piece wars: it lurks locally. Witness the bombed federal building of Oklahoma City, or the new 'gas chamber' made of the subway system in Tokyo, or the horrific massacre of little children in Dunblane, or the in-flight bombing of jumbo jets.

Mestrovic saves his praise for the long-ignored sociological writings of Thorstein Veblen. The *Theory of the Leisure Class*, published in 1899, has enjoyed a recent revival. It serves to underline some of the contemporary postmodernist criticisms of modern America and other modern cultures made by Baudrillard, and earlier by Riesman in the 1950s. Veblen, who coined the term 'conspicuous consumption', believed that barbarism and civilization co-exist. For Mestrovic, we witness all around us the 'postmodern barbarians', with their vicarious interest in 'wars' on a range of problems; in their use of drugs and other addictive substances.

But this is an oversimplification. How anarchic is it, really? Mestrovic (1991) again:

> Contrary to the rhetoric of rebellion and liberation, the postmodern body is tightly regulated, and in some ways, postmodern persons are more inhibited than the Victorians. Consider the ever-increasing aisle and shelf space in postmodern stores devoted to 'personal care products'. [. . .] postmodernism is merely an extension of the modern civilizing process. (Mestrovic, 1991, p. 26)

Power-dressing, manicured lawns, fad diets, high-performance cars, cosmetic surgery, body-building and immaculate complexions are all part of the care-cult; of image-management.

Modernity is intact, and is extended. Capitalism and democracy seem unassailable in the near term. O'Neill (1988), in his commentary on Bell, takes a similar line to Mestrovic:

> The curious thing, however, is that despite Bell's vision of the erosion of authority we have not seen any expansion of social revolutions other than in the name of the very bourgeois, nationalist and religious values discounted by postmodernism. (O'Neill, 1988, p. 496)

If postmodernism is not really new; if vestiges of modernity remain (and there is no shortage of examples of tightening bureaucratic control), then why does it seem like 'new times'. Whilst Mestrovic has a point when he asserts that Elias' civilizing process — that is, the increasing tendency to suppress affects and to regulate desires — is still very much in train, he would not, presumably, take issue with Bell's more general point that the consumer 'ethic' has come to prevail over the producer ethic. We have 'bought into' a consumer 'ethic'. Back to Bauman: 'This means that in our time the individuals are engaged (morally by society, functionally by the social system) first and foremost as consumers rather than as producers' (Bauman, 1988, p. 807).

To be sure, the consumption of pleasure ensures the continuation of capitalism: the soft sell is the emerging mode of regulation, at least for those (Galbraith's 'contented') who can afford to be consumers. Over the rest, at the margins of the wage economy, the state will keep a watchful eye, hoping that they will seek to contain themselves. And the 'contented' will shore up their property and their person with all manner of personal security paraphernalia, all of which nicely complement their burgeoning array of personal care products. The contented do indeed choose to care, but only for themselves. Others, so it seems, can choose what they like, and live with it.

To re-state: postmodernist culture is, for Bauman, symptomatic of a 'much deeper transformation of the social world — brought about by the logic of modern development, yet in a number of vital respects discontinuous with it' (Bauman, 1988, p. 812). Not so, argues Himmelfarb (1995). Moral decay is not the necessary price to be paid for material development. It is not the case that, as Marx argued in *The Communist Manifesto*, the bourgeoisie 'has left no other bond between man and man than naked self-interest, than callous "cash payment"'. She claims that the historical evidence supports her, for capitalism and the industrial revolution quite clearly did not have the consequences which Marx expected. On this she argues that the incidence of crime and illegitimacy in Victorian England was proportionately far lower than it has been in the last thirty years. Indeed, 'the Victorian "self" was very different from the "self" that is celebrated today. [. . .] This is truly a self divorced from others, narcissistic and solipsistic' (p. 256). In sum, postmodernist culture is not solely the necessary consequence of a post-Fordist economy. It is here that the response of critical theorists logically applies. On this, brief reference has already been made to the work of Bauman, but it is the work of Berman which provides an eloquent critique of the ideas of Daniel Bell.

Critical Theory and Postmodernism

Berman (1983), unlike Himmelfarb, is far from dismissing the insights of *The Communist Manifesto*. In *All That is Solid Melts into Air*, he eloquently points up the dilemmas of postmodernism: between a desire for stability and a desire for new knowledge and experience; between a search for our roots and our tendency to uproot everything; between our individualism and our search for national, ethnic and class identities; between our need for a moral standpoint and a desire to go to the limit (Berman, 1983, p. 35). Like Mestrovic, he is doubtful that much of this is news — merely more of the same — and indeed the very title of his book is based on an extract from the *Communist Manifesto*, by Marx:

> Constant revolutionizing of production, uninterrupted disturbance of all social relations, everlasting uncertainty and agitation distinguish the bourgeois epoch from all earlier times. All fixed, fast-frozen relationships, with their train of ancient and venerable prejudices and opinions, are swept away, all new-formed ones become antiquated before they can ossify. *All that is solid melts into air*, all that is holy is profaned, and man is at last compelled to face with sober senses his real conditions of life, and his relations with his kind. (Marx, quoted in McLellan, 1977, p. 224, my italics)

Berman has little time for Bell's analysis, referred to earlier. How, argues Berman (1983), could postmodernism be otherwise, given the logic of capitalism:

The one specter that really haunts the modern ruling class, and that really endangers the world it has created in its image, is the one thing that traditional elites (and, for that matter, traditional masses) have always yearned for: prolonged solid stability. In this world, stability can only mean entropy, slow death [. . .]. *To say that our society is falling apart is only to say that it is alive and well.* (Berman, 1983, p. 95, my italics)

It is the market itself which explains nihilism. Nihilism, a cultural condition, is not inseparable from the market, an economic condition. Bell separates them; Berman links them causally. Chaos and nihilism are *functional for* capitalism. But nihilism is not, as Mestrovic avers, a despair resulting from the inability of reason and science to attend to the heart rather than the mind. Where Mestrovic and Berman are in agreement is in their contention that we have been here before. Mestrovic sees it in the work of late nineteenth century *fin de siècle* philosophers, such as Schopenhauer and Nietzsche; and Berman cites Marx. All of them have in different ways anticipated much of the contemporary discourse on modern despair voiced by the likes of Baudrillard and Foucault. It is worth noting that whilst Berman sees Marx as providing powerful insights into the culture of modernism and (by implication) postmodernism, he was rather less persuaded by Marx's political insights on revolutionary change. Indeed, Berman has no truck with those who see the next crisis of capitalism as the one which topples the system. No. Capitalism produces and *needs* crisis and chaos: '[. . .] given the bourgeois capacity to make destruction and chaos pay, there is no apparent reason why these crises can't spiral on endlessly, smashing people, families, corporations, towns, but leaving the structures of bourgeois social and power intact' (Berman, 1983, p. 103).

In his work *Towards a Rational Society* Habermas (1971) provides us with ways of both seeing and interacting with the world. It is an account of 'human cognitive interests': these being the *technical*, which relates to the world of work; the *practical*, which relates to how we understand each other; and finally, the *emancipatory*, which relates to the matter of power. This scheme also represents a hierarchy, from the lowest technical to the highest emancipatory. Now, different forms of knowledge apply to each kind of 'interest': to the technical, an *empirical and analytical* form of knowledge; to the practical, an *interpretive* form of knowledge; and to the emancipatory, a *critical* form of knowledge. And, very importantly, *different types of problem or issue logically require the application of different forms of knowledge.* Thus, technical and instrumental issues logically require the *empirical* form of knowledge; practical issues to do with intersubjectivity logically require the application of the *interpretive* form of knowledge; and issues concerning the constitution and legitimation of the normative order logically require the *critical* form of knowledge. Habermas is concerned that ever more issues and problems in modernity are being defined *as if* they are technical, when they are not. That being so, we see, for example, the erroneous application of the empirical/analytical form of knowledge to matters relating to human interaction and understanding — to education, for example. This, for Habermas — and a theme developed very lucidly by Slaughter (1989) — is to commit a category error, an issue to be returned to in Chapters 5 and 6.

Thus we can say that modernity has seen the gradual infiltration of instrumental rationality into the public sphere — into the sphere of morality and aesthetics. It is as if all matters can fall within the ambit of scientific reason. Now whilst the application of scientific reasoning to the physical and inanimate world has indeed brought benefits (in surgical medicine, for example), nevertheless instrumental rationality has no basis for deciding, objectively, how that technology might be used: for whom, by whom, where, when; and so on. These are political issues. For example, who should receive a heart-transplant: the smoker or the non-smoker, the child or the adult? Science is in no legitimate position to make political and moral judgments. For Habermas, these kinds of questions are the proper preserve of the public realm. In the early phase of modernity, there was indeed such debate in the public realm about the life-world. Later that changed. Increasingly the state and its bureaucratic agencies intervened in matters moral and aesthetic. Thus it was, for example, that education and welfare have come to be largely under the control of the state. Of late, transnational corporations 'transform individuals from citizens and discussants of political and cultural events to culture-consuming spectators of political and media spectacles' (Best and Kellner, 1991, p. 235). And despite the current rhetoric of choice and diversity, these transnational corporations are doing much to structure consumption, with many product-labels becoming instantly recognizable throughout the world.

For the resolution of these kinds of moral and political questions, Habermas sets out a case for what he calls communicative rationalization: that is to say, we can reach agreement or consensus through open dialogue, freely arrived at. The centrifugal and fragmentary forces in postmodernist culture can thereby be avoided. Meaning can be restored. Normative values can be negotiated and legitimated in this way, so that rights and laws may be framed and legitimated consensually. (Let it be clear that Habermas is not saying that we should leave it all to philosophers to decide what counts as moral: 'Whether a norm is justifiable cannot be determined monologically, but only through discursively testing its claim to fairness' (McCarthy quoted in the introduction to Habermas, 1990, p. viii).)

All this requires agreed universal standards of discursive procedures — what Habermas calls an ideal speech situation. This does not mean that the outcome of the communication must result in consensus; it means that its very procedures are agreed and standardized, so that a consensus based on reason can be distinguished, say, from a 'consensus' which has been imposed (Villa, 1992, p. 715). Steuerman (1992, p. 107, p. 112) agrees, noting how Habermas dismisses both the pre-modern and the postmodernist positions. That is to say, Habermas not only rejects any fundamentalist or religious affirmation of values (the 'pre-modern' position, now adopted by some neo-conservatives), but he dismisses also the ultra-relativism of some postmodernists who see no difference between truth and illusion, or between good and bad.

Even so, the nub of the matter is the answer to the following question: 'Can there be agreed *universal* standards of discursive procedures?' If these 'standards' are context-dependent, then the quest for normativity, for the accomplishment of shared meanings in modernity, logically falls. As has already been implied, and as the postmodernists aver, Habermas's call for communicative rationality in order to resolve issues in the public realm may be either logically or politically impossible.

In all this there is a contradiction. We could say, on the one hand, that we are regulated by what Weber and Habermas regard as bureaucratic or instrumental rationality, but on the other hand we have also said that for Bell we are witnessing the fragmentation of the moral code — we are beyond taboos as we are said to wallow in unregulated hedonism. Archer points up the issue well:

> The former (Habermas) is struggling for an emancipation which the latter (Bell) finds rampant and dangerous, while the latter in turn longs for a return to religion which he believes dead. (Archer, 1993, p. 117; brackets added)

The critical theorists are equally at odds with the postmodern philosophers. Whilst they do not disagree with their thorough-going suspicions of all universalistic claims, they fall decidedly short of succumbing to the numbing relativism implicit in constant linguistic deconstructions, for it 'tends to obscure the continuing con-stitutive role of capitalism in the production and reproduction of contemporary social formations and splinters power and domination into an amorphous multiplicity of institutions, discourses, and practices' (Best and Kellner, 1991, p. 221). Whereas for Foucault we are trapped within the normalizing discourses of the disciplines, for critical theorists the explanation rests with the capitalist economy, with its bureau-cratic rationality and its homogenizing culture-industries which give the appearance of providing us with an identity, one which is merely bought, to be held for a while, until it no longer serves as a meaningful illusion. Whilst some postmodernists — Lyotard and Baudrillard — certainly do not diminish the importance of information technology as a determinant of postmodern societies, they nevertheless tend to lapse into a position of technological determinism, thereby avoiding questions such as: whose technology is it; who defines the messages of the media, and for what purpose?

Critical theorists such as Best and Kellner (1991, p. 269) eschew the 'overly culturalist' tendency in postmodern theory. They prefer a 'multidimensional critical theory' (p. 264), which emphasizes the relative autonomy of the component domains of society — the economy, technology, culture, politics and social developments — whilst nevertheless showing how they interrelate. In a similar vein, the postmodern notion of 'difference' may well serve to suppress the very similarities among hith-erto marginalized and under-privileged groups. Thus, whilst postmodern theorists can be commended for their continuous deconstruction of commonsense meanings, nevertheless it has been that very emphasis which has turned out to be the 'Achilles heel' of postmodern theory, for it has signally failed to attend to the *similarities* in the oppressed status of different groups. In short, critical theorists stress the sim-ilarities within differences (Kanpol, 1992, pp. 220–21), and it is these similarities which can form the basis of concerted political action, thereby setting aside the pessimism which prevails in much postmodern theory which has been informed by discourse analysis and anti-Kantian philosophy. The latter pessimists lurk in what Rosenau (1992, p. 141) calls the 'dark side of postmodernism'. They are sceptics, retreating from the political, enjoying the carnival of self-indulgence, devoid of commitment to the social. Theirs is an opted-out world, above the fray. But whilst their unwillingness to engage in the political process can be construed as apolitical — above politics, so to say — it is nevertheless an implicit political act, and a conservative one at that, for it leaves unquestioned the political order of the moment. In contrast are those whom Rosenau refers to as 'affirmative' postmodernists, committed to politics, but not necessarily to the traditional so-called emancipatory politics of the kind espoused by some critical theorists, namely a search for justice, equality and freedom. Not only did some of these former emancipatory movements lead to almost the opposite of what they were intending to achieve, but also the 'enemy', so to say, is now very difficult to pin down, to define. The new postmodern 'affirmative' activists lack the homogeneity of their 'emancipatory' forerunners: they are drawn from a broad cross-section of society; they seek short-term and limited goals; they lack — and do not seek — the formal bureaucratic organization so typical, say, of trade union movements. They come and go.

Marxist Theory and Postmodernism

Postmodernists such as Lyotard declare that no longer are there any absolutes, or universals. Habermas's advocacy of universal standards of discursive procedure has fallen on deaf ears. In a related way, as stated earlier, Bell and Mestrovic have lamented the fracturing of the moral code, and they have no truck with those postmodernists who celebrate the 'carnival' of postmodern culture — its playful, ludic aspects. Indeed, they would regard it as more ludicrous than ludic, if not even detrimental to the cohesion of the social order.

For those coming to postmodern culture with a Marxist perspective, much of this misses the point: the central question is that posed by Ross (1988, p. xv; italics in original) *'In whose interests is it, exactly, to declare the abandonment of universals*? Put another way, wherein lies the cause of postmodern culture? Is it, for example, simply the concomitant of a "post-industrial society" in which new technologies *themselves* have cultural consequences, as Bell argues'. Jameson (1984) dismisses the view that postmodern culture is somehow detached from capitalism; on the contrary, it is but a superstructural derivative of America's emerging military and economic domination. Here indeed is capitalism in its 'purest form':

Rather, I want to suggest that our faulty representations of some immense communicational and computer network are themselves but a distorted figuration of something even deeper, namely the whole world system of presentday multinational capitalism. The technology of contemporary society is therefore mesmerizing and fascinating, not so much in its own

right, but because it seems to offer some privileged representational short-
hand for grasping a network of power and control even more difficult for
our minds and imaginations to grasp — namely the whole new decentred
global network of the third stage of capital itself. (Jameson, 1984, pp. 79–80)

The message is clear. The 'linguistic' turn of some postmodern philosophers,
on the one hand, and the technological determinism of the post-industrialists, on the
other, have both fallen prey to reductionism, thereby assuming an autonomy of
language and of technology, respectively. In sum, there is no context for language
and for technology. Jameson purports to provide it.

But the Marxists are not as one in their interpretation. Like the postmodern
confusion which they themselves seek to explain, some of them are confused, even
equivocal. The confusion appears to turn on the admitted fragmentation of postmodern culture. Rosenau points up the important distinction between the *post*-
Marxists and the *neo*-Marxists:

> The post-Marxists give up most Marxist terminology and categories of
> analysis. They require adjustments in Marx's 'original axioms' in the light
> of contemporary political situations. [. . .] The neo-Marxists retain Marxist
> terminology but are willing to abandon certain less essential Marxist con-
> cepts. (Rosenau, 1992, p. 162)

Ross (1988) alerts us to the difficulty of applying traditional Marxist concepts
such as class to postmodern culture:

> The comforts provided by the totalizing, explanatory power of marxist
> categories are no longer enough to help us make sense of the fragmented
> and various ways in which people live and negotiate the everyday life of
> consumer capitalism. (Ross, 1988, p. xv)

Postmodern politics is a politics of *difference*, of continuous deconstructions
of hitherto commonsense constructs which had served to structure implicitly the
compliance of marginalized groups. But now these different groups each 'voice'
their own cause. This is no longer class-based politics, all neat and tidy:

> As a result, postmodernist politics has been posed as a politics of differ-
> ence, wherein many of the voices of color, gender, and sexual orientation,
> newly liberated from the margins, have found representation under condi-
> tions that are not exclusively tailored to the hitherto heroicized needs and
> interests of white male intellectuals and/or white, male workers. [. . .] On
> the one hand, this new field of difference brings with it a new arrangement
> of power and therefore new structures of inequality. (Ross, 1988, p. xvi)

In the face of this mix of interests, some of the certainties in the orthodox
Marxist position begin to look doubtful:

Nor can it be safely assumed, as both liberal and Marxist theorists are wont to do, that it is the economic, in the last instance at least, that comes to prevail. (Aronowitz, 1988, p. 57)

Much of this is to imply that Marxism has somehow to be tweaked — to be fine-tuned, so to say — so that it incorporates the postmodern cultural mix (the 'voices') but yet still retains the critical edge of the Marxist metanarrative. The result would be a babble of emancipatory voices, clamouring for their respective concerns to be heard and acted upon. This is the politics of come-and-go interest groups. It could lead to a politics of me-too individualism, thereby ensuring a goodness of fit with postmodernism itself, a politics of personal consumption and desire. In sum, as Cole and Hill (1995) aver,

Some resistance postmodernists try to have it both ways. They attempt a pick 'n' mix appropriation of postmodernist analysis and critical theory, derived from Marx. While accepting, for example, the celebration of dif- ference and diversity and acquiescing in the oppressiveness of metanarrative in general, they nevertheless approve of the notion in selected instances. (Cole and Hill, 1995, p. 172)

Hill and Cole have a point. Their telling concept of pick-and-mix theoretical eclecticism surely constitutes a good analogy to shopping-basket supermarket con- venience. Other Marxist theorists have desisted from incorporating postmodernist theory. Like Hill and Cole, they have refused to go the way of cultural studies, and to take a turn towards a distributionist analysis which deals only with questions of fair and equal allocations of the 'fruits' of capitalism to racial, ethnic, national and gender groups. Thus:

[...] class antagonism is bracketed out and the 'surplus value' is distributed more evenly among men and women, whites and persons of color, the lesbian and the straight. (Zavarzadeh, 1994, p. 94)

Even so, in a culture marked by the consumption and constant re-arrangement of items and identities, it should come as little surprise that theory-generation itself should to some extent reflect this amorphous and ephemeral mix. Furthermore, the re-formation of capitalism into what has been termed its global phase requires a more sensitive conceptualization than hitherto rather simplistic conceptualizations of social class.

From the Medieval to the Post(?)Modern: A Summary

In this first part of the book we have considered both the economic expression (post-Fordism and consumer capitalism) and the cultural expression (postmodernism) of postmodernity. And we have given rather brief consideration to the claims of some postmodern philosophers that the Enlightenment 'faith' in rationality and science is unsustainable. The grand narratives have had their day. All this, therefore, loosely comprises what we have referred to as the *condition* of postmodernity. Thereafter, we went on to discuss some of the sociological interpretations which can be made of that condition. That is, we analysed various theoretical *positions* which can be taken, not only to interpret that condition, but also to explain it. The explanatory power of these various approaches varied. For the neo-conservative sociologist Daniel Bell, postmodernism is but the consequence of changes in technology to be found in the so-called post-industrial society; for Stjepan Mestrovic, who also, like Bell, has Durkheimian leanings, the fragmentation of culture (and particularly the rise of nationalism) necessitates the revival or the replacement of the lost moral code. The critical theorist, Jurgen Habermas, like his neo-Durkheimian counterparts, has long despaired of the dangerously nihilistic and conservative tenor of the postmodern sceptics like Lyotard, Foucault and Baudrillard, for they have foresaken the emancipatory project born of the Enlightenment. The resolution of conflict and the establishment of consensually agreed norms of dialogue is the goal which Habermas has been loath to let go. But he has been criticized from even within his own critical-theory position by those who regard his search for universally agreed rules of public discourse as well-nigh impossible in a society rent by cultural fragmentation.

There are some critical theorists who are not entirely opposed to absorbing some of the emancipatory practices of the postmodernists, arguing that the process of deconstruction is a necessary, though not a sufficient, condition for a democratically emancipated society, free of a scientism which claims that the writ of instrumental rationality can run through all that it stands for, both in the material world and in the social and psychological worlds. (Their views will be considered more fully in Chapter 6.) Plausible and eclectic all this may sound, it nevertheless cuts very little ice with those, like Jameson, or Hill and Cole, who regard postmodern culture as but a superstructural derivative of the new consumer capitalism, a capitalism global in its reach, and all-encompassing in its commodification of both the material and the cultural. Indeed, for Hill and Cole, one suspects that postmodernist theory is little more than a dangerous, if superficially playful, diversion which will lead even once-critical intellectuals into consumer capitalism's warm embrace. They would doubtless endorse Berman's less-than-understated view of post-'68 Parisian postmodernists who 'appropriated the whole modernist language of radical breakthrough, wrenched it out of its moral and political context, and transformed it into a purely aesthetic language game' (Berman, 1992, p. 44).

But this summary has been something of an oversimplification. We need to be reminded that the concepts of postmodernity and postmodernism admit many meanings which serve many purposes. Speaking of postmodernism, Ross (1988) has argued:

> That it has achieved such diverse cultural currency as a term thereby demonstrates what has been seen as one of postmodernism's most provocative lessons; that terms are by no means guaranteed their meanings,

and that these meanings can be appropriated and redefined for different purposes, different contexts, and, more important, different causes. (Ross, 1988, p. xi)

Rosenau states that postmodernism is neither inherently Right nor Left. The term can be appropriated to justify the timeliness of free-market economics and consumer-driven public policy, or it can serve as a stage on the path towards emancipation for hitherto silent and oppressed groups. Moreover, there is no easy accord between a fractured postmodern culture and post-Fordist regimes of production. Indeed, Mestrovic is surely correct in saying that many of us (who can afford to) regulate our bodies and our affects to a degree in excess of our Victorian forebears. To be sure, part and parcel of postmodernism is an atavistic tendency to resurrect some of the pre-scientific rituals of a pre-modern age. Nostalgia can be marketed. And perhaps the most crucial paradox of all is that whilst capitalism extends its global grip, counter currents of nationalism wrestle within it. Equally, to say that the modernist forms of social organization, especially bureaucracy, are being flattened or dismantled flies in the face of government policies which are feverishly regulating social policy as fast as they are de-regulating economic policy. But even with respect to changing policy on, say, welfare benefits or on labour law, these too may come increasingly to be framed, in Europe, by supra-national legislation.

So there are limits to flexibility for nation states, be it to do with economic policy or public policy (of which education policy is a part). The increasing globalization of capital sets limits on national fiscal policy-making, and the emergence of pan-European legislation in other domains of policy-making may have an equally limiting effect. And finally, policy-makers and legislators are ever mindful of the political consequences of their actions, and it would be facile to adopt an overly functionalist notion of 'goodness of fit' among elements of policy. To elaborate upon the statistical metaphor: there are certain 'degrees of freedom' which can be extended by political action, particularly when policy is riddled with the ambivalent rhetoric of individual choice and central control. It may be here that the a-normality of postmodernist culture plays into the hands of fast-acting, short-life, issues-based, technologically sophisticated, loosely structured and articulate interest groups. They will be difficult to pin down. But — far more worrying — will be the political tactics of those beyond the writ of the state, in Alain Minc's *zones grises*.

There are, to be sure, strong currents of modernism and postmodernism at play, mixing and merging in a seemingly chaotic balance. Is this a chaotic *post*-modernity, or is it merely modernity coming to terms with turbulent times, wrestling with the paradoxes thrown up in late capitalism? So we are left with something of a contradiction, an aporia, namely: on the one hand, the cultural expression of postmodernity, postmodernism, is increasingly devoid of moral and aesthetic standards — it is self-centred and consumerist; but, on the other hand, a capitalist economy must attend to production as well as to consumption. In providing for the means of production, capitalism in this 'late' form cannot simply intend away postmodernist culture, for to some extent this culture is derivative of what has come to be termed by Offe as disorganized capitalism. Rather, capitalism must 'employ' postmodernist culture, both for consumption and for production. Using it for consumption is, as I have argued, not problematic, for postmodernism is a consumerist culture. But using it for productive purposes is quite another matter. Here capitalism may begin to appropriate some of the very consumerist slogans of postmodernism, among them 'ownership', 'reflection', 'diversity' and 'choice' — in Foucauldian terms, a new moral technology. By 'employing' some aspects of postmodernism on behalf of the employer, the worker is now empowered to 'own' the means whereby he or she will achieve the strategic targets of the employer. But no such ownership of the strategy is permissible. This is specified by the employer, who will monitor achievement. It is in the specification of the strategy, and in the close monitoring and publication of the performance, that the discourse of modernity is retained in all its bureaucratic splendour. Here the standardized procedures of checklists, performance ratings, budget specification and the strategic plans all come into play. Taylorism is being 'marketed' with a new image.

How is this mix of contradictions affecting contemporary education policy and practice? How is the play of these cultural, intellectual, political and economic currents affecting formal education: its curriculum, pedagogy, assessment and management?

Chapter 5

Curriculum

Curriculum — literally the course to be run — is not a *given*. There is no absolute, universally agreed curriculum. It is always a selection from a culture, a culture which is itself framed socio-historically. The curriculum — or should we say, a curriculum — is therefore always set within its socio-historical context. It is contingent upon, not 'above', that context. Given that a curriculum is but the consequence of a selection process, it begs the question of who shall do the selecting, on what grounds, and on whose behalf? Furthermore, a selection process implies a political process, especially in a democracy. And it is not merely the content of a curriculum which is at issue, but also its very form, and the means whereby the form and the content will be transmitted (the pedagogy). For example, will the curriculum be structured as short-run modules, as items, or as large not-so-digestible chunks?

This chapter deals with the relationship between a curriculum and its context. Chapters 2 and 3 have set out some of the economic, cultural, political and epistemological trends in what have loosely been termed the age of modernity and the age of postmodernity. Whilst this modernity–postmodernity distinction implies a break from the modern age, it was not the intention to interpret that temporal divide as constituting also a very stark cultural divide. Some aspects of the modern (and indeed of the pre-modern) are very much present in the postmodern. In order to underline this, it may be helpful to think of the postmodern as the post(?)modern. We may be on the way, but we are not there yet; and indeed, we cannot know how the 'there' would be recognized.

The broad purpose of the chapter will be twofold. The first part considers the modern view of the curriculum. In attempting to inform the analysis of the circumstances and ideas which associate with education at a given point, Hamilton's (1986) position is adopted, namely that:

> [. . .] educational practice lies at the intersection of economic history and the history of ideas. That is the pedagogical practices of an epoch are expressions of both material and ideological resources. Taken independently, neither technologies (material resources), nor beliefs (ideological resources) are sufficient to account for the practices of schooling. (Hamilton, 1986, p. 85)

Between, say, 1900 and the 1960s — with a few exceptions — the development of curriculum was framed by the following:

1 by bureaucratic rationality as a dominant style of thought;
2 by the emergence of structuralist theory: behaviourism (in psychology) and of social systems and marxist theory (in sociology);
3 by the continuing calls from liberal philosophers for a curriculum whose content turned on 'purely' epistemological (not, say, political or vocational) principles: what Jonathan (1995) calls the neutralist liberalism of modern philosophy of education; and
4 by the need of both industrialists and governments for trained and educated workers.

Thus the modern curriculum is set very much within the Enlightenment project. The managerialist and posivitistic rhetoric rooted in behaviourism and systems theory suffuses the curricular prescriptions of modernity. Aims and objectives, inputs and outputs, standards and specifications — all can be fixed, fast and securely, in the system-serving organization called the school. The family is said to be functional for the school, the school for the social system, a system marked by a liberal-democratic polity, and by a Fordist production process within industrial capitalism.

The second part of the chapter suggests that a postmodern curriculum is framed within a context marked by the following intellectual, cultural and economic conditions:

1 an emerging intellectual movement within philosophy which argues that the grand narratives of modernity have had their day. As a set of disciplinary metanarratives, they no longer can sustain the emancipatory message which they were established to deliver;
2 related to 1, the long-suppressed voices of those groups whose silence and ignorance had been tacitly managed by these disciplinary structures. For example, the modernist Cartesian view of the mind–body dualism has set reason against feeling, privileging the former, and by implication privileging patriarchy. These awakenings — this postmodernist reframing of what shall count as curriculum — have cast curricular debate very much into a political one. Curriculum is highly contested — those once excluded are no longer prepared to countenance the priorities of white, male, and otherwise privileged social groups. Curriculum has entered the realm of rights;

These two trends derive in part from the postmodernist epistemological critique which was considered in Chapter 3. This critique is itself partly an intellectualization of the emerging culture of postmodernism.

3 It was argued earlier that postmodernist culture has been described as devoid of a moral code. There are said to be no moral absolutes. Anything goes. There is freedom to choose, provided the 'cultural product' can be

paid for. For the poor, this means marginalization, if not incarceration. For the rest, there is a sense of impermanence, of drifting, of anxiety. There is, therefore, a cultural tendency which implies a never-ending quest to re-define the self, through the purchase of therapeutic illusions or products. But this in the 'end' may produce a weariness of 'having' constantly to be a consumer. As an antidote, it may be replaced by a consequent quest to become — to be. So individuals may come to seek a sense of permanence, of belonging, of engaging in the collective rituals of community rather than in the private preening rituals of the self. In sum, the quest for personal consumption and that for collective community are at odds, logically. But temporally, the exhaustion of (or the exclusion from) the former may precede the search for the latter. The curriculum may support one or the other tendency, or both;

4 curriculum will also be framed by the imperatives of global capitalism. In a sense, postmodernist culture is to some extent a cultural consequence of consumer capitalism. The freedom to choose is a maxim in both. But capitalism must attend to both consumption and to production. There must be efficiency and effectiveness, and especially so in the traditional capitalist economies whose grip has been loosened by the growing economies of the Pacific rim. In this endeavour, instrumental rationality is far from being defunct. It is being re-worked, re-tuned, made flexible, be it with or without human workers.

But first, a return to the pre-1960s 'era'.

Curriculum and Modernity

The early modern period saw the rapid urbanization of the population and the increasing mechanization of the production process. The introduction of mass elementary education in the 1870s has largely — though not exclusively — been attributed to capitalism's need of basic standards in the 3Rs, and of a demeanour in the pupil which would anticipate the repertoire of dispositions required of the factory worker. Schooling was to be efficient. Compliance was to be engineered — the raw material (the pupil) would be 'fashioned', just as an inert object would be manufactured.

In the first and second decades of this century, capitalism developed into its corporate phase. New non-manufacturing businesses required workers with a more general education, one less concerned with manual dexterity, more with numeracy and literacy. In 1912, the National Association of Manufacturers (NAM) in the United States defined three types of mind:

- First, 'the abstract-minded and imaginative children who learn readily from the printed page';

- Second, 'the concrete, or hand-minded children (who) [. . .] constitute at least half of all the children'; and
- Third, 'the great intermediate class' (quoted in Nasaw, 1979, p. 127, with brackets added).

A different type of schooling for each type of mind was recommended: college track, vocational track and general track, respectively.

Nasaw has persuasively argued that these three types of 'mind' are not universal and fixed; rather they are both an artefact of the types of worker needed by employers and are a statistical artefact of psychometricians whose tests gave an apparent objectivity to these needs of employers. Under various labels, this threefold typology is still in evidence, and is retained and explained on the grounds that it enables schools to be designed to meet the needs of pupils. For example, in Scotland pupils are today classified as falling into one of three levels in the third and fourth years of secondary education: 'foundation'; 'general'; and 'credit'. Indeed, the NAM's threefold categorization merely extends an earlier dichotomization of mentality such as existed between 1770 and 1850: the 'higher orders' were said to be endowed with an intellectual, abstract and verbal mentality, unlike the more sensual and concrete mentality of the lower ranks (Shapin and Barnes, 1976). Of course, in the 1920s in the United States, and in 1960s' Britain, the needs of the employers for these three types of worker had somehow to be reconciled to the democratic ideal that there be comprehensive education. The solution was the comprehensive school, with three different tracks.

American education in the 1920s saw the cult of efficiency reach new heights. The mix of stimulus–response behaviourism and the tenets of Taylorism stirred the minds of curriculum planners into a desire to rationalize everything about education, from the training of teachers to the purchasing of school supplies. Ellwood P. Cubberley, dean of the School of Education at Stanford, writing in 1916, asserted:

> Our schools are, in a sense, factories in which the raw products (children) are to be shaped and fashioned into products to meet the various demands of life. (quoted in Kliebard, 1992, p. 116)

'The great bane of bureaucracy is uncertainty', a dictum recently aired by Kliebard (1992, p. 122), but one long since part of the credo of curriculum planners who have succumbed to the certainties of scientific management theory. In this way of thinking, structures are good for education — better still: not so much structures, but rather a single over-arching, universal structure, fixed and predictable, where there is a goodness of fit among the form, the content and the function of education. As a guiding metaphor for curriculum planners, the 'system' knows no equal. It resonates with the instrumental rationality of the age. All of the components of the curriculum can be defined, assembled in good order, according to 'best practice', efficiently, predictably. The transmission of this curriculum can be monitored, objectively, continuously. A brave new curriculum? Not so. Kliebard again:

The bureaucratic model, along with its behaviouristic and technological refinements, threatens to destroy, in the name of efficiency, the satisfaction that one may find in intellectual activity. The sense of delight in intellectual activity is replaced by a sense of urgency. The thrill of the hunt is converted into an efficient kill. The wonder of the journey is superseded by the relentless pursuit of the destination. And to condition the victim to enjoy being conditioned is certainly less humane than open coercion or bribery. (Kliebard, 1992, p. 130)

The search for structure by American policy-makers during the 1920s is itself in need of explanation. On this, Franklin (1988) makes the point that not a few of them were raised in rural communities. Ralph Tyler, for example, the author of the seminal *Basic Principles of Curriculum and Instruction*, was raised in a small town in Nebraska. Franklin's speculation is interesting and awaits a fuller consideration. His general point that the city must have seemed a chaotic, confused, competitive and overly commercialized world, relatively bereft of warm interactions, is plausible. The urban schools needed a corrective: systematization.

For the anti-systematizers like Kliebard, Tyler shares more or less equal status with his one-time doctoral supervisor, Franklin Bobbitt, as the *bête noire* of American education. B.M. Franklin (1988) is keen to distance Tyler from Bobbitt on the grounds that Bobbitt was too wedded to Taylorism. Tyler, argues Franklin, inclined towards the softer regimes of human relations management. Hlebowitsh (1995) shares much of Franklin's analysis.

Tyler's approach to curriculum planning was elegant in its simplicity. He asks: what shall comprise the knowledge base and educational purposes of the school; what experiences can enable these purposes to be attained, and how can they be arranged effectively; and how is it possible to know if these purposes have indeed been attained? True to his modernist mentality, Tyler insists on stating the objectives at the outset. From these, all else follows. In arriving at what shall comprise these curricular objectives, Tyler casts a wide net, trawling ideas from subject-matter experts, from more general studies of life beyond the school, and from studies of learners. All this is then filtered further, with the aid of philosophical and psychological screens, to draw out the core objectives. The validity of this screening procedure has been a matter of some debate (on this, see Reid, 1993; Rubin, 1991; Hlebowitsh, 1995; Franklin, 1988 and Kliebard, 1992, 1995). But none of it detracts from the central point made by Cherryholmes (1988, pp. 25–6) that Tyler's framework is at root a structuralist one, by which Cherryholmes means one which is based on a 'systematic way of thinking about whole processes and institutions whereby each part of a system defines and is defined by other parts' (13).

Given the depth of instrumental and technical rationality as a mode of thought throughout much of this century, it comes as little surprise to be advised that the 'grammar' of schools — its underlying code — has been persistently bureaucratic (Tyack and Tobin, 1994). True, there have been some deviations — the Dalton Plan, or the mid-1960s open education approach — but they have been long on rhetoric and weak on implementation. In short, 'the mode of curriculum theorising that has dominated the field is rationalistic and closely aligned to modes of scientific management and analysis; curriculum theories are essentially prescriptive' (Goodson, 1994, p. 29).

In post-war educational theory, sociology, philosophy and psychology brought their respective gazes to focus on the educational endeavour. Sociology until about 1970 concerned itself with the 'political arithmetic' of education: that is to say, it calculated the relationship between the social attributes of children — especially their social class — at the points of entry to and exit from schooling. (There were, exceptionally, a few sociological studies of classroom processes (Waller, 1932).) Psychology gradually distanced itself from the dubious statistics of psychometry and rapidly embraced Piagetian developmental psychology. For its part, philosophy of education confidently set out its 'logic' of the curriculum. For Hirst, the doyen of modern philosophy of education, the logical structure of existing knowledge is 'one of distinct, unique, irreducible forms' (Hirst, 1974, p. 137). Each form — he defined seven: the physical sciences, mathematics and formal logic, the human sciences and history, moral understanding, religion, aesthetics, and philosophy — confers on the learner a particular way of making sense of experience, of understanding. This constitutes a liberal curriculum, liberal in the sense that its successful transmission will provide the learner with the wherewithal to distinguish 'true propositions [. . .] from false, valid arguments from invalid, and correct judgements from erroneous ones' (Pring, 1993, p. 49).

There is no pandering here to politicians, to business, to interest groups with whatever axe to grind: Hirst's rational curriculum has no truck with any of them. It is a curriculum based on logical considerations — no more, no less. So there is something rather timeless and fundamental about the logic of the curriculum, as first defined by Hirst, though it has since been revised by him, so that social construction prevails over purely logical construction (Hirst, 1993). It is important to stress here that the liberal curriculum movement laid claim to being politically neutral, and made a virtue of it, resting easily on the position that the very purpose of a liberal curriculum enabled the maximum degree of individual autonomy in the learner. Equally, it is also worth saying that until 1971, with the publication of MFD Young's critical anthology *Knowledge and Control*, this curriculum had enjoyed a remarkable degree of consensus during the post-war period, at least insofar as secondary education was concerned. But this was soon to change.

So much, by way of introduction, to the elements of the modern curriculum. Before we proceed, however, it is perhaps as well to remind ourselves that it is all too easy to lapse into a functionalist interpretation, such that we could simply think that the curriculum could be 'read off' as some kind of aggregative effect of these intellectual, cultural and economic trends. Indeed, insofar as we are dealing with postmodernism, it would be very incautious to refer to *the* curriculum, for we shall suggest that there are many dis-integrating tendencies afoot which could serve to fracture the rather cosy notions of *the* curriculum which has hitherto been the construction of modern philosophers of education. On the other hand, it would be equally incautious to assume that the postmodern epistemological critique voiced by the likes of Lyotard will also be given free rein. The metanarratives may, logically, have outlived their purpose in the eyes of the postmodernists, but never-theless there are powerful factions around who very much lament the fracture of meaning, the dissolution of the moral order, and who are ready and willing to re-assert a grand curricular narrative. True to their modernist mentality, they will seek a solution to the problem, perhaps even exaggerating the 'problem' in order to justify heavy-handed intervention.

Curriculum and Postmodernity

If the postmodernists are to be believed, then caution is warranted in the use of the definite article: *the* curriculum. Equally circumspect is the definite article in *the* culture. No longer can we be definite about either. All the same, the curriculum has never been fixed for very long. The advocates of this and that definition of know-ledge continually vie for position. Nevertheless, there have been times when the secret garden of the curriculum (a term coined by Sir David Eccles, Minister of Education in England and Wales during the 1960s) has been tended quietly and peacefully by philosophers of education, or by ecclesiastics, monastically seques-tered from the hurly-burly of politics. But these times have been relatively few, and they tend to occur when all is well with the economy, or when all paradigm wars are in abeyance, or when the moral order remains fixed. Prosperity and certainty pose no threats to the prevailing definitions of the curriculum. But, for the moment, these days are gone. Indeed the recent assertions by government of what is 'basic' in education is in itself an indication that all is not well.

What influences pervade curriculum as the millennium approaches? Four are suggested below. The types are not mutually exclusive, and they apply unevenly across countries. (For analytical purposes, pedagogy is considered separately in the next chapter, but it bears mention here that some pedagogical devices — informa-tion technology, for example — can have curricular consequences.) Even so, they incorporate a range of intellectual, political and economic trends which have come to prevail, for the moment. Out of this *mélange*, curriculum will emerge. The typology provided below is to serve as a heuristic device which may help to orientate our thinking about what might count as formal 'educational' knowledge in postmodernity. This emergent typology is as follows:

1 The ludic-rous curriculum;
2 Curriculum, culture wars and national identity;
3 Subjects of the self; and
4 Performativity and the curriculum.

The Ludic-rous Curriculum

In the phenomenological critique of curriculum which emerged in England in the early 1970s, there emerged a powerful movement against what came to be termed the 'absolutist' or 'received' curriculum, as defined on logical grounds by the likes of Hirst. Curriculum was seen to be 'external to the knower', 'imposed', having little connection to the commonsense understandings of pupils. The nub of this critique, drawing upon the social phenomenology of Schutz (1972) and the symbolic interactionism of Berger and Luckmann (1967), was that school knowledge was but a social construction, and could otherwise have been constructed. (The pedagogical implications of this sociological position were to be realized in the 1980s within the constructivist school of psychology.) So, curriculum was not a fixed, absolute reflection of reality, but rather was contingent, perspectival. An even 'wilder' version of this was ethnomethodology (Garfinkel, 1967). Its express purpose was to unsitate social actors in order to reveal to them that the nature of reality — their reality — was somewhat slippery, and could easily be disrupted. So, for example, a teacher might walk into a classroom where the children were expecting a lesson in mathematics. The teacher whom they normally have enters the room dressed in a kilt and plays a lament on the bagpipes. This has not happened before. What does it mean for the children? They become perplexed. The event reminds the children that the definition of the situation could be otherwise, that meaning can be disrupted, and must be re-made in order to make sense of the situation.

Whilst Derrida's linguistic analysis is intended to disrupt, it shares with phenomenology the notion that meanings are provisional and sedimented over a period of time. To repeat: in the early 1970s, curriculum in England was subjected to a through-going critique by phenomenologists. Like Derrida, they questioned the notion of essences and givens. The objective world 'out there' can be defined in as many ways as there are individuals to define it. That world, they argued, has no intrinsic meaning. Meanings are assigned to it, and those meanings will be framed by the conceptual scheme which the individual holds. All the same, although it is a logical possibility that the number of definitions of reality could equal the number of definers of it, nevertheless there are social and political forces at play. So, whilst logically I could decide on a given definition of reality, politically I might have a difficult time sustaining that definition in the face of powerful others who might see it all rather differently. And equally, I might put it about that water flows uphill, or that Newton headed the apple up into the tree, but in this I might be hard put to explain away evidence to the contrary. On the other hand, for thousands of years, the sun revolved around the earth, or so it appeared. Our conceptual frameworks permit us to see things this way, but not that. Things may be otherwise.

Taking issue with the very title *Knowledge and Control*, Pring (1975) reasserted the rationalist view of Hirst in his clever title 'Knowledge out of control'. In particular, he argued against the implicit relativism of the phenomenological position, and the worrying epistemological issues at stake if knowledge were simply to be the outcome of agreement. Snook summarizes the division between the factions:

> Our situation as human in a world is bounded by two ontological facts: we have different kinds of interests; and the world has different kinds of properties. [. . .] Although there is a logical and epistemological basis for

our knowledge of the world (the rationalist position), the number, division, and extent of disciplines is more a matter of power, influence and institutional support than of logic (the social constructionist position) [. . .]. (Snook, 1993, pp. 97, 99; with brackets added)

I use the term 'ludic-rous' here to mean absurd. The term 'absurd curriculum' was avoided so as to preserve the ludic notion — the playful notion — which has been employed by some postmodernists to subvert the taken-for-granted certainties of modernity. Even to arrive at the term 'ludic-rous curriculum' implies a fixed position which the likes of Derrida would not countenance. As for Habermas's advocacy of universal standards of discursive procedures, as for Hirst's forms of knowledge, or Tyler's basic principles of curriculum — all of these rest on assumed first principles, which themselves can be shown not to be transcendental, but partly contingent.

It should now be fairly obvious, not to say somewhat alarming, that the modern project — the Enlightenment project of reason — looks decidedly shaky. Has reason run its course? If the disciplines are but constructions, then gone are the certainties which they purported to convey. Rather than being emancipated, are we not therefore dangerously unsure of our position and direction? Is not education's endeavour to initiate the young into what is known thereby rendered superfluous? Is all to be cast to the wind in the hope that it will somehow fall into place again? Is order possible?

In reading the ideas of Derrida and of Lyotard, we are left with the conclusion that to talk of 'core' curriculum, or (as is fashionable in some quarters these days) of 'the basics', is to embrace false foundationalism. There is no objective core, there are no basics. Even so, the likes of Derrida appear to make the rather convenient assumption that we can screen off the world of politics and power. However much we may be persuaded by Derrida's linguistic analysis, the fact remains that people can be prevailed upon to act *as if* there really are basics to the curriculum, *as if* they really can be structured neatly into aims and objectives. If we are concerned to educate our children (and our teachers), then an awareness of postmodernist theory as a basis for critical professional practice might allow teachers and pupils to read the world-as-text critically, in search of gaps and the political spaces which they allow for. On this, Cherryholmes (1988, p. 142) reminds us that, for all its difficulties, 'If poststructural criticism teaches nothing else, it teaches us to be suspicious of argumentative, knowledge, and policy claims based on appeals to precision, certainty, clarity, and rigor'.

But to speak of power invites us to return to Foucault. For Foucault, knowledge and power correlate. In the modern age, the mode of governmentality has increasingly set aside sovereign power based on obedience and coercion. Power and knowledge are not seen as being separate. The modern endeavour has been the pursuit of reason, of progress, of emancipation. It is Habermas's 'project'. But rather than leading to emancipation, it has, according to Foucault, produced disciplined subjects: by being constituted by the disciplines, we become subjects who have been subjected to the subject disciplines. What Foucault calls 'programmes'

— discourses which set limits upon what counts as real or true — are but 'regimes of truth' which define us as subjects. As an institutional 'site' for these disciplines, education is thereby complicit in governmentality. Informed by Foucault's theory of discourse, Kiziltan *et al.* (1990) argue that,

> [. . .] public education, as an ensemble of statements and practices and as a space of intersecting discourses, is not a seamless unity. Rather, it is a historically specific articulation of dispersions which, in our estimation, is coming apart. (Kiziltan *et al.*, 1990, p. 357)

In particular, the human sciences, for all of their declared scientific rigour, their 'hard data', may never uncover the laws of the social, the economic or the psychological. Freud's unconscious drives, Marx's economic determinism, Parsons' systems theory, Watson's behaviourism have all been shown not to have been universal in their explanatory power. Each is partial in its explanatory power, each is a regime of truth which claims to have defined what counts as truth. But in matters of the mind and of the social, there is no truth; only a 'truth' which reigns for the moment, awaiting a 'successor'. There is another consideration. In the natural sciences, scientists form concepts about things; in the human sciences, scientists form concepts about 'things' which themselves form concepts (Silverman, 1971). The social scientists are dealing with representations, not essences. They, the social scientists, can never stand beyond the human world of which they are a part. Yes, they can see the numbers of people in a classroom; or how the classroom is spatially arranged; or what is said, by whom, to whom, when. And these can all be represented numerically, to be statistically treated; and so on. But what does it all mean?

Foucault refers to technologies of surveillance and to technologies of the confessional. Neither are overtly repressive, but nevertheless they are important modes of regulation. Educational discourse today is suffused with technologies of surveillance: national testing, appraisal, league tables; and equally, we see a proliferation of personal profiles, guidance counselling, therapeutic human resource management procedures. (We shall return to these issues in Chapter 8.) These technologies thereby reveal to us and to others yet more of ourselves. They do this either through direct surveillance, or through situating us so that we freely express, in a therapeutic and unthreatening setting, what we truly think. So the disciplines allow us to think this, not that; to be this, not that. They define what it is normal to know and how it is normal to act. But these norms have no real, grounded ontological status; rather, they are situated in time and space, in process, always. They could be otherwise, and history tells us so. Yet all is not lost. Lest we succumb to the view that their power is total, 'programmes' can have unintended consequences, producing 'gaps in our knowledge', so to say, which portend yet more disciplinary configurations to 'fill' them. The availability of these gaps logically allows those who hitherto have been silenced to have their voice, to expand knowledge, to fill the gap. Whether or not they do so, however, is a matter of politics, not of logical possibility.

From the foregoing, it follows that any notion of curricular foundations, of classifications, of sequence, forms no part of a curriculum informed by the ludic poststructuralism of Derrida or the 'regimes of truth' of Foucault. Any such notion is marked by too much closure, too much systematization, too little chaos. There seems little to counter the view that veridical discourses are but historically contingent. How then does one proceed? If one takes a 'purely' ludic-rous position, then the very notion of educating in the manner of modernity becomes redundant, for there are no arbitrary standards against which to decide upon competing knowledge claims. This is to lapse into solipsism. Alternatively, the curricular structure as defined, say, by Hirst could be preserved, but could be deconstructed from within, form by form, field by field. This implies that the forms and fields of knowledge must first be taught, each with their separate conceptual structures and ways of reasoning. That done, deconstruction could occur. To some extent, this has in higher education already occurred in the teaching of English:

> Texts can be read in many ways; each text contains within itself the possibility of an infinite set of structures, and to privilege some by setting up a system of rules to generate them is a blatantly prescriptive and ideological move. (Culler, quoted in Gibson, 1984, p. 100)

This implies the absence of closed, transcendental meanings in text. The purpose is to deconstruct the text, not to acquiesce in the fixed and final interpretation of it.

Quoting Eagleton, Cherryholmes (1988) states,

> Movement from 'work' to 'text' [...] is a shift from seeing the poem or novel [discourse practice] as a closed entity, equipped with definite meanings which it is the critic's task to decipher, to seeing it as irreducibly plural, an endless play [...] which can never be finally nailed down to a single, centre, essence or meaning. [...] The text [...] is less a 'structure' than an open-ended process of 'structuration', and it is a criticism which does this structuring. (Cherryholmes, 1988, p. 8)

The de-canonization of the classic great works has not, however, gone without some less than good-natured exchange of opinion. It began in 1981 when Colin McCabe, then an assistant lecturer in the Faculty of English at the University of Cambridge, was not promoted to the status of university lecturer. *The Observer* newspaper (1 February 1981) and *The Times Literary Supplement* (6 February 1981), among others, set out the reasons for this. One reason was that McCabe was a poststructuralist. Since then the debate within the humanities has gathered pace. The traditionalists contended that the poststructuralist notion of the 'subject' was but a fancy term for the 'individual'. But the 'theorists' viewed this reaction as no more than naivete: that is, the liberally and traditionally educated 'individual' was anything but free and autonomous. Liberal humanist education was but a con-text, a con trick, constituting framed subjectivities. Indeed, many American university

departments have dealt with postmodernist theory simply by extending this context: that is, they — the so-called 'traditionalists' — have appropriated the discourse
of the postmodernist 'theorists', even going so far as to rename the English department as that of 'textual studies', or as 'literary and cultural studies' — without
commitment to its very approach (Zavarzadeh and Morton, 1990, pp. 52–3; 1994).
Postmodernist theory has been accommodated. True to the image-making and consumerist quality of postmodern culture, these cosmetic and inauthentic changes
have been made with a view to attracting prospective students. It is a marketing
ploy. Far from offering the potential of a thorough-going critique of capitalism, this
appropriation of postmodernist theory has served to strengthen it.

This poststructuralist analysis succeeds chronologically earlier critical modes
of English teaching in British schools in the 1970s. At school level, English teaching became influenced by the various strands of progressive education which had
come to the fore, officially, as policy, in the mid-1960s. Here the notion of the
'active learner', the advocacy of 'child-centred pedagogy', and the view that the
previous attenuation between curriculum and commonsense should be bridged, all
came to the fore. Those who espoused what came to be termed the New English
were regarded as something like 'loose canons' (Gates, 1992) by the elitist didacts
of the classics at Cambridge. But they persisted in their attempt to shift the emphasis
from elite to mass access, from transmission to interpretation, from literacy to
oracy. But it did not stop there. The primacy of literacy is increasingly undermined
by the transmission of images as cultural and commodified artefacts (Birkerts,
1994).

In a similar vein, but drawing upon the new science, Doll (1989) calls for a
curriculum which appeals to disorder, to transformation, to disequilibrium, to incre-
mental not linear progression. In order to illustrate his argument, he draws on chaos
theory. Take the case, he says, of a pendulum which swings between two magnets
(A and B) in the same plane. The movement is predictable and repetitive. However,
add a third magnet (C), so that each magnet is equidistant from the others. If the
momentum of the pendulum is low, then it will swing between only two of the
magnets, ignoring the third. If the momentum is increased, then the pendulum
will swing between alternating sets, thus: A< >B, B< >C, or A< >C. And if the
momentum is increased even further, then the pendulum will swing initially as
previously; but, *at a critical point*, the movement will then appear to be chaotic,
'oscillating wildly' among the three magnets (Doll, 1993, p. 91). A small, seemingly insignificant local change, has brought about a change with far-reaching
consequences. On the face of it, there is an absence of structure, but Doll argues
that 'deep within chaos itself there is a universal structure' (Doll, 1993, p. 93).

What has all of this to do with curriculum? Doll puts it thus:

Closed systems, being centred, stable, and looping back on themselves,
in a mechanistic, cause–effect, 'negative' (equilibrium-seeking) way, find
disruptive qualities too decentering. Curricularly, these disruptive qualities
take time from 'the task at hand' and create 'noise,' which the system wishes
to overcome or eliminate as quickly as possible. The current curriculum

syndrome of setting goals, planning implementations, and evaluating results fits well within a closed systems model. Contrarily, open systems *require* disruptions, mistakes and perturbations — these are the 'chaotic mess' to be transformed. [...] Curriculum goals here need be neither precise nor pre-set: That should be general and generative, allowing for and encouraging creative, interactive transformations. (Doll, 1993, p. 14)

There is an implied reductionism in Doll's analysis: 'For the order that (under certain biological conditions) emerges from turbulence is self-organizing order' (Doll, 1993, p. 163). The concept of self-organization is important in Doll's analysis, because self-organization is occasioned only when there is a disruption to the stability of the system. For that to occur, the system must be open, not closed. Systemic closure leads to entropy. The curricular implications of this approach lead us to discard the orderly, modernist frameworks of Tyler and to replace it by a curricular structure which admits 'just enough' — Doll's term — disequilibrium, contingency and connectivity. The structure resembles a matrix, not a ladder or a set of hurdles. The pedagogical implication begins to resemble something not dissimilar to the child-centred pedagogy which came to the fore in the 1960s. Doll again:

In regard to daily lesson plans the focus would not be on closure but on flexibility for alternative yet productive pathways. Lesson plans would be designated to provide just enough disequilibrium that students would develop their own alternatives and insights. Disequilibrium and re-equilibrium would be intentional components of the lesson plan. (Doll, 1989, p. 251)

Whereas child-centred education drew on the philosophy of Rousseau and the developmental psychology of Piaget, Doll's (1993, p. 103) 'dancing curriculum' — that is, 'one where the steps are patterned but unique' — derives from paradigmatic shifts in science which leave behind Newtonian mechanics and embrace quantum physics and chaos theory.

So are Doll's ideas yet another 'determinant' of child-centred education? In the 1960s, it was the philosophy of Rousseau and the developmental psychology of Piaget which gave the intellectual impetus to child-centred education. In the 1980s, whilst child-centred education in primary education was rejected by government, it re-surfaced as learner-centred pedagogy in further education. It did so because emerging post-Fordist modes of management and a burgeoning service sector required of young people a more flexible, self-supervising demeanour. In other words, in the 1980s, learner-centred pedagogy was economically driven. Now there seems even further intellectual support for this kind of pedagogy. 'Local' knowledge creation — not the grand narrative and its search for transcendent principles — is a logical derivative of postmodernist theory. But — and this is the important point here — if also we consider Doll's analysis on the possible consequences for curriculum of chaos theory, then there emerges yet another intellectual support for something close to learner-centred education. The reason is this: chaos theory emphasizes the effects of individual, local perturbations which can have massive consequences for a system. Similarly, postmodernist theory also stresses the indeterminacy of knowledge: of knowledge creation rather than knowledge discovery. In both instances, the local rather than the global is important. There is an affiliation, therefore, between postmodernist theory and chaos theory insofar as they have consequences for curriculum. On this, Winter (1991):

> Rather, since the mutual feed-back relationships which constitute most of our experience are unpredictable even at the level of mathematical theory, our knowledge of a given situation is necessarily dependent upon continuous monitoring of its 'local' determinants. In this way, the 'Chaos Theory' of modern mathematics and computer science joins post-modernist cultural theory to support the arguments for decentralising the location of (and the authority for) knowledge creation. (Winter, 1991, p. 475)

Slattery (1995, p. 621), whilst agreeing with Doll, puts the crucial question, 'How is this postmodern vision possible within a bureaucratic paradigm committed to the principles of modernity?' How is the cultural code (postmodernism) to enjoin the efficiencies demanded by the economic code (post-Fordism)? And Zavarzadeh and Morton (1994) would surely refine Slattery's position by substituting 'capitalism' for 'the principles of modernity' in the quotation above.

Curriculum, Culture Wars and National Identity

'The right to *equality*, under whose banner all modern revolutions have been fought [. . .], is being replaced by the right to *difference* (Melucci, 1989, p. 177). It has already been argued that postmodernist theory is neither Left nor Right. Although the demarcation line between Left and Right is becoming less easy to discern, political alignments tend less to centre on class-based interests. (At the time of writing the Blair-led British Labour Party had shifted towards the Right onto ground which in the 1980s had been the decided domain of the Conservative Party.) All the same, there are political groups which pursue emancipatory goals, even though they are not explicitly class-based groups. Carlson (1995, p. 340) typifies these Left-leaning social movements thus: *identity politics* movements — racial, ethnic, gender — which have civil rights agendas; *body politics* movements — those to do with control over one's body, such as abortion or euthanasia; and *green politics*. In particular, the last two movements attract those new middle class groups whose material needs are well met. The danger is that this articulate professional and managerial class will engage in politics on its own behalf, thereby foresaking the cause of the poor, whose plight attracts merely aesthetic not ethical consideration. Of the social movements most closely associated with the Right, the fundamentalist Christian seeks solace in the pre-modern certainties of religious teachings, though they are not above using the imagery of postmodern techno-culture in order to disseminate their message, especially to the young. Carlson suggests that these Left-leaning social movements should demand and make curricular space for their concerns, and thereby counteract the emerging hegemonic corporate and funda-mentalist discourses which currently frame education policy.

This is easier said that done. On 19 July 1995 the *Daily Telegraph's* educa-tion correspondent published an article entitled, 'Curriculum chief backs Britishness'. It followed in the wake of an earlier speech made by the chief executive of the School Curriculum and Assessment Authority, Nicholas Tate, in which he had urged head teachers to instil a sense of British identity in all pupils, irrespective of their ethnic background. Tate argued for the transmission of 'our' culture and social cohesion. The article also implied that Tate had equated 'Englishness' to 'Britishness', which had not endeared him to the Scots, whose education system is separate and distinct from that in England. There the matter did not rest. On 19 September 1995 Tate again figured in the same newspaper under the title 'the "betrayal" of Britain's history'. This time, as the Education Editor, John Clare, put it: 'In a speech with apocalyptic overtones, he said a society that failed to hand on the "great tradition" from one generation to the next was "nearing its terminal stages"'.

Clare wrote that Tate had reportedly said that 'factual knowledge was being sidelined, narrative neglected, heroes and heroines debunked and nationalism regarded with distaste'. Tate was also reported to have noted the decline of narrative and historical content at the expense of a preference for source material. And that was not all:

> In its extreme form, the flight from narrative represents *doubts about the possibility of historical knowledge.* [...] The prime purpose of school history thus ceases to be the transmission of an established account of the past and becomes instead an induction to our brave new world of *relativ-ism and deconstruction.* (my italics)

For Tate, the postmodernists are allegedly making headway; and, for good measure, he also reportedly said that many teachers had rejected the idea of a 'literary canon to which pupils needed to be introduced'.

Tate, therefore, is mindful of the postmodern turn in curriculum theory and practice. Of importance is the way in which the term 'story' is used by both Tate and the traditionalists, respectively. Take Tate on stories: he was reported as saying that, 'The English Civil War was studied nowadays as an example of competing interpretations or as a lesson in handling evidence rather than as a part of *the nation's story. Yet national identities depended on stories*' (my italics).

Consider now Pinar and Reynolds (1992) on the themes of stories:

> The stories we tell in schools, formalized as disciplines, are always others' stories, always conveying motives and countermotives, dreams and night-mares. To understand curriculum as a deconstructed (or deconstructing) text is to tell stories that never end, stories in which the listener, the 'narratee', may become a character or indeed the narrator, in which all

> structure is provisional, momentary, a collection of twinkling stars in a firmament of flux. (Pinar and Reynolds, 1992, p. 7)

Herein lies the danger: we live for the moment, forgetting the history of moments which have preceded us. Even the progress towards democracy loses any meaning. For example, Touraine — no ally of Tate, one suspects — laments the way in which the bicentenary of that crucial revolution of modernity, the French Revolution, 'lost all meaning', becoming 'a piece of kitsch', constructed by the advertising agencies in whose hands the celebrations were placed. In sum, as he puts it, 'a foundational event was *officially* reduced to being a pure spectacle' (Touraine, 1995, p. 191, my italics).

Tate is by no means alone in his concerns about cultural relativism. The debate is particularly fierce in America, again especially over history. Catherine Cornbleth (1995) has reported and analysed the extremely acrimonious debate which took place over proposals to revise the history curriculum in the state of New York in order to reflect more fully its multi-cultural heritage. Cornbleth lists the ethnic distribution for the five largest school districts in New York State: white, 22 per cent; African-American, 39 per cent; Hispanic, 32 per cent; American-Indian, Alaskan Native, Asian or Pacific islander, 7 per cent. The reaction of what she calls the 'neo-nativist Opposition' was swift and heavy-weight. Arthur Schlesinger Jr., in an appropriately elitist classical jibe, reportedly warned, 'The national ideal had once been *e pluribus unum*. Are we now to belittle *unum* and glorify *pluribus?*' (Schlesinger, quoted in Cornbleth, 1995, p. 173). Here, argues Cornbleth, is a case of Ball's 'discourse of derision': not so much a ridiculous curriculum, but a ridiculed curriculum.

Consider a further attempt to deride. This time it was cultural studies which bore the brunt. A physicist, Alan Sokal, published an article entitled 'Transgressing the boundaries: towards a transformative hermeneutics of quantum gravity' (Sokal, 1996a). *Social Text*, the journal which published it, later discovered that it had been set up by Sokal (Sokal, 1996b). The article had appeared in a special issue of *Social Text* on the theme of 'Science Wars'. The issue's editorial suggested that whilst the 1980s had been witness to 'culture wars', the 1990s could see 'science wars' being waged between conservatives in the sciences against those broadly within the cultural studies community who argue that what counts as science is culturally grounded, not a universal absolute. It appears that Sokal had playfully — surely an appropriate strategy in order to lampoon some postmodernists — strung together a paper comprising a loose collection of critical/postmodernist terminology and linked them to the subject of quantum gravity. The media had a field day. Peter Jones, a lecturer in classics, published a piece in *The Times* with the header '(Peter Jones) aims a custard pie at practitioners of cultural studies and their pretentious gibberish' (brackets added). He went on to provide a 'self-adjusting guide to Getting Academic Articles Guaranteed Automatic Acceptance (GAA-GAA for short)' (Jones, 1996, p. 25). A more serious debate, including a response from the editors of *Social Text*, ensued on the Internet (Sokal Affair, 1996).

But opposition need not go as far as derision. Barrow (1995, p. 29), having agreed that 'society has lost it (sic) way morally' (p. 28), raises his concern about what he calls the 'tyranny of the group'. His main target are the Quebecois [Barrow's paper was published just before the wafer-thin majority won by the *Non* vote in the October 1995 referendum on Quebec's sovereignty] who have convinced themselves and many other Canadians that they deserve their independence. He goes on, 'In a similar way, the native peoples, the gay community, women, almost any loosely definable minority, in demanding redress for themselves seek, consciously or otherwise, to further limit the freedom of individuals' (p. 29).

In *The Closing of the American Mind: How Higher Education Has Failed Democracy and Impoverished the Souls of Today's Students*, Bloom (1987) strikes a similar chord, lamenting the lapse into relativism and particularism inspired by philosophers such as Nietzsche. He calls for a new core curriculum for the elite universities of America. The message is clear: recant. Forget relativism; return to reason. Appeal to the certainties which the disciplines of the Enlightenment have provided. Faced with cultural fragmentation, the wagons are being rounded up to protect the traditional curriculum.

But is there a case for a more mediatory and pluralist position within the 'culture wars' (Shor, 1986)? Graff (1990) considers this. He asserts that many universities speak of diversity — a 'liberal pluralist rhetoric' — which glosses over the inherent conflicts within that diversity:

> The iconography of the college catalog, with its juxtaposition of pastoral and technological imagery, represents the campus as a reconciler of contraries, where ivy and steel, the chapel and the laboratory, the garden and the machine need not clash (Graff, 1990, p. 826).

His stance lies neither with the neo-conservatives, who take issue with relativism, nor with the liberal-pluralists. Both miss the point. The point for Graff is that the conflicts of the culture wars should be expressed, not denied, in the curriculum. The conflicts should be taught in what he calls the 'dialogical curriculum'. This is to be no mere change in the content of the curriculum: it is also in its pedagogical form. In the days of modernity when the 'master discourse' was consensually agreed, it was appropriate for there to be a pedagogical homogeneity centred about the department, the classroom, the teacher and the text.

It is worth re-stating that the political Right is not alone in its concerns about the fragmentation of culture. There is a convergence of concern with the Left on this. Touraine (1995), for a long time a leading Left intellectual in France, underlines the dangerous co-existence between neo-liberal market economics and postmodernist culture:

> Neo-liberalism describes a society reduced to the state of a market with no actors (or one in which behaviour can be predicted on the basis of the laws of rational choice), and post-modernism describes actors without a system who are trapped in to their imagination and their memories. (Touraine, 1995, p. 192)

Wherein lies a sense of the social in all this? Can Touraine's 'absolute separatisms' and 'unrestricted multiculturalisms' (p. 193) lead to anything but culture wars and a growing politics of difference? Bernstein (1991). Suggests that,

[...] we seek for a type of reconciliation of pluralization and differences without ignoring or repressing the otherness of the Other. Otherwise we are threatened by a new form of tribalism in which difference and otherness are reified, and where there is a failure to seek out communalities and solidarities. (Bernstein, 1991, p. 313)

Let us return to the National Curriculum for England and Wales. This debate, as Whitty (1989) argued, has been cast as one between two factions within the Conservative government: first, the neo-liberals, who advocate a curriculum which is a constellation of consumer choices — a market-driven curriculum, beyond the regulation of the state; and second, the neo-conservatives, who argue for a one-nation, common curriculum which will provide the moral cement to bind together an increasingly fractured social order. Whitty is more concerned about the neo-liberals than the neo-conservatives: whilst we may not wholly approve of the way in which the National Curriculum was imposed through legislation, nevertheless its structure and content are common to all; and it will be a structure which will not be entirely objectionable to a future government of the Left. How the structure and content might be changed remains another matter, but at least the common structure will be there. Indeed, the Conservative party may well come to rue the day that it ever decided to *legislate* for the National Curriculum in England.

Goodson (1994) takes a different line on the National Curriculum. The issue for him is why the 1988 National Curriculum in its composition of subjects bears a striking resemblance to the Secondary Regulations of 1904. The much-aired view that technology be given far greater prominence has been largely ignored in the National Curriculum. It is hardly a curriculum for economic re-birth. What, he asks, is at risk? The nation? Or is it 'the elite and middle class groups that were perceived as "at risk"' (104–5)? It is these groups which have a traditional affinity for those subjects which have been re-asserted in the National Curriculum. The Establishment has re-staked its claim as the cultural arbiter in a post-war period which has seen its influence ebb. It is interesting to compare on both sides of the Atlantic the levels of vitriol in the political debates between what Cornbleth calls the 'neo-native Opposition' and the advocates of a common curriculum for all of the people. Little wonder, therefore, that history — and to a lesser extent literature — constitutes the curricular high ground which both sides seek to control.

The growing band of prophets of doom continue to remind us of the millennium. There is much national flagging of '2000'. In America, for example, nationalism and millennialism have been brought together with much pomp and circumstance in the National Education Goals statement issued by the White House Press Office on 31 January 1990:

1   By the year 2000, all children in America will start school ready to learn.
2   By the year 2000, we will increase the percentage of students graduating from high school to at least 90 per cent.
3   By the year 2000, American students will leave grades four, eight, and twelve having demonstrated competency over challenging subject matter, including English, mathematics, science, history and geography.
4   By the year 2000, US students will be first in the world in science and mathematics achievement.
5   By the year 2000, every adult American will be literate and possess the knowledge and skills necessary to compete in a global economy and exercise the rights and responsibilities of citizenship.
6   By the year 2000, every school in America will be free of drugs and violence and offer a disciplined environment conducive to learning.

All this was set in a discourse which referred to 'restructuring', 'revitalization' and 'renaissance'. True to its modernist impulse, the prefix 're' loomed large. Of note, too, is the re-affirmation of the separate status of 'history' and 'geography', not social studies. President Clinton's administration has taken this further with its *Goals 2000: Educate America* legislation in 1994.

Towards Subjects of the Self

So far, this chapter has considered what, if anything, shall count as educational knowledge in a postmodern age. This issue has turned on a debate between those who say that there is some universal epistemological basis to curriculum, and the postmodernists, some of whom give the lie to any logical possibility of this, and others of whom call for the expression of voices not hitherto heard in the construction of the curriculum. Added to this debate is a further consideration, one mindful of the fragmenting tendencies of postmodernism. That is to say, there are those who are concerned about the emergence of constellations or mosaics of cultural groups which have little affinity to each other except their common commitment to difference. In that state of affairs, the social bonding looks decidedly loose — dangerously so.

Reconsider Daniel Bell. For him, the three realms of industrial society — culture (the Protestant work ethic and technocratic thinking), polity (liberalism) and economy (capitalism) were for most of this century in a symmetrical, mutually supportive relationship to each other. Systems theorists like Talcott Parsons were able to superimpose on society an organic metaphor of interdependent roles within organizations, of interdependent organizations within the institutional sub-systems of society, and of interdependent sub-systems which in their totality comprised the social system. Sub-systems, be they instrumental or expressive in their function, were said to be mutually functional. All this is now long gone, if indeed it ever was. What has occurred — as we argued earlier — is that there is now a highly unstable culture (postmodernism) and an emerging neo-liberal or market form of capitalism. The Archimedean cultural fix is being replaced by a cultural flux. Touraine puts the risks we run very succinctly:

> What is an actor who is defined without any reference to rational action? Someone who is obsessed with identity, and who sees others only in terms of difference. At the same time, in a society which is no more than a market, everyone tries to avoid everyone else, or relates to them only through market transactions. The other easily comes to look like an absolute threat: it is us or them. (Touraine, 1995, p. 193)

These kinds of concern are now also being raised within what Ruth Jonathan (1995) calls the neutralist liberal position within the philosophy of education. She goes on,

> Modern procedural idealism stands independent of any moral and social commitments in requiring simply that in deliberation, judgement and action we maximise individual liberty by equally respecting the like liberty of all. As a guiding principle, this is both open-ended and even-handed, equally respecting the judgements of value made by each and ostensibly requiring none to be preferentially endorsed. There is ambiguity here, however, for though no *particular* moral or social commitments are required for the philosophical coherence of this principle, this does not mean that it stands above or apart from *any and all* such commitments. For without reference to *some* beliefs about the nature of man, the good for man and the good for society, we cannot cash out — or even make sense of — our procedural requirement of equally respecting the like liberty of all. (Jonathan, 1995, p. 105)

And yet at the same time as this cultural fracturing (and indeed the fracturing of the self, itself) proceeds apace, there are quests to limit the emerging disorder, both within ourselves and among others. As modernism is 'exported' to the emergent Pacific rim economies, leaving postmodernism in its western wake, there is already a search for salvation in the West. Here we can witness a government-imposed techno-bureaucratic fix being applied to the cultural flux. The national curriculum is a case in point. But the search for salvation does not end with the state. New forms of individual identity are rooted in conspicuous consumption. In other words, '[. . .] dependence on the defining gaze of the Other becomes the lifeline of personal survival' (Friedman, 1992, p. 358).

But that is easier said than done. We are all on short-term contracts with ourselves, and they run out rapidly. Permanence is thought to prevent self-fulfilment. We are as fragile as the image which others have of us, and when the fragility is too much to bear we re-imagine ourselves, at a price, if we can afford it. We re-sign ourselves. Or we can open ourselves up to the therapeutic illusions peddled by the psychotherapists. Note that all this is a matter of choice, voluntary, an artefact of the apolitical market, not a directive from government. These are modes — literally come-and-go fashions — of self-centring; a new 'governing of the soul' (Rose, 1989). Adrift, we seek roots, and they too can be experienced vicariously, again at a price, in the escapist nostalgia of 'theme' restaurants and week-end culture breaks.

If we are mixed up, we can re-mix ourselves. Enter what Lasch calls the narcissistic personality, devoid of empathy, unable to trust others, lurching between self-importance and profound self-doubt. But there seems a way out: 'Consumption [. . .] promises the very things the narcissist desires — attractiveness, beauty and personal popularity — through the consumption of the 'right' kinds of goods and services' (Giddens, 1991, p. 172). And yet although this 'hermeneutics of the self' (Rose, 1989, p. 247), facilitated by the therapists, purports to free us — to lead us to self-awareness, authenticity and fulfilment — it does no such thing. It only appears to free us, for with our freedom we choose to become complicit in the political, economic and social structures of our time:

> Their significance is less the fact that they extend domination than in their functioning, at the same time, as practices that promote the obligation to be free. We are obliged to fulfil our political role as active citizens, ardent consumers, enthusiastic employees, and loving parents as *if we were seeking to realize our own desires*. (Rose, 1989, p. 258, my emphasis)

How close is the curriculum to striking a chord with this narcissistic, self-reflexive tendency? Even a subject like PE, arguably very close to body-beautiful hedonism and image-awareness, is disliked, especially by girls, for it connects little with their consumption of postmodern culture. And it is not that they are all unfit. Some dance and rave, for pleasure, the real thing, emulating the perfect bodies which are associated with the advertisements. But all of this is far removed from the structured regimes of school-based PE (Tinning and Fitzclarence, 1992). This is no syllabus of desire.

But even if this endless consumption has no limits for capitalists, it surely has limits for us. That is to say, the constant instability may eventually put some of us into free-fall, among the down-and-outs, the drugged, the deranged and the depressed. And it is then we become vulnerable to the siren songs of the cultists, the chauvinists, the ethnic cleansers and other would-be messianists with Utopia up their sleeves. Indeed, all these therapies could well calm us down, for a while, but, sad to say, the logic of late capitalism will not allow us to rest assured for long:

> One part of the world is preoccupied with a defensive quest for its collective or personal identity, whilst the other part believes in nothing but permanent change, and sees the world as a supermarket which always has new products on display. (Touraine, 1995, p. 217)

Touraine's 'world as a supermarket' with its array of constantly changing material and media products relies, on the other hand, upon technical rationality for their effective and efficient production, whilst their consumption relies on the prevalence and proliferation of a culture of narcissism, hedonism and difference. Postmodernity is divided.

Equally divided is the self. The Enlightenment had set in train a process whereby the subject ceased to be the victim of custom, the will of God or of the sovereign. Rational thought would prevail over blind acceptance. We would come to have faith in science, not gods. But the writ of reason has run through us, curbing the passions, desires and feelings. Reason has been co-opted in the cause of production and consumption. The passions are managed, linked to products which claim to express them, but which serve to limit them, within reason. Reason and technology have not emancipated us. Our dilemma is that in order to be effective we must cease to be affective.

Recall Mestrovic's (1993, p. xiv) stark comment in *The Barbarian Temperament*: '[. . .] the modernist faith in the ability of rationality to contain barbarism has been severely shaken in recent years.' Gone is what he calls the 'healthy individualism'. In its place is an egoistical, narcissistic individualism. Echoing Veblen, Mestrovic believes that western civilization is both peaceable as well as barbaric, and that beneath the veneer of good manners and civility there lurks a dark side. The rituals which surround sporting activities are examples. Even nature programmes on television seem to be increasingly focusing on the conflict and killing of one species by another. So violence is lived vicariously, but only for those who can afford the goods and services which can provide it. For others, violence is a daily reality.

Consider this further. The affects have been contained, especially in those strata of society whose material needs are assured. In his two-volume work *The Civilising Process* (written in 1939, but of great relevance now), Elias argued that since the beginning of courtly society around 1600, relationships between people became based less on fear and aggression, and more on interdependence. What marked this civilizing process was that the individual came to prevent the expression of desires, impulses and passions. Good manners replaced bad habits (Hartley, 1993a). Desire was driven underground. In a similar neo-Durkheimian vein, Giddens (1991) refers to the 'privatisation of passion' (p. 162) and to the 'sequestration of experience' which 'refers here to connected processes of concealment which set apart the routines of ordinary life from the following phenomena: madness; criminality; sickness and death; sexuality; and nature' (p. 156).

What can be done to re-integrate us? Do we continually seek the quick fixes offered by the illusion-mongers? Do we withdraw into what we once knew as the basics? Indeed, the turn towards conservatism is everywhere evident. Tough-minded penal policies ('three strikes and you're out'; the revival of the death penalty; maximum security, retributive prison regimes where 'life means life'), the resurgence of ethnic and national ties, devil-take-the hindmost neo-liberal economics. But also there is a turn away from the party political process, perhaps born of a despair about the ability of national governments to change things for the better. Beyond that comes cynicism and the search for time-honoured remedies or 'alternative' life-styles.

In the modern age — especially during the early days of mass elementary education — the school had an explicit purpose in socializing the pupil into a moral order. Teachers were the new 'secular priests', as Durkheim put it. Social skills, as we might now call them, were explicitly taught through drills. Even subjects like art and embroidery could be used to make the messages and maxims of the Protestant work ethic. Once made, the signs would be displayed about the classroom, in neat rows, neatly spaced, framed. As the bureaucratic ways came to be instilled — to be taken for granted — the explicit, formal teaching of social skills fades into the background, no longer needed. Of course, there were always transgressors, but they could be coerced into line; or, later, could be the objects of Skinnerian behaviour-modification techniques. But it would be fair to say that the transmission of social behaviour gradually became the preserve of the hidden curriculum. That is not to say that there had previously been no hidden curriculum. There is always an architecture, a mode of assessment, a structure to the curriculum, all of which in their entirety convey tacit messages about conventional behaviour. Rather, it is to state that in those early days nothing was left to chance: social behaviour was taught explicitly *and* implicitly, in a mutually reinforcing manner.

In the early 1960s, there were attempts to alter the hidden curriculum of the school, particularly the primary school. As an ideal type, child-centred, progressive education was not new. It had been endorsed, for example, in the Hadow Reports of the 1930s. But then the time had not been right for the culture to absorb it, and it lay in waiting, so to say, for more propitious conditions. These emerged in the 1960s, at the point when some say that the dawn of postmodern culture was beginning. Indeed, the intellectual, social and economic conditions were such that progressive education might take hold. In intellectual circles, existential philosophy and social phenomenology assigned primacy and purpose — or agency — to the individual, who was no longer said to be the passive puppet of social forces, but who was indeed the very maker of them. In social terms, the post-war 'baby-boomers' took stock of the totalitarian and bureaucratic world they had inherited. Had not 'reason' led to mass destruction, and, with the bomb, to the fear of even more? Had not women and people of colour been for too long set aside? And added to this was an economy of low inflation, low unemployment and the prospect of continuing high growth. With tax revenues pouring into the treasury, the demands of the individual and of the oppressed could well be afforded, provided that the consumption of goods could be maintained, and expanded. But how to expand demand? Had not the hidden curriculum of the schools been to foster production, not consumption?

Child-centred education (or progressive education, or — in America — open education) seemed to resonate with all of these intellectual, social and economic conditions. Intellectually, its roots in Rousseau's romanticism implied the freedom to be playful, to be creative, to be free of the bureaucratic imperative. North American educators beat a path to the exemplars of progressive primary education in England. The Plowden Report of 1967 seemed to enjoy the status of a sacred text, and its slogans could be chanted at will by its proselytizers. Only a few distant voices in the Conservative party (then out of government) preached heresy, predicting chaos and demoralization. Elsewhere the 'hidden persuaders' (Packard, 1981) in the advertising industry, along with commercial television, promoted consumption. So here was a new educational discourse which spoke of choosing, playing, needs and freedom — music to the ears of those who were set upon commodifying the senses and the passions. This was an educational philosophy which could indeed mean business.

Or so it seemed. There were a few hitches. First, child-centred education was more or less confined to the infants school, not the secondary school. Second, it was honoured more in theory than in practice, for teachers could not easily intend away their own bureaucratic and didactic training. Third, and most important, the West in the early 1970s fell into an economic recession, no longer able to continue its expansion of the welfare state. On the face of it, the solution seemed simple enough: get back to moral and curricular basics; and do more with less.

But it was not to be that easy. High levels of youth unemployment posed a real risk to society. Within a very short space of time, optimism gave way to pessimism, from spending to cuts, from work to the dole queue. All this came, too, at a time when demographic factors — a rising level of so-called 'young people' in the sixteen to nineteen age-range — began to peak. Meanwhile, the advertising agencies had prompted demands for personalized goods and services which could not be met. To the east, Japan had re-tooled its factories and re-skilled its workforce. Both could multi-task and be re-programmed almost at will. In the face of this emerging lean flexibility, the British economy looked dated. More than this, the young were no longer willing for their part to kow-tow to coercion. They had to be coaxed into flexible but productive behaviour. The old hidden curriculum was 'delivering' the wrong message, and it was ill-received by many young people. More importantly, it was not the only message. They were increasingly exposed to the all-consuming multi-media, and correspondingly less to those old institutional purveyors of conformity: the family, the church, the factory and the school.

A new mode of regulation was required, quickly. It had to appeal to consumer culture, to flexible capitalism (both consumption and production) and to ensure democratic social order. New school *subjects of the self*, as I term them, were quickly introduced. The hidden curriculum was made manifest, as it had been in the 1880s. The expressive was to be instrumentalized (Hartley, 1985). These new person-centred, self-centred subjects ran under the banner of personal and social education (PSE), or personal and social development (PSD), or social and life skills. Their product was more in their process; indeed the process was the product. Experiential learning came to be the new pedagogical order.

This new learner-centred education was to some extent a re-worked child-centred education, but with a few important differences. Whereas child-centred education had been 'centred' mainly on children of primary school age, the 'new' learner-centred subjects of the self were mainly for the 14–18-year age-range, especially for those young people who were less than fully committed to a more didactic and academic education. Whereas child-centred education had appealed to romantic (uncompetitive) individualism, the subjects of the self rested more easily in the discourse of the 1960s' therapists, with its calls for self-esteem, empowerment, self-awareness and self-supervision. Here speaks the effective, socially skilled self who has been explicitly taught to be so. This is self-management. It is the formal acquisition of a repertoire of dispositions which will cope effectively with the new managerial regimes of the workplace and with the uncertainties of a life which demands flexibility and adaptation to change. This range of social skills is as crucial to living and working (or not working) today as the social skills which taught conformity to a standardized bureaucratic order were during the early part of the modern age. The mode of regulation is now different. Beneath these new school subjects there emerges a new hidden curriculum which is at one with them.

All this is entirely consonant with the new modes of regulation: what Rose (1989) calls 'governing the soul'. The purpose of therapy no longer seems to be the *treatment* of some pathology of the personality; rather it is to *educate* us into the skills of personal effectiveness and emancipation. This is self-regulation of a very high order. And it is very much in keeping with Elias's view that the civilizing process requires ever-increasing suppression and management of the affects. It resonates too with Mestrovic's view that total care of the self applies not only to the body but also to the personality. But there is a paradox in all this. Beneath the discourse of emancipation and self-management there is an attendant rise in the degree of doubt:

> [...] a constant self-doubt, a constant scrutiny and evaluation of how one performs, the construction of one's personal part in social existence as something to be calibrated and judged in its minute particulars. [...] The self becomes the target of a reflexive objectifying gaze. (Rose, 1989, p. 239)

This self-reflective self is a self which is prone not to reflect on the social structures which frame it. It is introspective; critical, but only of the self, and in relationship to accepted and given social conditions. The expectation is that children so educated will seek to locate the causes of the vicissitudes of life within only themselves.

Take an example drawn from the National Vocational Qualifications (NVQ) in England. The unit is about 'Personal Autonomy'. These units comprise 'elements' and 'performance criteria', an example of which is,

> **Element**: Identify personal strengths and weaknesses and set targets for self development in a range of applications and contexts.
>
> [Among the **Performance Criteria** are]:
>
> an appropriate and relevant range of evaluation and decision making frameworks for the identification of strengths and weaknesses is identified and accessed.
>
> an appropriate and sufficient amount of relevant personal data is collected and made available.

strengths and weaknesses are assessed within the limitation of the evaluation instrument(s) and are clearly prioritised for future action. (Jessup,
1991, p. 84; with brackets added)

Clearly, this 'personal autonomy' is very much framed by what counts as
'strengths' and 'weaknesses', and by what is 'appropriate'. This personal autonomy
with its echoes of therapy and empowerment is to be regarded very much as *functional* autonomy. These personal skills are perceived to be core skills for an emerging flexible workforce.

Will these subjects of the self persist as postmodernity comes to pass? It is
likely that, for a while, they will. Once, however, the disposition which they foster
comes to be regarded as natural, as commonplace, then the need for these formal
subjects will recede, just as formal social skills training in the modern age did so.
The sense of faking or managing fraternization (Ritzer, 1993) may eventually abate.
All the same, a matter so crucial cannot be left to chance, or even simply to these new
subjects of the self. What is occurring is nothing less than a required transformation
of the self in a society which is itself in a state of profound transformation: economically, intellectually, morally and culturally. Indeed, we have fallen to images, but
we cannot settle with any one image of ourselves. We must, so to say, be our own
iconoclast, ceasing to be static, constantly in process, thereby facilitating the transformation of society itself. These individual transformations are first and foremost
functional for economic revival and renewal, but are couched in terms of individual
reflection and renewal.

It is no accident that these new subjects of the self serve to combine and to
define the transformation of the self on behalf of the economy. There is no decep-
tion here. The ends of these courses are highly explicit. This is not so much the case
with the investment of funds now being made in guidance counselling: personal,
educational and vocational. The quest to articulate all levels of education into a
system comprising credit-laden modules, level by level, portends a need for a
corresponding expert system of guidance. In the words of the Scottish Office,
'[. . .] developing self-reliance in students through an *appropriate* measure of
responsibility for their own learning' (Scottish Office, 1992, p. 3; my emphasis). It
goes on, 'The process of guidance is a way of assisting the learner to become more
autonomous and self-reliant' (*Ibid.*). At the same time, however, guidance is also
what Foucault would call 'pastoral power'. Whereas in days past the church had
'exerted' the pastoral power of the confessional so as to ensure salvation in the
after-life, now the state, through means such as guidance counselling and the
emerging subjects of the self, is set on ensuring the individual's salvation during
life itself (Howley and Hartnett, 1992). Mentoring, self-appraisal, guidance are all
set upon allowing the individual to choose the *appropriate* course of action, or one
of the alternatives from a range established by the state. Without being seen to have
imposed it, normative behaviour and compliance are seen as the effects of a free
choice. At a stroke this new mode of pastoral managerial power accords with the
freedom of liberalism, the diversity of postmodernist culture and the imperatives of
production (flexibility) and of consumption (choosing).

But will these emergent subjects of the self serve to render pupils as social, or, as Durkheim would say, as moral? It seems doubtful. Referring to the United States, Wexler *et al.* (1992) put a stark assertion, 'The crisis of education is a crisis in the school itself, and that crisis is a crisis of society. [. . .] The education crisis is first and foremost a crisis of *public life*' (p. 155). Their ethnography of three American city high schools — in urban under-class, working class and professional middle class areas, respectively — provides a graphic account of 'society in reverse', and of the 'elementary forms of social destruction' (p. 110); of an education system which reverses the role which Durkheim saw it as having in modern society — in other words, of *de*socialization, not socialization. But this process of desocialization takes different forms, and these patterns relate to the social attributes of the students. Consider Wexler's findings.

In the 'under-class' high school, comprising mainly African-American and Puerto Rican ethnic groups, the students struggle to shake off the stereotype of a 'bad reputation' and to earn self-respect. These reputations could be earned by 'academic achievement, by dressing, by dancing, by fighting' (p. 79) in the face of what Wexler calls the institutional 'assault on the self'. These assaults on the self could be obvious and/or more subtle: of the former, there was the presence of 'professional sentries' (p. 102) who communicate by walkie-talkie radio, maintaining close surveillance of the corridors; of the latter were special education programmes, which attracted additional state funding, and access to which depended on students being regularly tested, but students regarded the testing as excessive and the programmes somewhat demeaning. In order to 'be somebody', Wexler argues that the students must constantly assert, 'I AM somebody' (p. 74).

In the 'working class' high school, a different pattern of desocialization obtains. Here was a school which had sought to reverse the permissiveness of the 1960s and 1970s, with a combination of both forceful leadership and bureaucracy. It also had a HELP programme, a compensatory programme which sought to maximize students' self-esteem, thereby providing an alternative regime to that of the principal. But the programme was under-funded and under threat. For the students, 'nobody cares':

'Nobody cares' is not only the result of cutbacks, inadequate professionalism and over rationalized administrative regulation on the teachers' side, and family neglect, mass media, poverty, materialism and general cultural 'backslide' on the students' side. The mutual noncaring — which comes from different sources on each side of the failed pedagogic relation — is a *closed feedback loop.* (p. 35; my emphasis)

Finally, desocialization takes on a different pattern at the professional middle class high school. Here was a school which was beginning to operate a more disciplined, less flexible regime, largely as a result of more working class families entering its traditional middle class catchment area, but due also to the anti-liberalism of the Reagan era. Its principal was distant, but civilized. The students performed well, and were pressured to do so. But there were few collective rituals: there was 'an absence of a social center' (p. 65). External management consultants came in order to facilitate communicative competence, but they could not provide it. Most of its teachers liked working at the school, but they too were 'departmentalized'. In sum, for the students it was 'success without society' (p. 41 *et seq.*)

Wexler's study, if generalizable, resonates well with the concerns of Bell and Mestrovic which were raised in the analysis of the culture of postmodernism in Chapter 3. As a sociological study it is of crucial importance, for on the one hand it reasserts the importance of social class in the structuring of identities, and on the other hand it lends empirical weight to the argument that schools cannot easily render us as social, and for reasons which are not solely attributable to the school. The 'subjects of the self' which are now emerging may be no more successful at rendering pupils as social than were the management consultants in restructuring a 'social center' in the school studied by Wexler. Indeed, the very fact that these new courses and consultants are needed is a sign of the concerns raised by him.

Performativity and the Curriculum

Jean-Francois Lyotard in *The Postmodern Condition* asserted that,

> The question (overt or implied) now asked by the professionalist student, the State, or institutions of higher education is no longer 'Is it true?' but 'What use is it?'. In the context of the mercantilization of knowledge, more often than not this question is equivalent to: 'Is it saleable?'. And in the context of power-growth: 'Is it efficient?'. (Lyotard, 1984, p. 51)

Elsewhere (p. 48) — and speaking of higher education — he believes that the transmission of knowledge will in future serve mainly functional, pragmatic, system-serving purposes. It will be instrumental for a purpose, not inherently worthwhile in itself, although it may make claims as such. The privileging of instrumental knowledge may marginalize both hermeneutic knowledge (or the knowledge which arises from understanding of the self and of others) and critical knowledge (which purports to question conventional thinking in all its forms). It will be traded, as information, at a price. And just as the transnational corporations have begun to reduce the ability of nations to make their own fiscal policy, so too will this new mercantilization of knowledge have similar consequences for those who would try to delimit academic knowledge. For its justification it will appeal to the need to compete globally.

This movement towards pragmatic performativity has been developed most fully in further education. In itself this is no surprise because further education has traditionally been closest to the world of work. Already in Britain there have been well-funded and coordinated initiatives to move the schools towards greater technical and vocational awareness (through, for example, the Technical Vocational Education Initiative, the City Technology Colleges and the Compacts Initiative). For the most part, these schemes have been taken up more by the lower academic achievers, and this has been especially so of the Compacts Initiative. What has emerged is a very elaborate model of education and training which employs an objectives/outcomes model not that dissimilar to what had been advocated in the 1920s in the United States. Jessup (1991, p. 150), one of the architects of the emerging National Vocational Qualification (NVQ) structure in England and Wales, claims his model is not wholly at one with the former behavioural objectives model (p. 150), but it is close enough, especially in its grand systemic structure. Where it accords profoundly with Lyotard's notion of performativity is in its structural isomorphism: that is, each module will comprise 'units', which in turn comprise 'elements of competence and performance criteria'; and these should:

> be stated with sufficient precision to allow unambiguous interpretation by different users, e.g. awarding bodies, assessors, trainers, and candidates;
>
> not be so detailed that they only relate to a specific task or job, employer or organisation, location or equipment. (Jessup, 1991, p. 17)

Here, if ever there was one, is a monument to modernity. Ironically, it replaces what Jessup himself calls a 'free market' in vocational qualifications, a 'proliferation of disparate schemes' (pp. 8–9). In sum, too much diversity and too much choice; a mess, ripe for rationalization.

Here emerges one of the apparent paradoxes of education in postmodernity. On the one hand, there may be established an over-arching, tightly specified, centrally controlled curricular structure, from pre-school to university, which would be modularized, credit-weighted, predictable and 'performative'. It will bear all of the hallmarks of bureaucratic, predictable modernity. On the other hand, there will be a rhetoric which resonates with the culture of postmodernism — the empowered, self-reliant, self-aware, self-supervising and autonomous learner, quietly mopping up the modules, sometimes impersonally through distance learning, on-line, whenever and wherever. It will matter little who provides the 'teaching' as long as the state centrally accredits the credentials, thereby ensuring quality and control. In combination, therefore, will be the modern bureaucratic curricular structure and the postmodern progressive pedagogy. It is what Goodman (1995) refers to as 'change without difference'. That is to say, notwithstanding the rhetoric of restructuring and the transformation of schooling — a rhetoric suffused with notions of choice, options, decentralization and learner-centred pedagogy — at root school reform continues to be underpinned by 'social functionalism', 'efficiency and productivity', 'individualism', and 'expertism' (p. 1). The metaphor of Robins and Webster (1989) is very apt:

> The wolf of technocracy is wrapped in the sheep's clothing of progressivism and individualism: flexible education for flexible accumulation. (Robins and Webster, 1989, p. 269)

This neatly encapsulates the dominant double code which comes increasingly to frame education: the one, which appeals to a democratic and consumerist rhetoric; the other, which resonates with the production imperatives of efficiency and effectiveness.

Summary

This chapter has considered the possible consequences for the curriculum of postmodernist theory, of postmodern culture, and of the new cultural products now marketed within capitalism.

Take postmodernist theory. There seems little purpose in opting exclusively either for what was referred to as a ludic-rous curriculum or for a curriculum founded on technical rationality. The profound paradox about education as it enters postmodernity is that, by its roots, education is supposedly about leading us away from where we are, but its effects may be to lock us into technical rationality as the only mode of thinking. In short, education ignores 'grounded' or 'ontological knowing' (Oliver and Gershman, 1989, p. 13), one which can include 'feelings, vague sensibilities, and inarticulable thoughts'. This is in contrast to what they call the 'technical knowing' upon which the modern school is based. They suggest that both kinds of knowing be seen as complementary, which would therefore be to add to our prevailing technical rationality another kind of knowing — ontological knowing — which can be expressed in the often imprecise realms of poetry, dream, drama and music. Here speaks the language of the unpredictable, of the imagination, of the passions, of feelings, none of which are objectively reducible to discrete, analysable entities, detached from those who feel them. Today, we are thirled to the metaphor of the machine, to the product, to the problem. This technical way of knowing — this search for certainty, this reason — should be integrated with the subject who feels.

An example of the privileging of rational thought over ontological knowing can be drawn from an article which ran in *The Times* on 25 May 1996 (Hawkes, 1996). Entitled 'Power of music extends across curriculum', it cited American evidence in the journal *Nature* (Gardiner *et al.*, 1996) that 'learning arts skills forces mental "stretching" to other areas of learning', in this case reading and 'visuo-spatial reasoning'. Indeed the very title of the *Nature* paper, *Learning improved by arts training*, implies a beneficial and causal link between what Oliver and Gershman define as rational and ontological knowing, the latter being a means to the former. In this sense, the arts can be seen as performative. It may well turn out that unless the arts can justify themselves in this performative-enhancing manner, they may come under increasing pressure to justify their inclusion in the curriculum.

Thus we have said that the certainties of the curricular canons have been undermined by the intellectual assault waged by some French postmodernists, who themselves seemed to have despaired of the emancipatory project of modernity. And this has produced its own backlash from those who cling to the safety of moral and epistemological basics born of modernity.

Consideration was given also to the relationship between postmodern culture and the curriculum. More than ever before, education seems caught within a maelstrom of cultural, intellectual and economic flux. The stresses and strains felt by those who work in education may be increasing, and they cannot be regarded merely as the result of innate psychologies. Capitalism, in its quest to establish insatiable demands, has commodified not just the material world, but the social and the psychological. Our identities are literally wrapped up in the packages which we buy. We display our identities, for a price, in style, a style whose life-span is short, soon to be re-made from the re-stocked shelves which lure us to them. Images are traded. Bodies are cared for. And we consume the info-products as easily as we consume those material products which are essential to our physical survival. The fix is quick, but it is fleeting. It all costs money. Those who lack it can 'choose' either to languish as non-consumers (and therefore as non-beings) or to steal it, at risk to themselves and to others.

And yet, whilst postmodernist culture is centrifugal, curriculum planners — despite the rhetoric of choice and diversity — withdraw to the centre, in a rearguard action, to re-group, not only themselves, but also the subjects of the curriculum, building in some personal and social development courses which will serve to integrate the fracturing self of the postmodern pupil, to set up the flexible demeanour of the future worker, and somehow to re-moralize society.

This is not all. Waiting in the wings will be new 'voices' seeking to upstage the old curriculum players. The voices belong not to the harbingers of ludic despair who bury their faces in text; rather they belong to those who see in postmodernist theory a means to a political end. That end is the end of their own domination, an end to what many of them had falsely felt was their destiny, ordained and overseen by the schools. About to enter — stage left — are a new troupe, a loose amalgam of critical theorists, postmodernists and feminists. Their play is about both pedagogy and curriculum, and how the one has meaning for the other. And their purpose is explicitly political.

Chapter 6

Pedagogy

In the previous chapter we began by considering briefly how the curriculum 'looked' in the modern age, highlighting the view that it was amenable to a good degree of consensus and certainty; and that, as a result, it could be broken up into its component parts (in modernist machine-like fashion) for efficient delivery. Thereafter, in our treatment of curriculum in postmodernity we considered how the curriculum might be changed by a range of intellectual, political and economic trends which are in train. A similar approach is adopted in this chapter. Before this, however, it bears mentioning that it is something of an over-simplification to divide curriculum from pedagogy, chapter from chapter, as here. In a sense, it is a typically modernist classification to make. But this analytical separation into two discrete concepts curriculum and pedagogy — implies that the two have little to do with each other, when clearly they are very closely connected. For example, if the form of the curriculum is structured into items which require little integration, each with the other, then clearly the teacher can lapse into an easy didacticism, delivering the curriculum fact by fact. The pupils will have been informed, but may not have understood. The 'Acts-and-facts' construction of historical knowledge would be an example of this. In contrast, let us say that the curriculum is to be taught in a way that not only provides facts but also allows for explanations to be sought and found. Then the pedagogical style will (or should) require more open-ended, discursive methods, with consequences for how time and space are regulated.

Pedagogy and Modernity

In his sermon on the 'Education of the Poor under an Appropriate System', preached at St Mary's, 28 Lambeth, June 1807, Dr Andrew Bell's pedagogical ideas were clearly framed within the metaphor of an efficient machine:

> Machinery has been contrived for spinning twenty skeins of silk, and twenty hanks of cotton, where one was spun before; but no contrivance has been sought for, or devised, that twenty children may be educated in moral and religious principles, with the same facility and expense, as one was taught before. (Bell, 1807, p. 17)

Here, therefore, is Bell's monitorial system for the education of the poor, a system based on both mechanistic and panoptical principles, a sign of its modern times.

It had mixed results. Horace Mann, the Secretary to the Board of Education for Massachusetts, reported unfavourably on the system after his return from a two-year study of European schools in 1844. Not having previously been in the 'old countries', he brought to his endeavour a certain anthropological strangeness. He notes:

I saw many Lancasterian or Monitorial schools in England, Scotland and Ireland; and a few in France. Some mere vestiges of the plan are still to be found in the 'poor schools' of Prussia; but nothing of it remains in Holland, or in many of the German States. It has been abolished in these countries by a universal public opinion. [...] one must rise to some comprehension of the vast import and significance of the phrase, 'to educate', before he can regard with a sufficiently energetic contempt that boast of Dr Bell, 'Give me twenty-four pupils of today, and I will give you back twenty-four teachers to-morrow'. (Mann, 1857, p. 44)

Mann's disillusion with the emerging cult of efficiency movement in education — now enjoying something of a renaissance — was tinged with eloquent sociological insight:

In the Europe of the nineteenth century, the incomputable wealth that flows from the bounty of heaven during the revolving seasons of the year, and is elaborated from the earth by the ceaseless toil of millions of men; — that wealth which is wrought out by human labour and ingenuity, in conjunction with the great agencies of nature, — fire, water, wind, and steam — and whose aggregates are amply sufficient to give comfort and competence to every human being, and the joys of home and the sacred influences of the domestic circle to every family, — that wealth, by force of unjust laws and institutions, is filched from the producer, and gathered into vast masses, to give power and luxury, and aggrandisement to a few. Of *production*, there is no end; of *distribution*, there is no beginning. (Mann, 1857, p. 188; italics in original)

The fourth edition of Mann's report — to which we have been referring — was published in the same year as Darwin's *Origin of Species*. Beyond that were advances in statistics. Francis Galton, a cousin of Darwin, and reputedly the definer of the 'normal curve', published *Hereditary Genius* in 1869, thereby combining the Darwinist survival-of-the-fittest notion with the rigour of statistical method. The psychometric movement had begun, and was to gather pace in America, especially in the 1920s. The population was tested, classified and rank-ordered according to normative criteria, thereby enabling an education best suited to the individual's needs, as inferred from scores on these tests. Here, therefore, was the scientific movement in full swing, 'progressing' from John Stuart Mill's *A System of Logic* (1930, original 1843), Alexander Bain's *Education as a Science* (1879), William C. Bagley's *The Educative Process* (1905), and beyond. (These and other exponents of the scientific movement in education are discussed in Smith and Hamilton, 1980.) The quantification movement did not stop there. Educational administration became established (in America, at least) in the same decade, and R.E. Callahan's (1962) *Education and the Cult of Efficiency* gives telling insights into the mind and methods of the forerunners of today's educational qualitariat.

All this constitutes a very brief and inadequate description of the early beginnings of the (mainly Anglo-Saxon) pedagogic process in the modern age. The process of instruction purported to rest on the weight of scientific evidence generated by the emergent discipline of psychology, a discipline no less useful to the educative process than to the manufacturing process. At one and the same time it systematized and individualized: through its behaviouristic and psychometric procedures it systematized the pedagogical process; through its mental testing procedures it rendered the individual as an objective entity who could be measured, isolated and compared. All this was enmeshed in an organizational structure for the school which, to a great extent, mirrored that of the workplace. Little, if any, of this pedagogical knowledge was generated beyond academe. Once teachers in training had been initiated into its discourse, they were left to apply it in the school.

That said, I now reconsider the cultural, intellectual, political and economic trends now in train, and then go on to ask what consequences these might have for pedagogy. Again, these trends overlap with, and contradict, each other, and it will also be necessary to stray beyond the bounds of pedagogy into matters to do with curriculum, assessment and organization. The argument will be as follows: despite the critiques raised by the postmodernists; despite the emergence of consumer culture, with its affinity for the virtual, the ephemeral and the fickle; despite the growing advocacy of post-Fordist work regimes — despite all this, there is a good deal of continuity with the modern endeavour. (The obvious one is that capitalism continues, albeit increasingly in a new 'late' form, though the adjective 'late' might prove to have been wishful thinking.) Only the type of 'link' between past and present is being redefined, and it is this re-formation which gives the appearance of there being an attenuation.

To repeat:

- First (for those who can afford it), postmodern consumer culture admits notions of play, pleasure, ownership and freedom. I consider this under the section: the pedagogy of pleasure.
- Second, the postmodernist epistemological critique of the grand narratives of the social sciences and humanities has included the parent discipline of pedagogy, namely psychology. Under the eye of the postmodernists, the notion of a unified, knowable self looks shaky, and so, therefore, does psychology in its modernist form.
- Third, I turn to critical pedagogy (it is here that the overlap with the previous chapter on curriculum occurs). I address two themes: the positioning of critical pedagogy in relation to the modern project of emancipation; and critical theory's appropriation of postmodernist deconstruction as a means of achieving that emancipation.

- Fourth, we turn to information technology, and consider critically some of the pedagogical claims made on its behalf.
- Finally, by analysing the discourse of a recent policy initiative for higher education, I bring together these four strands around one substantive issue.

The Pedagogy of Pleasure

The culture of postmodernism is said to be self-centred, not to say narcissistic. It is a culture where paradoxically the very term 'culture' (defined as a shared world-view) rests almost on a collective sense of meaninglessness. It is said that what we share is that we are different. We are, it is said, amalgamations of images — bought, experienced and discarded. We are in a hurry. Time is short. Reality is not represented objectively; rather it is played with. Soap-opera characters assume the status of real people, their trials and tribulations the object of coffee-break conversation — real gossip about virtual people.

Notions of play and fantasy are by no means new in pedagogical discourse. In their construction of childhood as a state of innocence, educators have thought to base their pedagogical insights on what children are said to do *naturally*: they play; and in their play they experience the world. They apprehend the world through all of their senses. This is not to say that they lack logic, but we adults may not regard them as being logical. For example, a colleague of mine was visiting her sister who has a 2-year-old son. They and the boy were in the garden. The little boy wandered into the flower-beds. He was told not to stand there. So he sat down — on top of the flowers. He was not being disobedient; he was acting 'logically', denying his education.

The history of nursery education makes much of children being allowed to be 'natural' — to play, in the fresh air, free of institutional constraints, giving vent to their passions. What counts here as 'natural' implies a definition of childhood which is universal and unchanging. Indeed nature is assumed to have its own internal logic. But this is a moot assertion. This notion of naturalness was to be given official endorsement in a range of reports on primary education in the 1960s, notably the Scottish Primary Memorandum (SOED, 1965) and the English Plowden Report (1967). The 'whole child' — not the whole *pupil* — was the object of these educational endeavours. The child was not to be named, shamed and blamed; rather, social control was 'oblique' (King, 1978). Bernstein (1977) refers to it as the 'invisible pedagogy'. Children would not be informed; they would discover, and in so doing they would begin to see the relationship among the different 'subjects'. And they could choose when and where to do something, although within the limits defined by the teacher, within reason so to say. Rather than suppress their affects, they were to express them. Much of this harks back to some of the ideas set out in Jean-Jacques Rousseau's *Emile*, published in 1762. Much of it, too, never came to pass in the classrooms, although the surface signs of it — open architecture, children sitting in groups, plants and animals in the school — were often to be seen.

The point in alluding to child-centred primary education is not to come to a view on its success or failure, but to put the question, 'Why did child-centred education as an ideal come to the fore *officially* in the 1960s?' (The first official endorsement had been in the Hadow Reports of the 1930s.) In other words, what were the intellectual, cultural and economic conditions which allowed these ideas to take root in the minds of the mandarins in central government and their political masters? It was suggested earlier that the economic conditions of the mid-1960s were relatively good: low inflation, low unemployment, and the prospect of long-term growth. People were beginning to get the feel of consumerism — advertising, credit cards and self-service; and so on. They reflected on their wants and called them needs, to be satisfied, through consumption. At the same time, existential philosophy and 'pop' psychiatry emphasized individual agency rather than structural domination. In sum, there was a fortuitous conjunction of intellectual, cultural and economic conditions which may have provided the space for child-centred pedagogy to stake its claim, with the approval of government.

The discourse of child-centred pedagogy resonated with the culture of consumption: choice, individual differences, individual needs, discovery and play. But it did not serve — at that time — the needs of production, for the processes of production remained decidedly bureaucratic and Fordist. The economic downturn of the 1970s meant the reversal of the 'gains' of the child-centred educators. But the discourse did not die. It was re-worked and re-applied, this time to the emerging disaffected teenagers whose commitment to didactic schooling and whose prospects for work edged lower and lower. Learner-centred pedagogy came to the fore. Its 'new' pedagogical status was broadcast into the far reaches of further education, and its slogans of self-awareness, self-control, empowerment and personal autonomy seeped into pedagogical discourse. With it came the rapid modularization of courses into easily-consumed packages. And through the attendant continuous modes of assessment, the young freely expressed their inner feelings to themselves and to their mentors. Here was a continuous cathartic coping process which at a stroke could simultaneously strike a chord with both the near-narcissism of postmodern culture and the emerging soft bureaucracy of (some) service-sector workplaces. But for the most part, this new pedagogy tacitly transmitted the so-called core transferable social and personal skills of an emergent post-Fordist economy.

There is nothing in this 'new' pedagogy of further education which appeals to the passions and playfulness of ludic postmodernist theory. What we see is personal development for a purpose, and the purpose is first and foremost not the real autonomy of the person but the real economy of the nation. It is the autonomy of the worker-to-be, the worker-in-work, the worker-in-waiting; and of the pleasure-seeking consumer. So there is an important difference between learner-centred pedagogy and child-centred education (Hartley, 1987a). It is that child-centred pedagogy did seem to accord with the postmodernist's critique of rationality as the one and only mode of understanding. All the same, even child-centred education's notions of naturalness, individual needs, play and freedom were all very much framed 'within reason', within convention, within the logic of both rationality and capitalism. Both progressive pedagogy and the new learner-centred pedagogy have, in theory, emancipatory potential which could realize desires (as individual needs), but curriculum has been carefully framed, defined and credentialized by central government, thereby making it safe for consumption.

The central point about this 'new' pedagogy is that it is presented as a pedagogy of pleasure. (Nevertheless, it has less than universal appeal, for there remain pupils, teachers and officials who are wary of it.) This is entirely consonant with the emerging mode of regulation in the capitalist system which 'deploys the pleasure principle for its own perpetuation' (Bauman, 1988, p. 808). This pleasure principle profoundly differs from the overt pressures of the 'production-oriented system' (as opposed to the emerging 'consumer phase'). Empowerment, nor repression, is now the 'order' of the day. That said, it may be predicted that the 'subjects of the self' which were referred to in the last chapter may gradually recede into the hidden curriculum. Having been used initially to engender the new demeanour required of postmodernist consumer culture and of post-Fordist work processes, these subjects — their job done, so to say — may quietly be subsumed under the hidden curriculum (Vallance, 1973).

There is another way of looking at this pedagogy of pleasure. Choosing and 'play' may well apply to the child's experience of learning, but what of the teacher's experience? Pedagogical 'style' is now being re-cast by officialdom in terms of competences which in their totality comprise a tool-kit that will enable 'good practice'. Efficient and effective performance is to be displayed. But where is the pleasure for the teacher in this emerging and empowered charisma-free zone called the 'competent' classroom? (This question has greater relevance in so-called 'distance' learning where impersonality is technologically wired in to the pedagogical transmission.) What now is the pedagogical relationship when contract replaces trust? In a provocative analysis, Erica McWilliam (1995) calls for a shift away from the 'safe terrain of quality, effectiveness and learner-centredness, and to talk about seduction, desire and pleasure' (p. 16), a project she terms '(s)education: a risky inquiry into pleasurable teaching'. Learning theory has been couched in the arid terminology of logical positivism, thereby dis-embodying pedagogy. Her focus is on the 'embodied nature of pedagogical work, that is, on teaching as traditionally an engagement some body has with other bodies in institutional spaces' (McWilliam, 1996, p. 3). This issue has so far been omitted in considerations of what it is to be an effective or ineffective teacher. All this, she argues, requires theoretical disruption, by 'theorizing pedagogy as an erogenous zone', and to focus not only on the desire of the teacher to teach, but also on the desire of the pupil to be taught. Clearly, as McWilliam avers, this is indeed a 'risky' discourse, but its initial effect is to disrupt and to look beneath the cool surface of the smug sensibilities of classroom competences on the part of both teacher and pupils.

Postmodernists, Psychology and Pedagogy

As we have seen, what counts as curriculum turns on many issues: the epistemological analyses provided by philosophers; the interests of powerful cultural and economic groups in society; even the so-called needs of the child, as imputed by educationists. How that curriculum is transmitted and how it is acquired also turns on many issues: the prevailing theories of cognition in the academy; the available technology; the ways in which curriculum is structured; and how learners are assessed. Here we consider the first of these: the prevailing theories of cognition.

It should be obvious by now that the postmodern turn in literary studies and in the social sciences is beginning to have an effect. From our earlier discussion of pedagogy in the last century and much of this one, it was clear that the behaviourist, chalk-and-talk, didactic approach of active teaching and passive learning held sway. Freire, in a neat phrase, called it the 'banking concept' of education: empty vessels are filled up. Faculties of education — especially in North America — have been dominated by psychologists, for it was they who claimed for themselves the last word on pedagogy. Their behaviouristic and psychometric paradigms sought universal appeal. Mental states could be 'grasped', measured and manipulated, objectively. Furthermore, psychological events could be explained by laws, universal and unchanging. Indeed we could say that modern psychology presumed to be able to uncover generalizable laws. Just as the natural scientists sought to discover the laws of the physical world, so the psychologists purported to discover the laws which governed the self.

Thus far, postmodernist theory has not yet encroached on the domain of the natural sciences to anything like the extent that it has the humanities and the social sciences. The central criticism which the postmodernists make of modern psychology is this: if the self is not knowable — if it has no unitary essence — then the search for laws governing the self is surely a misplaced and ultimately fruitless endeavour, however much psychologists continue to surround themselves with the scientific paraphernalia of laboratories and computers; however much they report their data in a hard, statistical format. So, if there is no unitary notion of the self, if there can be no grand narrative, if generalizable theory is not achievable, then modern psychology looks to be on unstable ground. No longer claiming to be hard science, psychology — if it is unable to deal with the postmodernist critique — will have to content itself with an altogether different notion of science and theory:

> The resulting image of psychological 'science' is in some respects more humble (aiming only for the production of 'local knowledges' that are more bonded and closer to the domain of practice), and [. . .] holding out the promise of only a shifting, fragmentary, and constructed knowledge, without the bedrock certainty of firm (logical or empirical) foundations. (Neimeyer *et al.*, 1994, p. 459)

Psychology — with its more traditional link to the natural sciences — was relatively slower than, say, sociology in adopting what is now called a social constructionist position. The roots of this position in sociology are well located in the symbolic interactionist studies of the Chicago School in the late 1920s and early 1930s, notably in the work of W.I. Thomas, G.H. Mead and Willard Waller, and it was this intellectual heritage which the 'new' sociology of education in the early 1970s drew upon.

But there were other influences, in particular the ethnomethodology of Garfinkel (1967) and McHugh (1968). For them, knowledge is but a construction which is devoid of objective meaning. We assign meaning to the objective world. We symbolize those meanings. But these meanings could be otherwise, and ethnomethodologists in their method deliberately set out to unsituate 'actors', thereby conveying to them that the nature of reality was not fixed, but changeable. For most of us, most of the time, this is a difficult notion to deal with, for it is usually the case that the recipes for dealing with the world which we had yesterday will serve us well today, and this is repeated, as we come to act out of habit — to act normally. It is only when our recipes for action do not have the expected effect that we have cause to be quizzical about what is going on. So, although the world out there seems to be objective — fixed and reified — it nevertheless can sometimes place us in a state of meaninglessness. What we tend to forget is that this objective world is no more than a social construction, an historical creation. That is to say, we, and others before us, have subjectively made sense of the world, but over a period of time that social construction takes on the status of the reality, an objective reality, which could not be otherwise, and which is natural for us. Berger and Luckmann (1967) in *The Social Construction of Reality* refer to this process as the 'objectification of the subjective'.

Whereas Garfinkel, and Berger and Luckmann, remind us that what we regard as real and objective is not inherently so, others take it a stage further. They would not disagree that the world is a social construction, but they would go on to say that, even if the world is a social construction, this prompts a crucial and necessarily prior question: how do we understand each other? Or, indeed, *can* we understand each other? Put another way: if we agree that reality is a social construction, this implies that we can know each other's construction of reality. But can we? In his book *The Phenomenology of the Social World*, Schutz (1972) sums up the problem thus: the only way in which you can know me is to be me. Anything else is an approximation. Our 'streams of consciousness' may, for a moment, come close, but they are never wholly at one with each other. Indeed, for much of the time our own actions do not seem to be known even to ourselves. That is, for most of the time, we act habitually, not intentionally. This does not mean, however, that we could not return to an habitual action and retrospectively assign an intention to it.

Even then we face problems. Yes, we could retrospectively have assigned an intention, a meaning, to a past action. But was that really our intention? Was it the real meaning? Some — Marxists or Freudians, for example — might say that we did not really know why we were doing something. For example, we could simply have been expressing an ideological misrepresentation (Marxism) or have been impelled by some unconscious sexual desire (Freud). In other words, it is quite reasonable for us to think that in an age dominated by *rational* modes of understanding that we should give reasons for providing a definition of the situation, rather than just feel it to have been the thing to say or do at the time. To agree with most of these ideas would be to question implicitly the claims to an objective knowing of the self. And it goes without saying that the representation of psychological or mental 'properties' may now seem rather less valid and objective than had been thought.

Take an example: Piaget. In post-war educational psychology, the influence of Jean Piaget dominates. Even before then his influence had figured prominently in the Hadow Reports of the 1930s. But it was in the progressive education of the 1960s that his theory of genetic epistemology was given official endorsement in the Plowden Report (1967). Genetic epistemology is defined by Burman (1994, p. 152) as 'the study of the origins and growth of knowledge'. The adjective 'genetic' underlines the structuralism of his approach, for his view was that children *progress*, or *develop*, *naturally*, from a state of *emotionality* to one of scientific *rationality*, in stages, linear-fashion, assuming that the experience in the child's environment allows for it. But, whatever the culture, the development is said to be the same. This privileges western culture — in the sense that Piaget's end-state of development is abstract logical thought — and this privileging needs to be rendered problematic (Siann and Ugwuegbu, 1989, p. 78). The terms above have been italicized because they are modernist terms. There is a further association with modernism: it is the practice of *monitoring* the child's stages of development so as to determine whether or not the child is 'ready' — a central concept in child-centred education — to proceed to the next stage. Despite the importance of 'play' in Piaget's work, his work is decidedly within the structuralist tradition. Burman (1994, p. 153) argues that Piaget's concern with the *general* knower, or epistemic subject, serves to distance Piaget from the *individual*, and therefore from psychology.

All the same, Piaget's work is not of a piece with the mechanistic and modernistic approach of behaviourism. That is to say, behaviour is, for Piaget, not simply a response, a reaction; rather knowledge of reality is the outcome of a dialectical relationship between subject and object. For Piaget, knowledge is a construction. The world of objects beyond us is *assimilated*: objects are worked into our existing cognitive structures. Objects are adapted (hence the biological analogy in his work) to what has already been made sense of. But it is not only a one-way process of assimilation. There is *accommodation*: if some objects do not fit — cannot be fully assimilated — then the very cognitive structures themselves will be altered so as to meet these new input-objects from the environment. These two processes (assimilation and accommodation) are part of an interactive, simultaneous and continuing process (*equilibration*) of knowledge construction. This constructed knowledge constitutes objective knowledge for whoever constructs it. So knowledge is not really a reflection of a pre-existing world-out-there.

> [. . .] knowledge results from continuous construction, since in each set of understanding, some degree of invention is involved; in development, the passage from one stage to the next is always characterized by the formation of new structures which did not exist before, either in the external world or in the subject's mind. (Piaget, 1970, p. 77)

Despite Piaget's departure from a mechanistic approach, his work has attracted criticism from those whose own work touches on postmodernist theory. Having referred briefly to Burman (1994), I deal here mainly with two others: Valerie Walkerdine (1984, 1993, 1994) and Joe Kincheloe (1993), in that order.

Walkerdine draws on aspects of Foucault. For Foucault, the disciplines of the Enlightenment — psychology especially — are said to 'constitute' us. That is, in the modern age — an age of the expert — we are all caught in the gaze of those who can lay claim to expert, discipline-based knowledge. We are cast within their interpretive frameworks, and are thereby rendered as objects for study. Our subjectivities are described, researched and analysed within these disciplinary discourses. But these discourses are not just academic. Those who own them can define those who lack them. Power is conferred on the knower. The power thereby 'wielded' is never total, never final; but it is nevertheless considerable, for we are little aware that we are being 'worked on'.

The notion of the developing child is not a representation of an objectively real child with essentially childish properties; rather it is a production, a production of Piagetian theory. This conceptualization of the developing child which claims to be universal and objective is but an artefact of a theory. It is a textual child, constructed within the framework of a disciplinary discourse. This theory itself is situated socially and historically.

Why was it, so to say, that this 'child' was to progress naturally from a state of emotionality to one of scientific rationality? Is it not rather convenient that this is the very path which European society has taken from the middle ages to the age of modernity: from emotion to reason, from the expression of affects to the suppression of affects. In other words, there is something rather teleological about this journey, as if history is unfolding according to some pre-ordained plan not of our making, as if we are expressing evolutionary inevitabilities, the end-state of which is 'a rationally ordered social order' (Walkerdine, 1993, p. 456). Spiecker (1984) puts it well:

> The interactions between mother and baby are determined to a large extent by the conceptual framework within which the mother approaches her child; it is this framework which needs further research. [. . .] Because he is spoken to *as if* he were already a person, the child, in his relationship with those significant other(s), becomes a developing person. (Spiecker, 1984, p. 204)

The irony in all this is that Piagetian developmental psychology has been tacked onto the romanticism of Rousseau in the literature of child-centred education. Implicit in Rousseau is the notion of freedom for the young child who should not be shackled by the institutional fetters of the school. But what freedom, what play? Developmental psychology's end-state of formal, abstract, rational thinking is no freedom, for it surely traps us in the modernist mind-set of rationality. Play has been incorporated, not released.

Moreover, Piagetian psychology privileges patriarchy: not explicitly, but implicitly. Here is the privileging of masculinity and rationality, and, by implication, the pathologizing of femininity, passion and sexuality. Walkerdine again:

> It is my contention that the naturalization of reason as the end-point of a stage-wise progression of development, places 'Woman' as constantly threatening this goal. She is constantly harangued for not reasoning, while equally being targeted if she does so. Her reasoning is seen to constitute a threat to reasoning masculinity. (Walkerdine, 1994, p. 65)

Walkerdine's analysis relates to a wider feminist analysis of ways of knowing, and which in turn relates to postmodernist theory. At issue is feminism's stance on what Sandra Harding (1990, p. 87) calls 'objectivism': that of the rational, value-free, truth-yielding scientific method associated with the Enlightenment project. Also at issue is feminism's stance on what Harding calls 'the loyal opposition to object-ivism', namely 'interpretationism', according to which knowledge is but a social construction, a perspective, with conflicting interpretations, all relative to each other, thereby leaving 'non-feminists' on a par with feminists.

The difficulty for feminists is that they are placed in a number of dilemmas. One such dilemma is this: on the one hand, they wish to retain the *emancipatory* agenda of the Enlightenment project; on the other hand, if they accept the Enlight-enment notion of the 'transhistorical, unitary individual' (Harding, 1990, p. 93), then implied here is the notion of one *unitary female gender*. If so, then this underlines but a single feminism, a feminism which privileges white, middle class and educated women. Other groups of women are thereby marginalized by their race, ethnicity, creed and class. There is a second dilemma, related to postmodernist theory. It is this: if, on the one hand, the epistemological critique made by some postmodernists has weight, then the search for 'grand narratives' and Truth becomes logically questionable. For this reason, postmodernist deconstruction has considerable attrac-tion for feminists, for it questions the privileged status of (masculine) rationality as the dominant mode of thinking; or, in Harding's term, it questions objectivism. On the other hand, if feminists go along with this postmodernist epistemological critique, then, logically, feminist theory itself cannot lay claim to the status of a grand narrative. Jane Flax (1990) puts it well:

> We cannot simultaneously claim (1) that the mind, the self, and know-ledge are socially constituted and that what we can know depends upon our social practices and contexts *and* (2) that feminist theory can uncover the Truth of the whole once and for all. (Flax, 1990, p. 48)

This view comes close to that put by Nancy Fraser and Linda Nicholson (1988) in their call for a synthesis between feminist and postmodern theories:

> Postmodernists offer sophisticated and persuasive criticisms of founda-tionalism and essentialism, but their conceptions of social criticism tend to

be anemic. Feminists offer robust conceptions of social criticism, but they tend, at times, to lapse into foundationalism and essentialism. [...] A postmodernist reflection on feminist theory reveals disabling vestiges of essentialism, while a feminist reflection on postmodernism reveals androcentrism and political naivete. (Fraser and Nicholson, 1988, p. 84)

Like Nancy Fraser, Jane Kenway is loath to let go of feminism's political agenda. Postmodernist deconstructions are a necessary but not a sufficient condition of the emancipation of women. For feminist teachers to confine their critique solely to the epistemological is to leave out of account the fact that women are framed structurally within the material situations of colony, capitalism and patriarchy. In sum, her position is that of the materialist feminist who 'articulates important insights from postmodernism with an analysis of social totalities. It articulates struggles over meaning with an analysis of struggles over other resources' (Kenway, 1995, p. 45; brackets added).

Now Kincheloe (1993). Like Piaget, he rejects the Cartesian dualism of mind-body. There is no objective reality: 'we can see only what our mind allows' (p. 111). But what concerns Kincheloe is that we seem often blind to our ways of seeing. What is this environment which shapes our perceptions and, by extension, our constructions of knowledge? 'This', he argues, 'is where critical postmodern theory collides with constructivism — hence, the etymology of our term, "critical constructivism"' (p. 109). He allies himself with those critics of Piaget who take issue with Piaget's privileging of disembedded, higher-order, abstract thought over personal experience. For both Walkerdine and Kincheloe, the point at issue is to look beneath the surface of this privileging of abstract thinking in Piaget's stages of development. In whose interests is it, and how has this come to pass?

But Kincheloe takes the critique further, drawing upon Derrida rather than on Foucault. First, the notion of a stable cognitive structure which gives primacy to abstract thought is at odds with the postmodernists' doubts about the very possibility to the stability of thought-systems, for these are said to be contingent and provisional. Second, Piaget's stage theory of cognitive development is a process rooted in a modernist concept of linear time and progress. Third, all this can hardly stand up to the historical record of the medieval period when thought-systems and notions of time were rather different, although this view would doubtless be countered by those who subscribe to a teleological view that all societies progress naturally to one in which rationality is the natural way of knowing. Indeed it is this very notion of 'naturalness' which reveals the common thread between Walkerdine and Kincheloe. Walkerdine argues that the child who 'naturally' develops cognitively through Piaget's stages is but a *production* of Piaget's theory; and Kincheloe reminds us that this privileged end-state of abstract thinking screens off the world of feelings and experience, and, by implication, serves to prevent us from looking beneath the surface of these experiences so as to hold up for scrutiny their determinants. In sum, we should deconstruct our constructions. On that basis, the term 'instruction' should itself be the object of 'critical constructivism'. The term 'critical' introduces now what is a growing corpus of influential writing in the United

States which can be loosely termed 'critical pedagogy'. How it seeks to appropriate some strands of postmodernist theory is now considered.

Postmodernists, Politics and Pedagogy

Postmodernist theory is sometimes classified into a 'sceptical' strand and an 'affirmative' strand. The former takes a pessimistic and nihilistic epistemological position, admitting no logical possibility of a universalist conception of knowledge. It is dismissive of the metanarrative, favouring local narratives which are historically contingent and provisional. But this is to dismiss all metanarratives with another metanarrative: 'The bottom line is this: if the rejection of metanarrative requires metanarrative, then metanarrative cannot (coherently) be universally rejected' (Siegel, 1995, p. 40).

There is another way. It is to appropriate the deconstructionist possibilities of postmodernist theory, but for a political purpose, one which empowers those groups who have hitherto lingered — powerless, oppressed and silent — at the margins of society. Let it be said that this latter appropriation of postmodernist theory by critical theorists and some feminists is not simply to re-make the pedagogical *style*; rather it has also profound implications for what should be selected as text in curricular knowledge, for it has the expressed intention of undermining and replacing what had previously counted as official knowledge. In sum, it has the intention to engage in cultural politics. These two extracts from Morton and Zavarzadeh give a flavour of the approach.

> In humanistic pedagogy, right and wrong are preordained, values and ideas are considered to be determined outside discursive practices, and language is therefore treated as basically an aesthetic category and not as an epistemological ensemble through which reality and values are produced. (Morton and Zavarzadeh, 1991, p. 7); *and*

> (Post)modern critical theory has decentered the humanist regime of truth and engendered a crisis in the philosophy and practice of its pedagogy. That crisis is too fundamental to be contained by such new humanist programs as those articulated by a reformist (post)structuralism or its seeming opposite, a nostalgic conservatism. [. . .] The serious question, however, is no longer how to save the subject by changing the courses in it, but *how to change the study itself.* (Morton and Zavarzadeh, 1991, p. 29; my emphasis)

This appropriation of postmodernist theory by critical theorists such as Giroux and McLaren has spawned a new vocabulary: 'oppositional postmodernism'; 'radical critique-al theory'; 'postmodern education', 'resistance postmodernism' and 'critical postmodernism'. They are appropriations of ludic postmodernism, not alternatives to it (Giroux and McLaren, 1994, p. 199). The indictment which they make of modernist schooling is considerable, re-affirming and adding to many of the critiques which both Marxists and critical theorists of the school have been making since the publication of Bowles and Gintis' *Schooling in Capitalist America* in 1976. That is to say, education purports to be meritocratic, but the same categories of children keep winning and losing. The social locations of the pupils — class, gender or ethnic — have, on average, more predictive power than their measured intelligence. Schooling reproduces the social order. It treats social characteristics as if they are natural, academically favouring some, demeaning others. The education system purports to be fair, but it is far from it. And the winners and losers learn to individualize their success and failure. They do not have an insight into the structural conditions which may have predisposed them to succeed or not. Added to all of this, the regimes of schools are far from democratic. The Enlightenment project is said to have gone badly wrong, and the education system to be deeply implicated.

But all is not lost. The injection of postmodernist deconstruction into the pedagogical relationship can, so the argument runs, reinvigorate the emancipatory vision of the Enlightenment. Few are more eloquent about this than McLaren:

> What isn't being talked about in today's educational debate is the desperate need in our schools for creating a media-literate citizenry that can disrupt, contest and transform media apparatuses so that they no longer have the power to infantilize the population and continue to create passive, fearful, paranoid, and apolitical social subjects. (Giroux and McLaren, 1994, p. 9)

McLaren draws on his study of Portuguese Catholic students in Toronto. He points up the 'inflated rationalism and logocentrism' of the classroom, and its carefully codified suppression of the affects. The students, refusing to deny their street culture, resisted this, thereby 'gaining power, celebrating pleasure through the shattering of sanctified codes' (Giroux and McLaren, 1991, p. 172). But more than this, these acts of resistance should not merely be recorded as unexplained events. Drawing upon the pedagogical tradition of Freire, both Giroux and McLaren recommend that 'Teachers would do well to tap the hidden utopian desire in those resistances' (p. 174). The appropriation of postmodernist deconstructionism can provide the basis of a methodology for teachers and pupils to make meaning together, to look beneath the surface of events, revealing their structural antecedents. Giroux and McLaren, however, are sometimes taken to task for writing at a high level of generality, far above the day-to-day practice of front-line educators (a point considered below). What other examples could illustrate the approach?

Graff (1992) suggests a way forward, though one which Giroux and McLaren might regard as overly pluralist and liberal in its *curricular* position. The sub-title of his *Beyond the Culture Wars* (1992) is a question which implies that the study of the humanities in American higher education is in need of some resuscitation: *How Teaching the Conflicts Can Revitalize American Education*. Though not as stark an indictment as Reimer's (1971) classic *School is Dead*, nor as conservative as Bloom's (1987) analysis, it nevertheless raises two related concerns: one curricular, the other pedagogical. Whilst welcoming what he calls the revisionist (as opposed to the traditionalist) view of culture, Graff asserts that to focus only on the curricular content which supports these positions is to miss the point, which is that:

> In the heat of today's antagonisms it is easy to get so caught up defending one or another proposed list of books to be taught that one forgets that for many students it is *the life of books* itself that is strange and alien, regardless which side gets to draw up the list. (Graff, 1990, p. 823)

What is missing is a re-definition of *pedagogy*. In the sequestered setting of the classroom, students, armed with the book-for-the-course, do not become party to the intellectual conflicts which are aired by 'other voices' in 'other rooms': that is, the faculty members in the faculty common rooms. Within a course, students learn to read and repeat the paradigm of the professor; they must learn to distinguish these 'voices'. No risks are taken. Graff's solution is the curricular theme or 'multicourse symposia [which] would concentrate on common issues across the courses raised by the common texts and on exemplary points of difference and convergence over them' (p. 836). Drawing upon the analogy of teaching a foreign language, Graff argues that just as a student of a foreign language will learn best within the foreign country so also will students of the humanities better understand an academic or intellectual culture if they are part of it. Change must be both substantive and structural. On the other hand, Hill (1994, p. 140), in a commentary on Graff, reminds us of the 'extraordinary attractiveness' to the 'academic psyche' — especially that of the male — of the cocooned and sequestered domain known as the classroom. In these days of bureaucratic interventions and politicking, the retreat to the certainties of this domain is not something which is to be disturbed easily.

Much of this talk of themes and collaborative teaching will seem somewhat *passé* to 1960s primary school teachers in Britain. It adds to the range of reasons which have been raised to explain progressive pedagogy: Piagetian stage theory (psychology); Rousseau's romanticism (philosophy); the 'new' 1980s pedagogy in further education (management theory); Doll's (1989) consideration of the implications of chaos theory. For the most part, higher education has so far been literally above these debates, but as it attracts more disparate groups — as it becomes massified — its traditional curricula and pedagogy will be under both epistemological and cultural pressure to change.

Kathleen McCormick (1994) provides an example. Her approach is illustrated in a course on 'Western Heritage' which she taught to a class with a 'vast array of ethnic and class backgrounds'. The students were asked to contrive different 'reading positions' or interpretations of a text which she gave them to read. One was the 'humanist position' which assumes meaning to inhere in a preordained way, and that there are transcendent human qualities shared by all. Another position was a 'social-constructionist' position which sees texts as historically contingent, devoid of a universal meaning. The text in question was about a black woman who 'achieves happiness and societal respect' by being a hard-working servant.

How was the text read? Most of the white males adopted a humanist position, whilst the rest sided more with a social-constructionist approach. The atmosphere in the classroom became racially charged. The issue was risky, and the students were resisting the analysis. McCormick then asked the students to find press articles on multiculturalism which best accorded with their own individual 'reading position'. They worked in groups, and they decided upon the papers which typified their group's position. The papers would thereafter be set aside for general distribution. In doing so, the students were able to see structurally their own subjectivities. McCormick makes the important point that approaches which align themselves to critical theory may easily produce, unintentionally, a sense of powerlessness in students no less damaging than the very didactic, humanist approaches which they seek to supplant. She argues further that no viewpoints held by students should be dismissed or overly managed by the teacher, for if they are then the students may deem themselves to be worthless, not worth hearing. The mere assertion of the need for the voices of the long-silenced to be heard is not enough. The students must be given the space actually to listen and to be heard.

Elisabeth Ellsworth (1989) had anticipated McCormick's concerns in an important review of Giroux's approach. She puts the question: 'Why doesn't this feel empowering?' First, she asserts that notions of empowerment, voice, dialogue — even the very term critical — are 'repressive myths that perpetuate relations of domination'. Who, she asks, is this 'generic critical teacher'? The 'generic' teacher tends to be a 'young, White, Christian, middle class, heterosexual, able-bodied, thin, rational man' (p. 310). If Ellsworth is allowed this assertion, and if we admit the postmodernists' argument about the provisionality and situatedness of knowledge, then the concept of the generic critical teacher looks even less admissible.

Critical theorists are not unaware of the postmodernists' arguments against epistemological certainty. McLaren (1989, p. 233), for example, is out to underline epistemological uncertainty when he advocates the practice of 'pedagogical negativism', the doubting of everything. (This presumably includes his own views on pedagogical negativism.) Moreover, advocates of critical pedagogy do not subscribe to the nihilist tendency which obtains among some postmodernist theory. Derrida, for example, is said to be ready to cast aside the project of modernity, particularly its democratic concerns. In fact, he states, 'I try where I can to act politically while recognizing that such action remains incommensurate with my intellectual project of deconstruction' (Derrida, quoted in Kearney, 1984, p. 120).

Wright (1995) returns to Giroux's concept of border pedagogy. Giroux's concern is to bring together the diverse emancipatory projects and to unite them in a common cross-border democratic cause. However, far from facilitating 'border crossings' in common cause, critical pedagogy can result in border wars and retrenchment. Giroux's error, argues Wright, is in his very 'border' metaphor. Like Ellsworth and McCormick, she is concerned about the hierarchy of emancipatory causes, and how dominant and assertive causes are played in the 'messiness' of the classroom, producing unintended consequences which are far from emancipatory

for some. The paradox is that those who produce critical theory are placed hier-
archically above those — teachers — who put into practice a pedagogy which
seeks to undermine hierarchy. Advocacy needs to be metaphorically incorporated
into pedagogical process, not separated from it, not above it.

Wright, drawing upon anthropological work in Africa, prefers a 'crossroads'
metaphor. Crossroads in many African societies are seen as enchanted sites, unpredictable, uncertain, dangerous, where evil spirits are warded off by sacrifices to
the gods (p. 73). 'Crossroads' pedagogy captures the unforeseen twists and turns
of teaching which no carefully structured lesson plan can accommodate: 'As in pedagogy, the outcome of working at the crossroads is at once up to us but at the same
time somehow beyond our control' (74). The notion of crossroads is one of more
openness and uncertainty, a metaphorical space where entrenched positions behind
fortified borders are difficult to sustain. Crossroads are figuratively open, but the
outcomes — the directions — are not fixed. Wright's recognition of the 'messiness'
of teaching is well taken, but invites the question — metaphorically — where do
the roads which meet come from, and why were they constructed? If a voice cannot
travel to the crossroads — the new agora? — then it will not be heard. On the other
hand, the course-correction to Giroux's border crossings made by the likes of
Ellsworth and Wright are important, and help to reveal the complexities of the
journey towards emancipation through pedagogy.

There are further criticisms of critical pedagogy. Misgeld puts one of them:

> There is absolutely no point to attempting to 'politicize' these populations
> such that they first and foremost respond to issues of sexism and racism.
> They simply will not respond as long as they have some hope to attain a
> better and more secure future. (Misgeld, 1992, p. 129)

This is an important point, for a number of reasons. First, it raises the question
of just which long-silenced groups shall be a party to this communicative dialogue.
Who decides? Could it all turn out to be a polyphonic babel; or even a war of
separatists, each seeing its own cause as central, as some kind of universal particular? (It bears noting that we are dealing here with what Giddens (1991) terms
'emancipatory politics': that is, the politics of justice, equality of opportunity and
democratic participation — all of these being arguably political causes of the modern
age. He suggests, however, that when a satisfactory degree of emancipation has
been achieved, then political causes come to be centred upon what he calls 'life
politics': that is, the politics of lifestyles.) The important issue to address, therefore,
is how this critical pedagogy can be undertaken in practice. On this, Giroux
and McLaren have been said to be weak on grounding their approach in actual
situations (Bowers, 1991, p. 244; Misgeld, 1992, p. 132; Weber, 1993, p. 298). As
stated, both McCormick and Ellsworth alert us to the unintended consequences
of this kind of teaching. The critical dialogue which 'the' critical teacher initiates
assumes a kind of open and equal access to the arena of free discussion. But, even
with such a commitment and intention to an open communicative dialogue which
is devoid of symbolic violence, there are prevailing asymmetries of power, not just

between teacher and student, but among students themselves; and it is the playing out of these power asymmetries which can lead quickly to the expression of the very 'isms' which the teacher seeks to educate away. 'Teaching the conflicts' — to use Graff's term — may produce even more conflict.

Perhaps this is inevitable, to some small extent. It does, however, have an educative (transformative) potential if, once expressed, the basis of these differential power relationships can be made explicit and analysed. The importance of Giroux and McLaren is that they call for a 'pedagogy of the popular', a critical dialogue of the media of popular culture, and in so doing they go some way to meeting Ellsworth's critique, whilst advocating an approach broadly similar to that described above by McCormick. In a more recent paper, 'Right wing pedagogy', Giroux (1995) raises concerns about the rapid spread of talk radio in America which serve mainly as media platforms for 'conservative public intellectuals'. The power of talk radio lies in its reduction of complex issues to impassioned commentary, a blend of what Giroux calls 'right wing ideology and pop culture'. The appropriation of popular culture in this medium by the Right requires progressives on the Left also to 'arouse the language and passion of hope through an appeal to the possibilities of what it means to live in a democracy'. Progressives, he implies, must appropriate the culture of postmodernism (including its technology) in order to reach a wide range of audiences by a diversity of media. This is a more pro-active approach. Giroux is calling not just for a critical dialogue *of* the media in popular culture, but rather for a critical dialogue *within* the media in popular culture. In sum, Giroux and McLaren use postmodernist theory as a means to an end. They politicize postmodernist theory. They do not subscribe to its nihilistic extremes.

Despite these important reservations, the critical postmodernists and some feminist theorists have not fallen to the fashions of postmodernist nihilism. Although the disciplines and metanarratives of the Enlightenment can no longer lay claim to Truth and certainty, this is not a justification for losing sight of, or abandoning, the important democratic gains which the past two centuries have realized. And critical postmodernists appear not to countenance the wayward tendencies of technical rationality: they retain some commitment to Habermas' notion of communicative rationality. Even so, it is an adherence to technical rationality which is often uppermost in the minds of policy-makers, and it is appropriate now to focus on those who believe that the way forward for education lies in the path of technical efficiency, of a 'technical fix' (Robins and Webster, 1989).

Technology, Performativity and Pedagogy

For Lyotard (1984) it is the very technological sophistication of the computer which provides the demarcation line between the modern and the postmodern. The computer allows new forms of social networks to emerge, networks which are ephemeral, local and international. Insofar as pedagogy is concerned, the following two quotations from *The Postmodern Condition* are instructive:

> The moment knowledge ceases to be an end itself [. . .] its transmission
> is no longer the exclusive responsibility of scholars and students. The
> notion of 'university franchise' now belongs to a bygone era.

He goes on to state that:

> To the extent that learning is translatable into computer language and
> the traditional teacher is replaceable by memory banks, didactics can be
> entrusted to machines linking traditional memory banks (libraries, etc)
> and computer data banks to an intelligent terminal placed at the students's
> disposal. (Lyotard, 1984, p. 50)

The pedagogical consequences of the digitalization of knowledge have been
seen in some quarters as favourable. For example, Reid (1994, p. 5) asks, 'What
are some of the promises of CBE?' Computer-based education (CBE) provides the
following advantages (I have re-ordered Reid's items. The italics have been added):

> * *accelerated* learning * *reduced time* required for instruction * *accom-
> modates differing rates* and styles of learning * more effective use of
> lecturer *time* * increased *flexibility and timetabling*

(This category focuses heavily on time management as it operates in the post-
Fordist workplace, with its notions of just-in-time delivery and flexibility of
treatment.) Consider further items in Reid's list:

> * more pleasurable learning

(This resonates with the notion of pleasure and play in postmodern culture.)

> * automated collection and analysis of student performance data * im-
> proved understanding of student progress * simplified remedial effort *
> simplified prescription of courses of learning

(Here, too, the tenets of post-Fordism are writ large, with its concern for zero-
defects and closely-monitored quality control, much of it automated in the
computer's log.)

> * *improved* understanding and performance by students * *improved* ef-
> fectiveness in teaching * *improved* communication between students and
> lecturers * *improved* student attitudes to learning * ability to teach student
> attitudes to learning

(These 'improvements' seem like something of a wish-list; or, as Reid terms
them, a set of 'promises' of CBE.)

In total, the list is a technicist's tale. Reid is aware of pitfalls, but they seem to be few. The values implied in this technology are not discussed, and the implication is that the technology is value-free. The implications for the content and form of knowledge are not discussed. Perhaps most importantly, this technology of pedagogical treatment generates its own hidden curriculum, a panopticized pedagogy. But Reid's itemized list — its appeals to simplicity, automation, progress, systematization, efficiency and effectiveness — comes close to constituting a powerful hidden curriculum which Broughton (1984, p. 104) calls 'programmatic lucidity', by which he means: 'the pragmatic virtues of cognitive order, organization, and systematicity, characterized by clarity, nonambiguity, nonredundancy, internal consistency, and noncontradiction'. There is something in all this which accords with the certainties of Taylorism and the social efficiency movement criticized by Kliebard (1992). Here looms an efficient mix of systems analysis, instructional packages and information technology.

What is also striking about the list is the extent to which its discourse accords with the performativity principle: that is, with the maximization of the system's efficiency. It is this principle which was said by Lyotard to be a crucial facet of the postmodern condition. Knowledge, he argued, would increasingly be rendered digital and saleable. Those types of knowledge not so rendered would be pushed to the periphery. How would this knowledge be transmitted? Not, he thought, by the 'professor', for the university would fast lose its monopoly on the generation and transmission of knowledge. And new information technology, with its enticing multi-media image could be at one with, first, the performativity principle; and, second, with *laissez-faire* economics. These points are considered next.

Take performativity. Information technology allows for cost-savings. A virtual school or university can be open at any time. It can be accessed from wherever there is a land-line or cell-phone link. It requires hardly any laboratories, residences or classrooms. It has a potential global market. It can monitor the log of activities whilst a student is on-line. True, its start-up costs — especially the writing of software, the hardware and the initial cabling — can be very high, but thereafter the cost-savings could be considerable.

Is there another price to pay? In the history of education there has been a tension between efficiency and democracy. Efficiency and performativity now have the upper hand. Educational issues tend to be re-cast as technical problems, thereby to be solved by technical solutions. Information technology is said to provide some of them. I have already said that there is a tendency for the curriculum to be rendered digital, which could mean that notions of humour, feeling, intuition and wisdom will tend to be sidelined. In the dedication of Abbs's (1987) *Living Powers: The Arts in Education*, the late Louis Arnaud Reid writes:

Children are stuffed with cognitive facts, and in these days particularly, facts of highly specialised knowledge the acquisition of which is supposed to qualify them for jobs. Bored with school and starved there of emotional satisfaction, they turn for it to the stereotypes of commercial entertainment and are stuffed instead with wholly false conceptions of the human condition.

But, he goes on, will information technology:

> ease much drudgery of factual learning, releasing time and energy for more 'creative' insights into the understanding of both fact and value — including as a major field the arts. The crucial question for humane education is, 'Will it?' (Abbs, 1987)

If very high cost-savings are being sought, then both economies of scale and machine-intensive modes of production will both figure. The implication of this for education on-line is that software-production costs should be minimized whilst the sale of software should be maximized. In order to facilitate low software-production costs it makes sense to standardize the content so that it fits culturally the widest possible audience. So, for example, in a country like Canada, it would be extremely tempting for provincial ministries of education to buy cheap, off-the-shelf software from the United States rather than to produce their own. For similar reasons, the Scots may be tempted to buy curricular software packages from England.

The rate at which this is emerging varies, but it seems to be a trend for the foreseeable future. One of its tenets is to reduce the expenditure of government. The cost-savings on buildings and personnel have been mentioned. But, furthermore, the temptation for government to allow business to merchandise its software and hardware will be difficult to resist. The education budget in the USA is estimated at over 280 billion dollars a year, a vast amount. And just as government looks to cut its costs, at the same time the corporations are continually on the lookout for more cultural products to define and to market. The cultural product called education offers huge markets for business. Already, there are business-school links, be they the sponsoring of chairs and research in universities, or the mere distribution of vouchers-for-computers in supermarkets. There are others one could mention.

But there are reports of it having gone further than that. On 17 August 1995 the Toronto *Globe and Mail* carried a report of the first school opened under the Edison Project, a for-profits company presided over by a former prominent Ivy League academic. The school, George Washington elementary school, is located at Sherman, near Dallas, Texas. Each child has an Apple computer to take home, with e-mail capabilities which enable pupils, parents and teachers to communicate. The teachers have Apple laptops. At 205 days, the school year is thirty days longer than normal, and the school day is eight hours, one-and-a-half hours longer than normal. The owners receive the standard *per-capita* costs of the school district (about $4500), for which Edison pledges to improve test scores. Other schools are to be opened. Their success or failure will turn on their profitability. It bears noting that the majority of the activities are not computer-driven, reportedly only between 10 and 15 per cent of them being so. In the same issue, it was reported that the Canadian province of New Brunswick had become the first province to implement a 'virtual campus' with the aid of the on-line Microsoft Institute. The on-line courses are accredited by the provincial ministry, and students are charged a fee by Microsoft for taking it. This certified course is available from home using a modem link.

All these are beginnings. A number of issues remain, but they are more to do with legitimating these technical fixes than with the software and hardware itself. In order for economies of scale to be effected, a standardization of curricular content will be required. In the United States, there is no national curriculum. Education is a state, not federal, responsibility, but the debate about the national curriculum grows (Ravitch, 1995). In England, but not in Scotland, there is a legislated national curriculum, so the standardization of content broadly exists. In higher education in Britain, there is no parallel to the National Curriculum which exists in the schools. What may occur — and there are signs of it already — is that academics may be funded to produce common curricular packages. In these days of diminishing resources, it is difficult to resist bidding for such grants; and there is a great deal of intellectual and social collaboration, which brings its own intrinsic reward. Equally, it can symbolize what Olson (1989, p. 505) calls one's *avant-gardisme*, and when institutions market themselves it may do no harm to portray to potential students and pupils an impression that a school is already well ahead along the information superhighway. Witness the proliferation of university home-pages on the World Wide Web. One may well expect to see further signs of these government-funded collaborative curricular ventures within academic disciplines. And government will surely deem it appropriate to enlist wherever possible the expertise of the Open University, which has a deservedly international reputation in these matters. All the same, government funding of education seems as uncertain as the culture in which it is based. If, and when, these collaborative curricular packages have been produced, then they can be held up as academically respectable standards of excellence, ready for transmission. There is a further issue, related to performativity. It is to allay the fears of professionals that all this information technology could undermine their very livelihood. Oft-quoted assurances suggest that all this will 'free' the academic to research or to give more individual attention; it will not replace the teacher, but rather will enhance the teacher's role. It will, in other words, 'support' the teacher.

Nevertheless, the introduction of new technology in industry has had effects which can hardly cause the 'modern' teacher to rest easily. In the long run, when the financial audits are conducted, the efficiency gains brought about by the introduction of information technology could be great. It is too early yet to say: the costs of own-ing or licensing software and of accessing data-bases, not to mention the very short product-life of hardware, may not produce the gains expected. But what of the democratic audit of such software, nationally produced, or even commercially produced? One of the things which in the past the universities in particular have escaped is the imposition of knowledge. (In the professions, the professional curric-ulum is accredited, but not by the government. The exception is the professional curriculum for teachers, which is to be defined by the government's Teacher Training Agency.) On the other hand, the advocates of on-line information technology argue, correctly, that it widens access by allowing the resource-limited system to admit more students than would otherwise have been the case. This egalitarian benefit may be so. But access to what? Whilst there may be broader access to the institutions of higher education, it may also be the case that the range of knowledge provided has a variety which is far less than that now provided.

All this rests on the assumption that there is a compatibility between a given theory of learning and the new technology. Some of the software rests on a behaviourist approach. It simply informs. How to make sense of all this requires conceptual frameworks. In an age of technical rationality, other forms of knowing — hermeneutic, intuitive, critical — could be marginalized if it can be shown that the very logic of computers excludes these non-rational forms of knowing. As we have seen, postmodernists and critical postmodernists are endeavouring to undermine the implied certainties of technical rational thinking. Postmodernists — in particular those of a Foucauldian persuasion — will also raise questions about the normalizing effects of a supposedly value-free technology which privileges abstract rational thinking and the power of the image over the word. Critical theorists, too, will raise questions: will it mean the exclusion of other forms of knowing apart from instrumental rationality; who has access to these technologies; who logs their users' activities; why, now, are they gaining currency; who creates and owns the software?

Papert, however, has claimed that educational computing can be based on Piagetian cognitive psychology, allowing for individual differences so that '[. . .] the computer allows us [. . .] to match the subject matter and learning style to the personality type' (Papert, 1984, p. 425). What slips into Papert's claims, however, is that this computer-aided pedagogy enables the child *naturally* to move to the end-state of logico-mathematical, abstract cognition. This supposed *natural progression* — as I argued earlier with reference to Walkerdine's critique of Piagetian developmental psychology — is a 'naturalness' which is produced by the theory itself, and its final stage — rational and abstract cognition — just happens to fit very conveniently into the dominant mode of thinking today, namely instrumental rationality.

There are other claims for CBE. For example, Hodgson (1993) sees no contradiction between the use of computers and what is now defined as a learner-centred pedagogy which embraces notions of choice, ownership, empowerment and collaboration. All these notions were said to have been enabled in a computer-mediated communication system running a conferencing software called 'Caucus'. The system was used as part of a pedagogical repertoire in the teaching of a part-time MA programme. Hodgson sees this as not dissimilar to the principles underlying Habermas' ideal speech situation to which we referred in Chapter 3. At times, the fervour is almost Utopian. Harking back to Illich, and speaking of the Internet, Pickering (1995, p. 10) states that the 'post-Fordist dispersal of production will be mirrored by the dispersal of post-modern education (sic). [. . .] Instead of a curriculum there is the Internet catalogue.'

I referred earlier in this chapter to the pedagogy of pleasure, one which speaks to notions of self-fulfilment and empowerment. The pedagogy of pleasure, however, can be regarded from another perspective. With the development of broadband fibre-optic networks, the link between pedagogy, entertainment and technology will be forged. As stated, the nexus between business and education already presents a massive market opportunity, especially so if neo-liberal economic policies hold sway. In 1995, the Department for Education in England published *Superhighways for Education*, a consultation paper on the introduction of broadband communications. (Broadband communications allow for interactive video along fibre-optic cabling; intermediate band uses ISDN — Integrated Services Digital Network — which allows for graphics and limited transmissions of video-conferences.) The term *superhighway* is part of the metaphorical repertoire which translates the esoteric high-technology terminology into a familiar, everyday discourse. That is to say, it merges transport and communication into a common discourse. But not only does it appeal to the freedom of the open road, it dissolves the notion of boundaries through the concept of network. It opens up virtual communities. Unlike the roads, it is safe — no physical contact, anonymous. But is it that safe: will credit-card fraud and on-line harrassment be possible? Its imagery is both hard and soft: the macho 'superhighway', the 'search engines', 'surfing the Net'; but the World Wide Web is non-hierarchical, and allows for random links and strands of thought (Kenway *et al.*, in press).

There is, too, a correspondence between postmodernist epistemology and the digital media: both stress multi-linearity, webs, links and networks, all of which open up the possibilities of chaotic complexity and emancipatory spaces. The digital 'text' allows the reader to interact with it, manipulating its form and content, re-ordering its sequence, to produce what Peters and Lankshear (1996, p. 68) call 'reader constructed inter-texts'. They argue, moreover, that designated educational spaces — the textbook, the classroom, the school, the curriculum — need no longer be enclosed institutional domains. The digital text allows us to go off-limits, creating links, finding texts which we did not seek, all of which by-pass the gatekeepers of convention in education. Admittedly optimistic — 'surfing on the side of optimism' (67) — they are mindful of the darker side to this techno-driven Utopia. Here they are in agreement with Rheingold (1994, p. 280) who notes the 'invisible digital trail' which we leave in our wake as we participate in the virtual community. This trail can already be mapped, and our surfing on the World Wide Web may soon be filtered and processed, unknown to us (Graham-Cumming, 1996). The collection and collation of these trails itself produces a commodity, which could be sold for marketing purposes, but it also could be used for political purposes:

> The great weakness of the idea of electronic democracy is that it can be more easily commodified than explained. [. . .] The Net that is a marvellous lateral network can also be used as a kind of invisible yet inescapable cage. (Rheingold, 1994, p. 289)

What now follows is a consideration of a grander scheme for the application of CBE in higher education. In particular I shall bring together some of the pedagogical, curricular and structural consequences of this approach. *Teaching and Learning in an Expanding Higher Education System* (The MacFarlane Report) was published in 1992 by a working party of the Committee of Scottish University

Principals (CSUP). Its introduction begins with the declaration that 'The effective and efficient support of the learning process is the key to the maintenance of high quality, and the containment of costs, in any successful expansion of higher education' (CSUP, 1992, p. 1).

A clue to how this might be accomplished is provided in the cover of the Report. On it there are three photographs, arranged vertically. At the top is an old sepia-coloured photograph taken around the turn of the century. It shows three male students in a chemistry laboratory. Two work at the laboratory bench, a third leans languidly against a door. The fashion is the tweed suit, the winged collar and the slicked-back hair style. The atmosphere is relaxed and uncrowded, befitting the male, leisured elite at study. The next photograph is in black and white: it shows two male students who are seated together at a desk, taking notes. Behind them are serried ranks of other students, crowded together, fading into the distance. No one is talking. The scene would be typical of many universities today. The third photograph is in colour: in the foreground is a female student sitting before a colour monitor on which there is a technical graphic; in the background are three groups of students, each group conferring before a monitor. Each monitor has the same screen-image. Some of the students are seated, others stand. These three photographs depict chronological, organizational and pedagogical change. The pedagogical means — the 'technology' — is associated with different forms of social and spatial arrangements. What appears to link the three photographs is a curricular content which seems to be science- or technology-related. This is the case with the sepia and the colour photographs. The academic subject to which the black and white photograph refers is unclear, though it may also be a technology-related subject, given the absence of female students in the photograph.

The MacFarlane Report makes three central recommendations. First, it recommends that the three higher education funding councils in Britain should jointly create a national body, entitled the Teaching and Learning Board. Its remit would be to generate and manage a programme in higher education to:

> foster the large-scale production of shareable resources; stimulate innovation in teaching and learning support systems; generate and support a research and development community in the fields of teaching and learning support; create and oversee arrangements for the quality control of the shareable resources which it endorses; establish national arrangements for the dissemination of teaching materials; for the maintenance of development and delivery systems; and for the creation and maintenance of the associated support infrastructure required in individual institutions. (CSUP, 1992, p. 42)

Secondly, it recommends that the higher education funding councils should require individual institutions to publish a detailed teaching and learning development strategy related to their institutional plan, this strategy to be assessed as part of the overall quality assessment process. Funding would reward innovative and effective teaching developments, and the production of widely shared resources.

Each institution would submit an annual statement on its teaching and learning strategy, to include:

(i)   plans for its implementation, including the relationship to quality assessment mechanisms;

(ii) plans for staff development, including: promotion structure in respect of excellence in teaching; financial and other rewards for commitment to teaching and learning within an institution; and encouragement to staff to collaborate on the production and/or use of shareable resources; and

(iii) plans for funding developments to maintain quality of teaching and learning from grant-in-aid resources (CSUP, 1992:43).

Thirdly, it is recommended that the higher education funding councils should take a strategic, long-term view of their arrangements for the development of teaching and learning in higher education.

The MacFarlane Report provides a mainly technical solution to an economic problem, using education as its medium. The Report is a sign of its times. It is driven by an economic imperative rather than by any intrinsic set of educational principles. Indeed the Report states that higher education now has a 'new set of expectations'. These include:

- a perception that higher education should serve the UK economy more effectively, and be more receptive to the needs of those who employ the graduates of degree programmes and other higher education courses;
- a demand that higher education develop and sustain closer links with industry and commerce, and that institutions encourage and reward a spirit of enterprise among staff at all levels;
- a new emphasis on the auditing of quality and performance in teaching, with concomitant attention to enhancing quality and increasing efficiency. The search for efficiency in teaching is complemented by a concern for standards and excellence. (CSUP, 1992, para. 1.2)

It goes on (para. 1.3): 'Increasingly the question is being asked: how far can new technology and distance education help universities adapt to their new role?' The 'new role' advocated in the MacFarlane Report goes largely unexamined, and rests less on educational principles, more on 'instructional principles'. The Report does, however, call for greater access to higher education, but the means whereby this might be accomplished — shareable resources, economies of scale — may themselves reduce the diversity of knowledge and opinion which is so central to the preservation of academic freedom. The greater the coordination, uniformity and standardization of the knowledge base, the more likely it will be that systems thinking will ensue. In the arts and the humanities, for example, where knowledge cannot be rendered objective and empirically verifiable, it would be unreasonable to substitute competence for culture, skill for wisdom, facts for feelings, certainty for doubt.

The Report is a grand design, with a staged, evolutionary pattern over a twenty-year period, and is very much a symbol of the transition from Taylorist and Fordist modes of mass production to what has been termed 'flexible capitalism'. Its discourse appears to be logically contradictory. On the one hand, it speaks of mass provision, monitoring, articulation, standards, long-term strategies, efficiency and instrumental relevance to the needs of the economy. Much of this accords with the tenets of F.W. Taylor's (1947, Original 1911) scientific management theory which had much currency during the first two decades of the twentieth century, especially in America. On the other hand, the MacFarlane Report refers also to notions of autonomy, virtuality, flexibility of time and space, urgency, innovation, diversity and choice — all notions which are arguably at odds with the standardization and rigidity implied by Taylorist management theory.

That the Report's answer lies in a 'technical fix' is implied in the very comprehensive appendices, of which there are five, the last four referring specifically to matters of technology. These are: *Overview of current technology in education*; *Survey of use of new technology in UK higher education institutions*; *Benefits and costs of computer-based learning*; and *Teaching and Learning Technology Programme*.

The first appendix, 'Student learning and instructional principles in higher education', draws on the extant research. The ordering of the Report's chapters is such that the impression given is that these research-derived instructional principles provide the academic, research-driven basis for the techno-bureaucratic solutions contained in the rest of the Report. That is, the chapter 'Instructional Principles and Practice' precedes the other chapters, namely: 'Developments in Technology-based Learning'; 'Teaching and Learning for Mass Higher Education'; 'Policy: Organisational Structure'; 'Policy: Benefits, Costs and Implementation'; and 'Recommendations'. It could also be argued, however, that the very timing of the Report rests not so much on the extant academic research but more so on economic imperatives, or 'doing more with less' during a period of fiscal overload within the welfare state.

In a number of ways the MacFarlane Report accords with the emerging culture of postmodernism: first, in its recognition of virtual reality, of the image, the simulation; and secondly, in its recognition of the new autonomous, flexible self. Take the first of these. The new cyber-space may replace, eventually, the physical space; the virtual may replace the real. Secondly, the instructional principles declared accord with the culture of postmodernism. Cognitive psychology has itself largely replaced behaviourism and the 'surface', passive learning which it implied; instead, learning should be 'deep' and experiential; the student should be taught to learn how to learn, to take responsibility, so to say, for his or her own learning. Thus the Report rejects the modernist discourse of behaviourism. It calls for a learner-centred pedagogy. This pedagogy has in the past been regarded as being expensive, but the Report takes the view that, through a systems approach to teaching and learning, a 'deep' approach to learning can be reconciled with impending 'logical and fiscal constraints' (para. 2.3.4), provided that information technology and other means are used appropriately. It does not argue for the wholesale adoption of technology, and is mindful of its limitations (para. 3.1.4), concluding that a 'mixed economy' of conventional teaching methods and the application of technology is the way forward. On balance, it is to be expected that computer-based learning will take root first in the sciences, where it will be possible to simulate experiments and demonstrations which hitherto would have been based in expensive laboratories.

In sum, the logic of the Report seems to be as follows. There must be an increase in the numbers of students in higher education; the unit-costs of higher education should be reduced by more use of information technology and shared resources; cognitive psychology underpins what formerly was called child-centred pedagogy, but, with reference to higher education, is now called learner-centred, 'deep' learning; information technology is compatible with the research in cognitive psychology, though not (yet) wholly so; a systematic approach to implementation should be adopted, with national structures for strategic planning, and local institutional plans for implementation. Thus there emerges a judicious mix of central control, on the one hand; and progressivism, individualism flexibility and information technology, on the other.

Vocation and Voice

In the modern age, teaching was said to be a 'vocation', a calling to serve others, to be trusted. Born and educated to a mentality of modernity, educated and trained in an ethos of professionalism, most teachers of more than ten years' service now face profound dilemmas. It is not that teachers have never had to deal with dilemmas (Berlak and Berlak, 1981), but those which now confront them are of quite a different order than those hitherto. Teachers face a rhetoric which appears to be contradictory, and therefore confusing.

On the one hand, teachers are being advised that they are to be empowered, with a sense of ownership of their endeavours. On the other hand, the manuals governing curriculum, assessment and appraisal — to name some — pile up on their desks. There is an increase in the monitoring of teachers and in the monitoring of their pupils. Audits, assessments and inspections follow. The qualitariat swarm around them. Much of what they had previously done at a private, implicit, informal level is now rendered public, explicit and formal. Professional and collegial accountability is replaced by public accountability. Trust gives way to contractual obligation. Stress levels rise (Cooper and Kelly, 1993). What permits central government to declare that the education system is indeed less bureaucratic is that local government is being by-passed, an issue to be returned to in Chapter 8. Local management of schools and grant-maintained schools (or charter, or self-governing schools) devolve to schools some of the tasks hitherto performed by local government. This does not mean that the educational bureaucracy is reduced; it simply means that it has been moved from local government, and intensified, at school level. The emergence of the 'management team' in most schools is testimony to this shift. When things go wrong, it will be the school, as implementer of policy, which will bear the brunt of the criticism. The government — way above the fray — can claim not to be culpable, for it will reason that it is not the policy *per se* which is at fault, but the manner in which it is executed. In other words, teachers now feel an increasing bureaucratic weight bearing down upon them: the first, system-defined curriculum, assessment and appraisal; the second, management-team defined tactics which will serve to implement system-defined goals; the third, increasing procedural controls and monitoring. All this is no post-bureaucratic, empowering professional culture. The discourse of legitimation may be empowering, but the lived experiences of the discourse are not. Far from being empowered, classroom teachers may become the bearers of the will of their line-managers. There seem to be few, if any, recent changes in education policy and practice which have their origin with classroom teachers — hardly an indication of empowerment.

Teachers also face other intrusions into their professional space. Not only are teachers increasingly enmeshed in bureaucracy, but they are simultaneously being taken to the market, in search of pupils, often in tow with business. Image becomes the essence. This is a significant change in the teacher's theatre of operations. For a long time, the school could keep its environment at bay, both architecturally and theoretically: architecturally, because the physical space of the school was largely off-limits to the public; and theoretically, because teachers were seen to have eso-teric pedagogical content knowledge to which parents did not have access. This is changing. Assessments of schools are made public; and many parents — especially in the middle class — have access to the pedagogical discourse of education. They know the score.

Teacher educators, too, for long at the margin of the academic and political centre in universities, now find themselves even more so, for a number of reasons, not the least of which is the content and theoretical basis of the curriculum within faculties of education. There has been something of a last-ditch attempt (Shulman, 1987) to define the knowledge base of teaching. Throughout the modern period, fac-ulties of education have sought this base, a base to which we could all withdraw, safe and sound, exuding intellectual certainty, admitting none except the initiated. Perhaps, privately, the advocates of 'the knowledge' realize that the game is up; perhaps, pragmatically, they seek to portray to the public the *impression* that all is well-founded on the rock of value-free hard data. In sum, perhaps they publish their hard-backed texts in the vain hope that the iconoclasts will not open them.

This seems wishful thinking. Labaree (1992, 1995), in a perceptive analysis of the emergent discourses contained in the American Holmes Group publications (*Tomorrow's Teachers* [1986]; *Tomorrow's Schools* [1990]; *Tomorrow's Schools of Education* [1995]), reveals the shift from claims to intellectual rigour in 1986 to a media-minded, 'profoundly anti-intellectual' piece of journalese. How curious it is, however, that whilst the parent disciplines of education — philosophy, soci-ology, psychology — are in some disarray, fending off the postmodernists who are bent upon undermining them, there are some in teacher education who retreat into an inner sanctum, hoping it will all go away. As I have argued elsewhere (Hartley, 1993b), the demise of positivism in teacher education occurred in the early 1970s, with the phenomenological turn taken by some researchers, a turn which has since become mainstream constructivism. What it did was to focus on what we had all been missing: the taken-for-granted commonsense knowledge of teachers. But this approach has not always served teacher educators well, for its theoretical under-pinnings have at times been weak, or non-existent, such that personal narrative purported to count as theory itself, an intellectually superficial version of 'grounded theory' (Glaser and Strauss, 1968). But grounded theory must be adequate at the level of meaning (it must accord with the commonsense, first-order constructions of actors) and be causally adequate (it should be comparable to similar situations, and, though provisional, should be able to establish its claims to be more adequate than other explanations of the data). The lapse into narratives which speak for themselves has not enhanced the academic status of teacher education in the academy. Indeed constructivist theory appears to have taken hold in American teacher education (Burch and Imig, 1996).

Government is stepping in, removing the epistemological uncertainty, en-coding pedagogical reform in a knowledge base of its own making, not that of the academy. In England and Wales, the government-appointed Teacher Training Agency is set to prescribe the course content for the training of primary school teachers in the teaching of English and mathematics, a clear infringement of the curricular autonomy of the university by the state (Clare, 1996). Similar trends are in train in the United States (Burch and Imig, 1996, p. 8). In the main, government has not even bothered to engage the teacher educators; it has simply gone around them, directly to the school, in the same way that it is by-passing local government. To survive financially, faculties of education are forced to do deals with schools, and the deals involve knowledge as well as money. There is a transferral of funds, but with it comes a transformation of professional identities. Increasingly, with the emergence of alternative modes of certification, teacher education can become dis-persed across a multiplicity of providers who are in a market relationship to each other. Now, both teachers and teacher educators inhabit a more common ground. And into this space also there is the possibility of parental involvement. The mixing of these academic, practical and parental registers of concern open up possibilities, not only of mutual understanding, but thereafter of concerted political alignments — in other words, of a network.

The danger for teacher educators is that the greater emphasis on school-based initial training may have unintended political consequences for faculties of educa-tion within their own universities. At a time of fiscal cut-backs, beating a path to the school, albeit for sound pedagogical reasons, may turn out in hindsight to have been to play into the very hands of administrators who are in search of academic activities which are less than central to the mission of the university, and which are therefore expendable. Teacher education could be one of them. Equally, this applies to in-service education, for as budgets are devolved to individual schools the tend-ency for head teachers to focus only on their pragmatic concerns may increase, and university-based award-bearing courses of a more general educational nature may decline. As universities continue to target so-called 'non-viable' courses — that is, those courses which attract few students — this shift in in-service priorities could have a knock-on effect on the curriculum in faculties of education, an effect dif-ficult to curb, and one sure to weaken even further the academic standing of teacher education. At a time when faculties of education should be engaging in both political and academic alliances *within* their universities, their efforts seem to be spent wholly in forging new partnerships with schools and system administrators. 'School links', though long overdue and necessary in the 1980s, may have been overdone, but the new re-institutionalization of teacher education portends turbulent times ahead for teacher educators. Ironically, teacher educators have spawned a welter of research which allows *classroom* teachers to give 'voice' to their concerns, but they have been almost silent in sounding their own collective voice. Indeed, to take this further, university academics in general, long used to having a one-to-one 'quiet word' with colleagues, are perhaps unused to forms of collective action.

This scenario is surely less than optimistic. But all is not lost, for in these changing times new agendas can be constructed (Hargreaves, 1994a; 1995b). The sub-heading of this section is 'vocation and voice'. As mandarins and marketeers 'recall', so to say, the notion of teaching as a vocation, demeaning its moral status, many teachers may be lamenting having taken up their 'calling' in the first place. For them, they see moral obligations being replaced by measured obligations. A re-worked behaviourism 'stimulates' their performance. Their public esteem and their self-esteem seem to be ebbing away, their normative involvement in tension with what Etzioni (1975) called calculative involvement. Speaking more generally about economic strategy and new modes of control in the public sector of Britain, Hoggett (1996) makes a perceptive point:

> [. . .] what we seem to be heading towards in both private and public sectors in the UK is the development of a high output, low commitment work-culture in which trust has become a value of the past and where quality counts for far less than quantity. (Hoggett, 1996, p. 28)

Earlier in this chapter, in relation to critical postmodernism and the work of Giroux and McLaren, the notion of 'voice' was considered, in particular the politics of giving vent to concerns. Part of what emerged in that analysis was that there is no single voice of the oppressed. Whilst different groups share the status of being oppressed, the form it takes differs, according to context. Analysing the now-extensive research on teacher reflection, on teachers' biographies, and on teachers' experience and voice, Hargreaves (1994b, p. 27) is surely correct in asserting that, 'The teacher's voice has been made into a romantic singularity claiming recognition and celebration'. These voices may well be valid for those who project them, but they are not representative of teachers at large, and nor are they the result of an authentically negotiated position arising from among all those with an interest in schooling.

The blurring of spatial boundaries in postmodern culture opens up the possibility for teachers to 'travel' into domains long regarded as off limits. These domains are intellectual and political; and, in a way, personal. In other words, the fickle, fluid fashions of postmodernist culture can ease the passage of outsiders into the school, and vice-versa. The strict insider–outsider demarcations are now easier to breach, and it is the concept of network which allows for this. But these gaps may not be that easy to bridge. For example, whilst there has always been a generation-gap in the modern age, the inter-generational gap today is of a different order. It turns on the fact that children today possibly 'know' a great deal more about the adult world than their parents know of theirs. I say 'know' because much of the young's knowledge of adults is vicariously acquired through the media. On the other hand, parents — especially those who work long hours — have little firsthand access to the non-school world of the young. Furthermore, this 'world' of the young is not as homogeneous as the unitary term 'world' implies. The culture of consumption is fragmented, both for young and old. Notions of time and space in postmodern culture hardly accord with the bureaucratic spatial and temporal arrangements of a school which may reflect the mentality of the modern (and even the pre-modern) mind. For teachers, the question of how to appropriate this culture is of crucial concern, a concern not dissimilar to the clergy, some of whom have incorporated the 'holy disorder' of postmodern culture in order to woo back the young into their congregations. But for some teachers that kind of approach may be a bridge too far.

Towards the Curricular, Pedagogical and Technical Fix

In this and the previous chapter a range of intellectual, cultural and economic changes have been discussed in relation to curriculum and pedagogy. These are now brought together, as a summary.

1 Intellectually, *postmodernist theory* has effected a sustained critique on the rational curriculum of the type advocated by Tyler. And both Piagetian developmentalism and constructivist learning theory have attracted a postmodernist critique. Indeed, within the teacher education community, constructivism has taken the high ground, though it seems set to be under-mined by governments who seek politically to suppress it in favour of a re-assertion of much that the postmodernists are railing against.

2 *The culture of postmodernism* has itself attracted attention from a range of perspectives: liberal pluralists (Graff); critical theorists (Giroux and McLaren); and marxists (Zavarzadeh and Morton). All three of these approaches define a firm interrelationship between pedagogy and curric-ulum, though their political orientations differ, with Giroux and McLaren engaging in culture wars, unlike Zavarzadeh, who retains the sharpest focus on social class. And whereas Graff seems more at ease with having the culture wars expressed intellectually, the others wish to engage in them politically. All the same, there seems to be no dispute among them that the culture of postmodernism is fractured. The issue is where these lines of fracture fall, and whether or not the factional elements shall be regarded as a mere mosaic — as just different from each other — or as a stratified set of inequalities which must be contested through radical pedagogy and through a radical curriculum. Here disputes do arise: whose cause shall prevail; how can equality of access to the new dialogical arena be ensured;

are all subjects in the curriculum amenable logically to critical postmodernist approaches — is science, for example, above the fray?

The culture of postmodernism has prompted not only an emancipatory discourse, but also a conservative one. Stunned by the speed of the onset of postmodernism and its uncertainties, voices on the Right are fast seeking a *cultural fix* to stem the panic: the National Curriculum in England, for example; or the backlash from the Right in America, not to say Canada, against multicultural education. This cultural fix seems to centre more about literature and history than the sciences; and its extent ranges also into religious education, with the less-than-hidden preference for Christian religions over, say, Islam. And at the same time there are courses on personal, moral and social education being devised for quick dissemination, again with the intent of fastening the minds of the young to a new moral Archimedean point.

Even so, whilst both Left-leaning critical postmodernists and the Right-sided conservatives are pushed in different curricular directions, neither has yet resolved the question of pedagogy. Giroux *et al.* meet opposition from some who regard them as long on theory and short on practical application; and equally the advocates of what is termed here as the *pedagogical fix* are resorting to the tried-and-tested didacticism so dear to Korea and Japan, but so long-forgotten by those who were professionally nurtured in 1960s and 1970s progressivism. To be sure, whilst the Left seem caught up in a multicultural *mélange*, the neo-conservative Right lament the dissolution of the cultural order.

The political difficulty for the Conservative Right is that it is split between what Giddens (1995) calls neo-conservatives and neo-liberals, the former wedded to the ideals of authority, allegiance and tradition, the latter to market-driven choice, change and disruption. How the Right's curricular and pedagogical fixes will be effected provides one of the more interesting scenarios before us. Will it be cast within a discourse of postmodernism: empowering, reflecting, owning, individual; or will it appeal to latent fears of uncertainty, or to jingoism and 'our' long-hallowed traditions; or will these rhetorics all be served up as a suitably postmodern collage, with something for everyone?

3 Global capitalism and post-Fordist work processes present education with an *economic* context far more turbulent than has been the case for much of the twentieth century. In the face of budgetary controls, education has been called to account. Attempts in Britain to vocationalize the curriculum have been less than successful. The great academic/vocational divide remains. In England, the academic 'gold-standard' of the A-level examination still has more currency than the baser metal of the National Vocational Qualification (NVQ). So curriculum has arguably been little affected in its very content by these economic shifts. However, although its very subject content has not been much altered, the details and structure of that content have been fixed. And now there are signs that the 'excesses' of

progressivism are set to be trimmed. A more didactic, back-to-good-teaching movement seems to be in the offing.

Once officialdom has defined *what* shall be taught and *how* it should be taught, then the way forward for Webster and Robins' *technical fix* (based on information technology) will be open, logically if not politically. Though efficient, it would not be democratic, except in the sense that it might cheapen and broaden access to education. Though efficient, its didacticism would hardly transmit a hidden curriculum suited to post-Fordist work regimes. Though efficient, its narrow prescriptions for 'work' and 'discipline' would be decidedly at odds with the flux, flow and fickleness of the culture of postmodernism. At best, it seems no more than a holding operation — a quick fix.

Chapter 7

Assessment

Few are the days when the media gives no attention to standards in education. In the 1980s, research into assessment and school effectiveness in education has been a growth industry. Terms like competence and effectiveness are likely to have few detractors among the general public; after all, who would wish our children to be incompetent and our schools to be ineffective? But studies of school effectiveness require measures of effectiveness: first, there must be an objective way to measure the progress a pupil makes at two points in time — usually on admission and on leaving. The 'value added' to the pupil can be read off, and can be used as an effectiveness indicator; and second, there must be objective measures which will allow schools to be compared to each other.

There exists, however, a prior question to be put: why, now, have the issues of measurement and effectiveness come to the fore? A possible answer is to locate these issues in a broader one: the political commitment of a Conservative government to re-structure the education system along market principles. The logic runs thus: markets can only thrive on competition; schools must compete in order to attract the funds to function; these funds follow the number of pupils; the number of pupils will — by this argument — turn on the effectiveness of the school, assuming that parents will want 'the best for their children'; in order to make the choice the parents must be informed about the products on offer, and this information should be accessible, reliable, objective and allow for between-school comparability; between-school comparability requires measures of school effectiveness, which in turn require standardized assessments, the results of which are made public. The market, however, is not wholly a free market, for government retains the reins of quality control: it sets the standards for credentials; it measures the product, independently. As we shall see, what Callahan calls the 'cult of efficiency' movement is by no means a recent phenomenon. For example, in the 1860s, a government, strapped for cash in the aftermath of the expensive Crimean War, introduced the Revised Code and its attendant payment-by-results; in the 1920s, in the United States, quality control also carried the day, as it does now.

This chapter first deals briefly with the mode of assessment during the period up to about 1970, a time when the methodology of assessment and testing portrayed a sense of scientific certainty and rigour. I then turn to the insights and possible consequences for assessment which postmodernist theory suggests. I divide this latter discussion into three strands:

1   The first strand draws on Foucault. I consider the trend to panoptical surveillance of the self, in connection particularly with profiles and records of achievement (sometimes referred to as 'authentic assessment'). I link this with the emerging practices of reflection, self-assessment and personal development, drawing upon the ideas of Elias and Giddens.
2   The second strand deals with the postmodernist critique of representation and validity, and I relate these theoretical insights to the 'authentic' assessment movement.
3   The third strand refers both to Lyotard's performativity principle and to his insights on information technology, in relation to assessment.

Finally, as in the chapter on curriculum, I weigh the theoretical insights of postmodernist theory against the *political* power of central government to re-assert control of assessment, not just in response to a perceived fracturing of the culture, but also as a strategy to reduce public expenditure on education by introducing market-driven, post-Fordist managerial regimes.

Assessment and Modernity

Is education an art or a science? Is its discourse to be couched in terms of humanism or rationalism, value or fact? Does pedagogy rest on universal, scientific principles whose validity and reliability have been tried and tested? Is what counts as curriculum reducible to the cool logic of analytical philosophy? Can we abstract education from its cultural context — from its time and place — and see it, pristine and pure, in all its essence? When we speak of educational theory, do we mean description, explanation or prescription; or some mix of these? When we seek to generate a theory *of teaching*, do we turn only to the discipline of psychology; and when we theorize *about education*, are we more likely to draw upon sociology, economics and philosophy? These questions probably have exercised the minds of students of education ever since education became a university subject in the second half of the nineteenth century. But these very questions are themselves socially situated, contingent. One doubts, for example, that either Plato or Erasmus would have been much bothered by the question of whether or not education is a science. They were more interested in prescribing than in explaining. Erasmus, for example, thought that education (for boys only) should be about teaching civilized behaviour: curbing the passions, being polite; a gentleman, not a barbarian (*De Civilitate Morum Puerilium* — 'On Civility in Children', published in 1560).

In the modern period, education — or, more correctly, schooling — has fallen to the gaze of the disciplines. Children have come to be examined, both in what they know and in how they behave. It is commonly held that the first *written* examinations in England were held at Oxford and Cambridge between 1750 and 1810, building on a tradition of oral examinations (Hoskin, 1979). But the emergence of the written examination — of close monitoring — may be explained sociologically as the symptom of deeper social transformations. For example, in the wake of the success of Calvin and Luther in Europe, the Jesuit order sought to 'seize hold' of the soul by educating it. The Jesuits maintained constant supervision of their pupils, not only to prevent unruly conduct, but also to observe the pupil in order better to manage him, as an individual. And it was they who instilled a powerfully competitive system, causing the pupils to be ever mindful of their actions, lest they be caught out:

> Camp challenged camp; group struggled with group; pupils supervised one another, corrected one another, and took one another to task. [. . .] Everyone was thus kept constantly in suspense. (Durkheim, 1977, pp. 102–3)

So effective was this method that one teacher could oversee classes of two or three hundred pupils (p. 103). Here was a form of 'overseeing', or supervising, which would come to be formalized in the work of Jeremy Bentham. In his 'Panopticon', published in 1791, he set out his plans for a new mode of regulation. No longer would coercion itself be relied upon, but inmates of schools, factories and prisons would have their compliance elicited through the very architecture of the building, a building where the surveillance of sights and sounds *could be* (but was not always actually) constant. Inmates had to assume that surveillance was occurring, for the architecture was such that the possibility for constant surveillance was a feature of the building. This 'demanded' a degree of self-regulation. In sum, surveillance was rationalized in a very discreet way. It became more hidden, built into the very fabric of the institution: inmates came to behave in a more measured and rational way.

It is often assumed that this rational form of schooling is a derivative of the needs of capitalism — what Bowles and Gintis (1976) referred to as a correspondence principle. This means that the mode of regulation of the school anticipates and is functional for the mode of regulation in the capitalist workplace. This is said to occur not so much through the formal curriculum but through the hidden curriculum. Nevertheless, whilst there are good reasons to accept the existence of this correspondence, it is an oversimplification to regard rationalized schooling as solely an epiphenomenon of capitalism. The reference to Jesuit education above and the fact that in Germany and France rational modes of regulation anticipate the onset of industrial capitalism both give the lie to the interpretation that capitalism itself was the sole cause of rational schooling (Hoskin, 1979, p. 146). All the same, there seems to be a strong case to put that capitalism, wherever it found rational schooling, incorporated it into its structures of schooling.

Take an example: Scotland. In a Foucauldian analysis of the 'measures of schooling' in mid-nineteenth century Scotland, Fiona Paterson (1988) argues that:

> [. . .] state intervention into elementary schooling in the 19th century can be understood as part of more general programmes of power directed at transforming patterns of social relations to make them compatible with those of industrial capitalism. (Paterson, 1988, p. 283)

She provides a discourse analysis of state papers on elementary education between 1839 and 1872. Much of what we now take for granted was then only emerging: the specification of time (the 'school day' and the 'school year'); the ways in which time was 'accounted' for; the construction of a national 'system' of time-allocation in schools; the keeping of 'registers' of attendance; the definition of 'model plans for school buildings for which grants could be paid' (p. 283). More important was the position of the *individual* pupil in relation to the system: that is, measures of individual performance in written examinations against system-wide standards; the careful documentation of admission and withdrawal of children to and from a school so that academic progress and geographical movement within the system could be monitored. Here, therefore, is the emergence of policy based on Benthamic principles of examination, hierarchy and normalizing judgment. Thus we have the expression of mental and social states as numbers, to be classified, to be compared; and to be monitored and inspected, with funds to follow, if performance-levels so warranted them.

I suggested earlier that the 'modern school' which has developed these mid-nineteenth century practices has been remarkably resilient to change. Apart from the occasional upwelling of progressive rhetoric, the structures of modern schooling have remained more or less intact. Exceptions would be the 1960s non-graded school movement in the United States, and the more broadly-based so-called open education movement which drew inspiration from some child-centred schools in England. But in the main these were aberrations whose rhetoric was found appealing, but whose practice was limited (Sharp and Green, 1975); and understandably so, given the broader bureaucratic backcloth of education systems. In a society marked by competitive individualism and the systematization of a normative order, there could be no truck with protecting children from failure, with asserting their innocence, or with allowing them the free rein of their emotions. Such a society required — and got — the educational practices deemed functional for it: norm-referenced written tests (often stressing the multiple-choice), selection and predictability.

It would not strain credulity to concur with Goodman's (1995) recent assessment of American education:

> [. . .] throughout this century, schools in our society have been based upon a model of the efficient and productive business organization. Test scores have become the product of schools, students have become the workers who produce this product using the instructional programs given to them by the organization, teachers have become shop-floor managers who oversee the students to make sure work gets completed correctly and on time, school principals have become 'plant' supervisors who manage the school's personnel [. . .]. (Goodman, 1995, p. 11)

Goodman's summary may not strike so strong a chord with the pupils and teachers of primary schools, and others may wish to take issue with the implied cold efficiency of relationships within schools; and there is still arguably a good deal of traditional charismatic authority and ritual in schools. Perhaps schools have been based on the template of instrumental and bureaucratic rationality, but the good-ness of fit between the template and the actuality is less than firm. All the same, pupils are indeed tried and tested, individually, usually in writing, and the test-results have traditionally been made public (on notice-boards) and in rituals (prize-giving ceremonies) which also have a distinctively pre-modern aspect to them (as in the cap-and-gown graduation ceremony in some high schools).

Validity and Representation

The examination — whatever form it takes — is a measure of the mastery of a canon, a body of knowledge, handed down, structured into ways of seeing the world. Aims and objectives must be made known to pupils. There is a certain sequence in which learning must occur, and the extent to which learning has occurred is tested. The pupil begins a *course* of study in a state of deficiency and is expected by the end of it to have made it good. This course has a presumed linear and sequential structure. The test score is the objective indicator of this. But is it? In their controversial study *Pygmalion in the Classroom* Rosenthal and Jacobson (1968) argued for a 'teacher expectancy effect' whereby teachers' prophecies or expectations of pupils could in some circumstances be realized. More recently, Doll (1993) has reminded us of Werner Heisenberg's Uncertainty Principle: that is, the accuracy of any measurement can be compromised by the very measurement process itself — the observer's subjectivity and presence can have an effect. An examination is a social interaction in a cultural setting. The symbolizations of the pupil and the teacher — whether intended or not — will be interpreted subjectively by both, and they cannot be ignored away, or controlled for, completely, however much the ritual of rigour is played out, however certain the 'final mark' looks.

But if assessment is about measuring the mastery of a canon, what are the consequences for assessment if there are no canons anymore? Much of the post-modernist critique has argued against any epistemological fix or certainty. There are said to be no transcendent principles. Knowledge is not awaiting discovery; it is said to be indeterminate and to be created. That being so, how can we talk about 'making up the deficit', so to say? If there is no universal body of knowledge, if there are no grand narratives, then what we are left with are local knowledges, negotiated. And if that holds, then the days of the *norm*-referenced, standardized test look 'numbered'. Moreover, if we are beginning to admit that there are other modes of understanding the world apart from the rational, then this re-enchantment may lead us to bring in creativity, subjectivity and intuition from the cold. Assess-ment will become authentic, meaningful, local, and not necessarily logocentric.

One of the most important concepts in traditional modes of assessment is that of validity. Does a test actually measure that which it purports to measure? This implies that the assessment instrument is valid for the individual being assessed. It implies that the form and substance of the assessment methodology have a meaning for that individual which accords with the intended meaning of the assessor; and, furthermore, if the assessment is to be norm-referenced, then there must be an assumed mutual understanding between the assessor and *all* of those being assessed, *and* among all those who will interpret the results. If the interpretation is not common, then comparisons — norm-referencing — should not be made.

Postmodernist theory homes in on validity and the standardized approaches to assessment which it lays claim to. The issue is that of representation, and the appearance of validity. Patti Lather (1993) sets the scene:

> Contrary to dominant validity practices where the rhetorical nature of scientific claims is masked with methodological assurances, a strategy of ironic validity proliferates forms, recognizing that they are *rhetorical and without foundation, post-epistemic, lacking epistemological support.* (Lather, 1993, p. 677; my emphasis)

Her analysis is intended as a more broadly focused consideration of validity in the social sciences. It disrupts what counts as normal science, drawing on Lyotard's practice of paralogy, one which seeks to sow the seeds of dissensus in consensus, to think the unthinkable, to tolerate difference and complexity rather than to reside in the comfort of conformity; to seek to destabilize, to distrust linear logic, always, everywhere.

Traditional assessment practice is undertaken under the canopy of the normal curve. Occasionally tests are 're-normed' if the data do not fit the form. But an assessment process informed by postmodernist theory would not set aside data which fell beyond the pre-specified categorization; it would not, alternatively, try to force them into these categories in the interests of conceptual neatness and convenience. Rather, it would celebrate the abnormal; it would not discard it, or rework it, so that it 'becomes' normal. It would regard the examination questions as texts unto themselves, arranged in a certain form. These examination papers may themselves attract a superimposed text, written in the hand of the candidate, but not part of the formal answer script — an examination of the examination, unofficial, a silent off-the-record discourse constructed by the candidate, unexamined, yet meaningful, at the margin. It seeks the deviant — though not the standard deviation. It would say that assessment (if we allow the gaze of one to be cast over another) is to be done *with* another, not *to* another; and it would recognize that this endeavour can never achieve objectivity and universality; it is situated, political and local — a little assessment narrative, for the moment, whose outcome can never be anything more than a socially constructed representation, partial and provisional.

Foucault and Self-assessment

Curriculum models based on modern visions of Newtonian physics attempt, like a clockwork universe, to impose uniformity. Every lesson, every goal and objective, must conform to predetermined principles, cultural forms, social structures, or curricular guides. The postmodern curriculum, on the other hand, is based on a new science: a complex, multidimensional, kaleidoscopic, relational, interdisciplinary, and metaphorical system. (Slattery, 1995, p. 623)

In a society which purports to be meritocratic, there has to be a universally agreed notion of what counts as merit. The public education system purportedly ensures the fairness of the competition. The examination system constitutes the basis of a fair competition. In most modern education systems — especially at secondary school level — examinations are set by a central agency and are externally marked. If there is an element of continuous assessment, then the examining is moderated by officialdom, so that comparability is assured. For the most part, these examinations do not serve a diagnostic purpose: scripts are not returned to the candidate (itself an interesting term, deriving from the Latin *candidus*, meaning white, the colour of the supplicant). There is no dialogue, and there is no diagnosis. It is all about selection, about sorting pupils: some 'make the grade' and progress to the next hurdle; others don't, and leave the race. Examinations are therefore a way of 'getting the measure' of someone.

Since the development of statistics, it has been possible to arrive at a statistical notion of the 'norm' (a term not dissimilar to 'normal') and of the 'deviation' from the normal (the term 'deviant', like 'normal', being applied also to a notion of what counts as conventional behaviour, or the absence of it). No test is worth its salt until it has been *standardized*. The distribution of scores on standardized achievement tests or on personality tests has been used to compare, say, Blacks with Whites, females with males; and so on. As Kamin in *The Science and Politics of IQ* argues, not only is there a science of IQ, but also a *politics* of IQ. This politics of intelligence has its roots in the nineteenth century eugenics movement; and, under the influence of Francis Galton, it did much to confirm 'objectively' the racial prejudice against non-White races in the early years of the testing movement. And more to the point, the psychometric movement made the dubious correlation between intelligence and morality. All this is not to say that all psychometricians labour on behalf of the political far-Right and that they subscribe to a 'nature' (as opposed to 'nurture') explanation of intelligence (Harwood, 1979).

A central preoccupation of assessment in the modern era, therefore, has been that of the norm, which is both a statistical and moral artefact. Implicit in this is the view that a norm is that which an individual is measured against. Assessment heretofore has been individualized. Few teachers can get away with assigning a communal mark to a class of individuals. Collaboration among pupils would attract the charge of cheating. Knowledge must be kept private, not shared. For a teacher to allow otherwise would be to break the pedagogic code. Moreover, assessment has tended largely to be written, a process which appears to give the answer a certain objectivity and permanence. There must be rigour. And there must be objectivity, preferably represented numerically. In its extreme form, testing of this kind generates right/wrong answers chosen from a pre-specified range: the multiple-choice test. How the pupil might have interpreted the question and its pre-defined responses, or how the pupil came to a decision about the choice, are of no concern. Here, therefore, is curricular knowledge in its most fragmented form, with a testing procedure to match it.

Nevertheless, although this seemingly rational, objective and timed process has all of the hallmarks of modernity, it also has signs of the period which preceded it. The examination room — silent, almost monastic — seems to enact a contradictory ritual: the pupils are all together in order to reveal their differences. The candidates are engaging in a (w)rite of passage. And beyond the examination is the almost medieval prize-giving ceremony which reveals success and failure. Gowns and graduation certificates await those to be initiated.

In the 1960s, this code began to crack a little, in the wake of the child-centred education movement, and also as a result of a motivation crisis which loomed among those young people of low achievement who had to remain at school until the age of sixteen. For them, the rigours and routines of assessment were to be rendered more palatable, thereby inviting less resistance. Continuous assessment and records of achievement emerged. Building on this — and compatible with it — was the development of what has come to be termed authentic assessment, one which eschews the rough-and-ready rituals of formal, norm-referenced testing in favour of a more sensitive and non-threatening assessment experience. As I argued earlier, there emerged in the 1980s a series of new 'subjects of the self'. They focused on generating a repertoire of social skills. Initially, they were intended for those pupils who had failed to master the hidden curriculum which had been in place throughout this century. 'Destined' to be the peripheral workers of the service and manufacturing sectors, these pupils had to be taught explicitly (not through the hidden curriculum) how to cope with unemployment; or, if in work, how to behave flexibly and to interact with the public. These courses, therefore, were both thera-peutic and instrumental. The assessment of the kinds of affective outcomes which these courses required was problematic, not lending itself easily or logically to traditional modes of assessment. It was in order to deal with this problem that the introduction of profiles and records of achievement seems to have been made.

These and other new modes of assessment have come to be termed 'authentic assessment' (Torrance, 1995), or performance assessment. Fischer and King (1995, p. 3) refer to authentic assessment as that which 'examines students' ability to solve problems or perform tasks that closely resemble authentic situations'. In their early development they were heralded as an important step to maximize the motivation of the pupil and to document in a leaving statement what the pupil had done.

Take, first, the matter of motivation. It is worth stating that records of achieve-ment (ROAs) gained official endorsement with the publication of *Records of Achieve-ment: A Statement of Policy* (DES, 1984). The early 1980s was a period of very high youth unemployment, a time when the traditional causal relationship between an education and a job ceased to have meaning for those teenagers who found themselves in the lower achievement levels of their school. Their motivation was ebbing, their commitment to the traditional pedagogy relatively weak. In order to re-awaken their commitment, the pedagogical sentiments first expressed in the 1963 Newson Report *Half Our Future* were re-asserted, and built on. Part of the new edifice was the record of achievement, which was to replace the record of failure. ROAs had a second purpose: they were to be very explicit, detailed and formal statements which officially 'documented' far more of the pupil than letter-grade examination results had done. Third, ROAs give academic recognition to personal qualities — imagination and creativity, for example — which, though not amenable to being assessed in written form, are nevertheless not without importance for employers when they come to a view about applicants for jobs. Thus, whilst ROAs not only record academic achievement, they can also, if required, record revelations of personal qualities. They obviated the need, therefore, for potential employers to bear the cost of such detailed screening.

But there are important ethical and methodological issues involved here. On ethical grounds, the formalization of the pastoral domain of schooling opens up for public scrutiny what are private thoughts which are often made in the seemingly secure setting of the friendly interview, or which are recorded privately in a diary. This prompts two questions. How far has the school the right to probe (or to facilitate the therapeutic expression of) the innermost thoughts of pupils? Who confers on the school the right to retain the record? These are questions of profound significance. At best, they require a formal code of ethics which will guide — but which could hardly govern — the construction, ownership and dissemination of the pastoral ROA. Hargreaves (1986, pp. 209–10) is not convinced that these ethical safeguards will be provided, for the categories which structure the record (and indeed the available pre-worded range of responses) are pre-defined by officialdom, with employers in mind.

Hargreaves' reservation points up the tension between, on the one hand, the 'ownership' which the pupil was said to have of the contents of a portfolio and, on the other, the external control over it held by the teacher (who may also be mediating control on behalf of a higher order). Indeed, despite the consumerist rhetoric and the appeals to pupil autonomy, the very terminology of portfolio/performance assessment is itself riddled with the metaphors of production and control. Fischer and King (1995, pp. 12–14), for example, produce a typology of portfolios: *working*; *showcase*; *and record-keeping*. Each contain *samples*: *process* samples of works in progress; *product* samples of work completed. Each contain 'teacher *observations*'. The evidence within the portfolios is by no means restricted to the written, but can include, for example, audio- and videotapes, computer disks, computer shows, simulations and photographs. This panoply of multi-media representations, under the 'ownership' of the pupil, marks a break with the age of norm-referenced testing. And this assemblage of assessment evidence — this collage — even has space for the truly personal: for evidence which falls beyond the official rubric which frames the collage. It is called the *wild card selection*. This is said by Fischer and King to:

> provide students with autonomy, accommodating a wide variety of learning styles, and encourage creativity and variety. [. . .] a place for students to include other items that are not on the menu but are products of which they are particularly proud. (Fischer and King, 1995, p. 15)

Authentic assessment prompts methodological concerns. They relate to validity. Where there is negotiation between pupil and teacher about the criteria which structure the record, then validity will seem high, for it will have meaning for both. But if validity is taken to mean adequate coverage of the curriculum, then it is not. And if comparability among pupils is important — and it is — then the reliability of ROAs for making rank-order judgments of pupils within a class is weak (Brown and Black, 1988, p. 85). Moreover, the reliability of authentic assessment for public accountability purposes (and increasingly for funding) is also weak. The reliability of assessment procedures requires a shared agreement among assessors across schools. But, as schools come into ever-greater competition for funds, then the common culture of assessors may fracture, reducing the reliability claims of authentic assessment. Thus, despite the validity of authentic assessment within a school, their reliability across schools could weaken. Government, therefore, may push for a return to more restricted and controllable modes of testing in order to justify the reliability of its own decisions when allocating funds.

Authentic assessment lays claim to greater validity, but runs the risk of reduced reliability. (Some postmodernists, however, would reject the very possibility of any validity claims.) It accords with the emerging reflexivity of postmodern culture. Its discourse resounds with consumerist and (information) technological allusions. It is said to reward achievement rather than publicize failure. It forms no part of the traditional assessment procedures which celebrate differences among pupils. Formal, written and public examinations resulted in very public, immediate and humiliating ejection from the education system. The 'cooling out' period (Clark, 1961) was very short-lived. Profiles, however, are portable: they have 'currency' beyond the here and now; credit-transfer systems can mean that documented achievements are never wasted. Indeed, it is now possible for a person to defer almost indefinitely the point of exit from the education system. The dire consequences of a failed school-leaving examination no longer face pupils. Another chance awaits them. Continuing education means that all is never lost; that access to more credentials remains a possibility. The strict hierarchy of credentials is now blurred, the sense of failure deferred. The future remains provisional and indeterminate. Bourdieu (1979) puts it well:

> Everything takes place as if the new logic of the educational system and economic system encouraged people to defer for as long as possible the moment of ultimate crystallization toward which all the infinitesimal changes point, in other words, the final balance-sheet which sometimes takes the form of a 'personal crisis'. (Bourdieu, 1979, p. 156)

So, profiles make explicit more about the pupil than do mere examination marks. They require an open attitude of mind on the part of the pupil. And the reflexivity which they require of the pupil could be turned to sinister purposes. For what could emerge is an auto-opticon, continuously surveying the self, habitually. This invisible and self-regulatory process would obviate the need for external surveillance and coercion. In Elias's phrase, the 'battlefield has moved within us'; it is no longer me versus them. On the other hand, the contemporary world becomes ever more complex; the future appears more and more unpredictable; networks proliferate, but are often short-lived. All this suggests an existential uncertainty for us. To be taught to reflect continually on one's position within this changing complexity may be no bad thing. Whether or not our reflections should be recorded — and thereafter possibly owned and administered by others, for purposes not of our making — is quite a separate concern.

Foucault's notion of the 'confessional' logically lends itself to profiling. In this way the state 'exerts' pastoral power: the self must be known by the self, and by the state; a truth-telling process whose product is apprehended by the state (Howley and Hartnett, 1992). In many levels of the education system, this 'truth-telling' has been steadily emerging: in the form of pupil-profiling; in the form of teacher appraisal; and in the many internal 'audits' which are made of departments and institutions. Here, therefore, is a deeper form of surveillance — human resource management, no less. The more management knows of its workers, the greater the degree of precision with which it can assign tasks to them. Rarely are these truth-telling sessions conducted among workers who are in the same stratum of the hierarchy. Even so, these self-assessment sessions consume time and money, and there may come a time when the costs out-weigh the benefits. One could well envisage a time ahead when the statementing of reflexivity ceases to be a requirement: once reflexivity becomes habitualized, then it need no longer be rendered formal and visible. Meanwhile, authentic assessment appears very much to be a sign of the times, and there is something of a (very pre-modern) missionary zeal about the 'movement'. Bateson (1994) refers to it as a 'revolution':

> [Teachers] have wholeheartedly joined the authentic revolution. Although the established processes and methods of standardized, paper-and-pencil, black and white, selection-type testing have been researched and developed well and have served the purposes of making policy decisions about groups at relatively low cost in the past, the present mushrooming of interest in authentic performance, and portfolio procedures dictates that the focus of resources, training, and research in the testing/measurement/evaluation community must change. (Bateson, 1994, p. 239)

Performativity, Post-Fordism and the Assessment of Competence

In the *Postmodern Condition*, Lyotard considers the interrelationship among knowledge, science and technology. In the modern period, he argues that two grand narratives, or metanarratives, were legitimated: that, first, there is a justification for an idealist, speculative type of knowledge — that is, knowledge for its own sake; and second, that knowledge can be produced for emancipatory purposes. But, as time passes, we cannot continue to have faith, so to say, in these two rationales. In its quest to win approval, science has come to rely on technology in order to produce empirically supported proof of its statements. This technology is very expensive, and can usually only be acquired if funds from government or industry are forthcoming. Funds will tend to be granted if they maximize systemic performance, particularly economic performance. There develops, therefore, a nexus between science and economic efficiency. Put another way, there emerges a close relationship between what counts as knowledge and economic power. Those who choose not to 'buy into' this 'language game' will find themselves at the margin, unrecognized, if not silenced.

What is the connection between Lyotard's concept of performativity and the recent fashion for competence-based assessment? In a simple sense, a competence statement is a 'can-do' statement, which logically requires no gradation of 'can-do-ness': a task is either completed, or it is not completed. If the task is performed, then competence can be inferred. The National Council for Vocational Qualifications (NCVQ) in England and the Scottish Vocational Educational Council (SCOTVEC) have for some years been itemizing, defining and arranging the competences required of many occupations, from the simple manual to the professional. It is a grand design, born of the modern mind's quest to itemize, specify, standardize and systematize, all with the goal of optimizing performance. Lyotard's assertion, made in 1984, that the important criterion which would come to legitimate knowledge within postmodernity is its use-value, its commodity status.

Whilst it is important to stress that competence-based assessment is more likely to be found in further education (whose remit has traditionally been vocational), there is a case to be made that practices which have taken root rapidly in further education — modularization, learner-centred pedagogy, transferable skills and profiling — have tended to permeate other levels of education, thereby leading to an emerging structural isomorphism within all levels of the education system. The logical outcome might be an articulation of these levels within a single validation and accreditation board. This consolidation can open up the possibility for multiple providers of education at all levels to provide 'choice' for informed consumers. Quality control would be maintained at the centre, whilst 'delivery' could be left to 'players' in a voucher-driven marketplace of approved providers. In sum, the performativity principle may come to have two important consequences for assessment policy and practice: first, as with authentic assessment, there may be a shift away from the written form of assessment towards a range of indicators of competence and understanding; and second, government may reason that cost-savings can accrue if it centralizes assessment and privatizes provision.

A central feature of Lyotard's postmodern condition is the computer. The computer allows capitalism to monitor us beyond the workplace into the marketplace (including the home). The digital trail left by credit-card users enables patterns of consumption to be constructed. Data-bases can exchange information. This information can itself be harvested, sifted and sold as a commodity. Banks now encourage children to open accounts with bank-card access to their funds, and with telephone access to information about their account balance.

As children progress through school — and as computerized information systems become common — they will leave their digital 'marks' on the computerized records. These records will be kept because they are efficient ways of showing the development of the pupil, not only in relation to themselves, but to others in their own school and elsewhere. As information technology develops, this single record could comprise digitalized written, visual and oral representations, not only of the pupil, but also perhaps of the pupil's family. The nature of the 'file' would change: from index card to computer file, continually up-dated, electronically portable, instantly retrievable, its content limited only by the number of 'fields' which its structure contains. What comprises the portfolio — the file — can already include evidence to be presented in a digitalized format (Fischer and King, 1995). As information technologies converge on a digitally encodable format, then what counts as authentic assessment evidence may come to be structured by the available technology through which it can be revealed. Evidence which cannot be encodable in this format may come to be marginalized. It will be off the record, technologically *not* authentic.

If on-line pedagogy develops, the pupil could be continuously monitored and assessed through interactive feedback. The pupil's connection could easily be captured in a log file, a 'learning log', which could be backed-up, for future access. The record would be continuous. Indeed, 'continuous assessment' would literally be possible. The 'profile' of the pupil could be mined for information, with samples extracted for different purposes, using search engines, as is now the case on the Internet. Whilst assessment under this new regime might appear to be under the 'ownership' of the pupil in its *construction*, its availability — its *distribution* — would be for others to decide upon, and hidden from the pupil.

In this sense, the insights of Lyotard and Foucault emerge as complementary. Computerization and performativity (Lyotard) generate the means and ends respectively for a new mode of regulation (Foucault). The performative, instrumental ends of education can be transmitted in a multi-media format which is flexible (in time and space), non-hierarchical and non-threatening in its modes of (technologically aided) assessment. The burgeoning bureaucratic structure of the NCVQ in England with its closely defined, itemized competence 'elements' seems no less modernist than the increasingly maligned multiple-choice test of yesteryear. Whereas in the age of the objective test, a student's academic identity could be reduced to a grade-point average, now, argue Usher and Edwards (1994, p. 110) 'Through their inscription in the NVQ system, persons become a bundle of competences; in effect they *become* their NVQs'.

In sum, authentic (or performance) assessment seems to have much contemporary appeal. Its claims to validity are strong. Its processes appeal to the senses — to experience, not to the abstract. It is flexible, non-threatening, allowing for self-monitoring. There is an accord between it and just-in-time (JIT) production processes: there is no waiting around for the next round of tests — performances can be assessed when the individual pupil is actually ready, not when everyone is supposed to be ready. As in postmodern culture, spontaneity and immediacy are part of the very structure of authentic assessment, or so it seems. Implicit, too, is a further link with post-Fordist practice: zero-defects production. That is, on being assessed at relatively short intervals, rather than by being inspected at the end of a long batch-run, so to say, the student can be more easily diagnosed as having difficulties, which can then be put right, immediately. And its discourse accords with consumerism (ownership; 'showcase samples') and to humanism (autonomy; rewarding achievement rather than ritualizing failure). Students are taught to market themselves, both virtually (through the computer-based media) and in written symbolizations. Even the 'wild card' sample — where it is allowed — resonates with the cult of choice and diversity, unbounded by convention.

Playing for High Stakes

Slattery (1995, pp. 620–21) sets out a postmodern vision for the curriculum, one which 'encourages chaos, non-rationality, and zones of uncertainty'. But, to repeat, is it possible to realize this vision 'within a bureaucratic paradigm committed to the principles of modernity?'. I suggest here — as before in the discussion of the curriculum — that this will be no easy endeavour. There appears to be a logical contradiction. On the one hand, we have the systematization and optimization of resources according to the *economy*-serving performativity principle; and on the other hand, the emerging *culture* of postmodernism which seems to fly in the face of such a rigid bureaucratization of assessment. The first is an economically driven position; the second, a cultural. But there is yet another consideration. Both the postmodernist epistemological critique and the paradigmatic ructions which are beginning to stir in science both combine to undermine the 'one-answer-fits-all' approach in competence-based assessment. Notions of competence imply a universally agreed outcome (and perhaps an assumed universality of understanding which underpins the competence), but these would logically fall if this postmodernist epistemological critique is admitted.

And that is the issue: the *logical* position of the postmodernists can be overidden by a *political* credo enacted by government. All the same, government does not merely impose its doctrine; it purports to legitimate this by appeals to consumer culture and to a liberal discourse. I have suggested elsewhere (Hartley, 1987a) that there exists a striking similarity between the rhetoric of 1960s child-centred education and that of the 'new' learner-centred in further education in the 1980s. And the 1980s was a time when government were seeking a return to more didactic pedagogy in primary education. If so, why did it appear to introduce a version of child-centred education in the 1980s? In the 1960s, child-centred education turned on a short-lived conjunction between the realm of ideas and the consumerist needs of a booming economy. That is to say, Rousseau's romantic individualism and Piaget's developmentalism both resonated with the consumerist messages put out by the advertising agencies: needs, freedom, play, choice. In the 1980s and 1990s, learner-centred education has appropriated this humanist discourse for an instrumental purpose, for performativity. So, post-Fordist work regimes and a service sector economy require flexibility, self-supervision, negotiation and problem-solving skills, and this re-worked progressive pedagogy can prepare the pupil for it.

The government generates a double code: an over-arching, bureaucratic systematization of assessment and credentials, and the criteria for awarding them;

and a legitimating discourse which appeals to postmodernism by weakening the temporal and spatial contexts in which assessment occurs. Assessment which is continuous, non-logocentric, non-threatening is arguably more agreeable than the discrete, time-limited, norm-referenced, written tests held in the awesome confines of the examination hall. That said, the introduction of continuous assessment has not been even: high-status courses required at various selection points in the education system remain more rooted in the more traditional mode of assessment than do those courses which appeal to the lower-achiever. Even so, there is an increasing amount of continuous assessment at all levels.

What is now emerging as a unifying assessment discourse — authentic assessment — raises the question, 'Authentic assessment for what?'. Beneath the appealing, even playful, rhetoric of authentic assessment there lies an important instrumental purpose. This purpose — undeclared — is fourfold: first, authentic assessment — particularly where it relates to what can be termed the pastoral element — reveals and records aspects of the personality of the pupil which should have no place in the public domain of a democracy. In an era of increasing 'marketization' in education, it would not be too far-fetched to suspect that schools, strapped for funds, might succumb to selling these records to market-research companies and employment agencies who seek to target their customers at an early age. The second aspect of this instrumental purpose is that authentic assessment anticipates the post-Fordist managerial regime which some — not all — pupils may be exposed to in the workplace. Third, authentic assessment, with its emphasis on performance, may serve to drive the curriculum towards a narrow instrumentalism. And fourthly, information technology, if and when it becomes available throughout the education system, may well take root more effectively if, before its introduction, the hidden curriculum — which includes authentic assessment — has laid the groundwork by loosening the regime of the school to allow for it.

In other words, in authentic assessment there is an implied playfulness which denotes the greater pleasure to be derived from being assessed in this way. It is thereby motivating, for the pupil. Authentic assessment, however, seems to be logically distant from high-stakes, paper-and-pencil testing. Indeed, the very reliability problems which it spawns appear to render it inadmissible as a way of rank-ordering pupils (and, by extension, their schools, which are themselves rank-ordered in public league-tables). Schools still select. For pupils who aspire to higher education, the stakes remain high. It is not sufficient to say that we have entered the age of mass higher education. The 'mass' in universities is not statistically representative of all the social strata (Parker and Jary, 1995). For schools in a quasi-market environment, the stakes are also high. And for this market to function, government knows that the 'customer' in search of a school will wish to be informed by objective and comparable evidence of its worth compared to other schools. To be sure, the 'play' of authentic assessment is at odds with the 'high stakes' involved for both pupils and schools.

One way of dealing with this would be to limit authentic assessment to those who have all but selected themselves out of the race, or at any rate to those who might wish to defer their education. Authentic assessment — in the form of ROAs and profiles — was introduced for that very category of pupil who found traditional modes of assessment difficult. It was in further education that its procedures were tried and refined. It is further education which is closest to work, and for whom performance indicators of competence are arguably most appropriate. This is not to say that authentic assessment has by-passed other levels of education. Unless, however, its reliability can be assured, it may remain as a complement to more traditional high-stakes modes of assessment. For the moment, high-stakes may mean high status. In an education system marked by performance-related funding, government will tend to favour assurances of reliability over assurances of validity. Indeed, its willingness to implement a low-validity indicator of school effectiveness (namely attainment levels, rather than 'value-added' measures) underlines this. Universally applied authentic assessment will only be countenanced if it maximizes high-stakes competition.

Chapter 8

Management

Classroom 'management' is part of a teacher's pedagogical style. In Chapter 6 it was argued that this style is moving away from a highly didactic and bureaucratic regime towards what is known as a learner-centred pedagogy. Learner-centred pedagogy is said to serve a number of functions.

- First, it is functional for the emergent service sector and 'culture' industries;
- Second, it seeks to foster personal reflexivity — self awareness — in the pupil, and to enable the pupil to take greater responsibility for his or her own supervision. That is, 'super'-vision (from above) is replaced by 'intro'-spection (from within); and
- Third, the new pedagogy engenders flexibility. It does this at two levels: by reducing the strict demarcations of time, space and task in the school; and by opening up the possibility in the pupil's mind that life beyond the school will no longer take a single-career route, but rather that pupils can expect not only to change careers, but also to be unemployed at times.

In this chapter, management is also at issue, but at levels above and beyond the classroom. Management theory itself is contingent upon the academy, the culture and the economy. But more than this, education policy and practice are increasingly couched in terms of the discourse of management theory. Gone are the days when notions of equality of educational opportunity, or of individual needs, or of a liberal curriculum, held sway. Part of the reason for the rise of 'managerialism' — a term which for many has a pejorative ring to it — is that government has sought to prune the welfare state. It must do this in such a manner that it assigns a sense of 'choice' and 'ownership' to those who will be affected by the 'cuts'. That is to say, both the professionals of the welfare state and their 'clients' must in a sense psychologically 'buy into' these policies. In sum, management practice must resonate with the emerging culture of postmodernism; it must be grounded intellectually; it must be seen as effective, as system-serving, as 'performative'.

- First, I shall consider briefly the modern management of education.
- Second — as a basis for the main discussion of the emerging management approaches in education — I shall refer again briefly to the main cultural, economic and intellectual shifts which are in process, and how they relate to recent perspectives on organization theory.
- Third, the 'new managerialism' in education is analysed.

Modernity and Management

The metaphor of the machine has been an important one for social science; and management theory, which draws upon the social sciences, has been no exception. Production involves both technology and people, with the former sometimes defining the ways in which the latter are efficiently organized at work. Early management theory was heavily influenced by engineers, the most famous of whom was F.W. Taylor. It was the engineer who was gradually assigned the task of dealing with the day-to-day management of the factory, on behalf of its owner. Understandably, he came to manipulate people as he did materials and machines, as if people were inert. Little was left to chance: time, space, materials and workers were all subjected to supervision and specification. Everything was to be costed, nothing to be wasted. This mentality eventually took root in the broader culture. For example, we make lists; we leave in-house memos; we measure our petrol consumption; we become upset if we or others are late. Cool reason frames our passions, in the interests of impersonal efficiency. Moral problems attract technical solutions.

The school is a monument to modernity. Virtually everything is arranged rationally, including space, time, curriculum, assessment and discipline. Children are classified according to a range of criteria. The curriculum is rationally ordered, replete with aims, objectives and performance criteria. Rules regulate us. There are set procedures. A hierarchy of roles in the schools is deemed almost as natural. Schools are places where reason prevails over the emotions: be sensible, not silly, is the message. In its bureaucratic form, the school has sought to be a purveyor of distance education — not distance education in the geographical sense, but in the interpersonal sense. Lapses have been few, short-lived, having been defined as too unwieldy for our tidy-minded modern ways.

Organization Theory, Postmodernists and Postmodernism

In Chapter 3 it was argued that the culture of postmodernism turns on a number of trends: *consumerism* and the increasing commodification of culture; *ephemerality* marked by the ever-quickening flow of information, and by the movement of commodities and capital across the globe (Lash and Urry, 1994, p. 31); *reflexivity* of systems (for example, institutional audits) and of the self (facilitated by people like therapists and colour consultants); the widening divide between what Galbraith calls the 'contented' (whose concerns centre upon issues of lifestyle) and Alain Minc's *exclus* (whose concerns are very much to do with survival, and with emancipation from oppression based on gender, race and ethnicity); the *compression of time and space* enabled by the digitalization of modes of communication and, related to this, the greater cultural awareness made possible by the multi-media and tourism — an *internationalization* of cultural awareness; a trend for ethnically cohesive societies to assert *claims for nationhood*, as witnessed in Eastern Europe, Catalonia, Corsica and Quebec; the growing importance of what Lash and Urry (1994, p. 201) call *emotional labour* (in addition to, or sometimes instead of, manual and mental labour). Most of this applies particularly to that segment of the middle classes whose work requires the manipulation of symbols rather than of things. Furthermore, lest it be thought that this consumerist culture has lapsed into 'pure' hedonism, it is worth re-stating Mestrovic's and Featherstone's insight that this 'hedonism' is very much calculated, and indeed that there is a near-obsession with the cult of the self — with 'care' products, fitness and diet; again, for those who can afford them.

Re-consider the intellectual movements afoot. The culture of postmodernism was for Marxists (like Jameson) the 'logic' of late capitalism being played out. Capitalism had moved into the commodification of culture as a way of fueling demand, and for compensating for the prospect of a dried-up demand for material goods. Choice, diversity and immediacy were the clarion calls of the advertising media. For Bell and the neo-Durkheimians, the decline of the Protestant ethic in favour of the no-taboos 'morality' left many floundering, in need of a sure identity-fix which no drink, drug or shopping-spree could provide. Solace could, Bell argues, be found in the integrating rituals of religion.

Not a few post-1968 French theorists — Lash and Urry's 'semiotic left', Foucault among them — pointed up the nexus between knowledge and power. The disciplines of the Enlightenment, which had been premised upon progress, had enmeshed us in a textual cage even more confining than Weber's iron cage of bureaucratic rationality. We were ruled by these 'regimes of truth', these disciplines, our souls governed without us realizing it. But the litany of despair did not stop there. The world was said to be indeterminate; there was no essence waiting to be discovered. There were only simulacra, images in-the-making, not true representations of the objective world. As for science and rational understanding, it was said to have gone beyond its remit, so to say, applying itself to realms — the moral and the aesthetic — where it had no place to be. In so doing, it had thereby re-defined moral issues as amenable to a technical fix, in the interests of efficiency.

These cultural and intellectual trends have implications for organization theory, and therefore for schools, colleges and universities. Beyond Bentham, modern organization theory has gone through a number of phases: the 'engineering' of consent in factories based on panoptical principles in the late nineteenth century; the fine-tuning of production occasioned by F.W. Taylor's *scientific* time-and-motion studies; the emergence in the 1920s of Fordism, whereby control was not simply based on bureaucratic compliance, but also inhered in the ability of the speed of the moving assembly-line to be adjusted; the development of a 'softer' bureaucracy, which resonated partly with the romantic notion of happiness, and partly with the Durkheimian concept of the collective consciousness — that is, the human relations approach. Later still — inspired by Parsonian systems theory — organization theory finally recognized the importance of the environment. Open systems theory set in train a move towards more sophisticated cybernetic 'feedback-loop' approaches which purported to keep organizations in a state of dynamic equilibrium as they responded to contingencies both within and without their formal boundaries. Nevertheless, what unites these approaches is a firm belief that organizations can be rendered knowable, predictable, formal, systematic, rational and functional; that workers are in the final analysis beholden to the formal goals of the organization, and that their own 'needs' would be very much circumscribed by those of officialdom.

The postmodern critique of modern organization theory can be structured along three broad (but intersecting) lines:

- first, a critique derived from a 'strong' postmodernist epistemological approach;
- second, a critique which can loosely be called a social constructionist approach; and
- third, a critique which suggests that the efficiency gains of Fordist management approaches had reached their limit, and required very considerable refinement, along the lines of 'total quality management' approaches.

Organization Theory and Postmodernist Theory

The critique of systems thinking is by no means new. The First World War was to shake the notion of 'progress' to its very foundations. Weber, whose ideal-typical concept of bureaucracy informed much of organizational theory this century, remarked:

> I may leave aside altogether the naive optimism in which science — that is, the technique of mastering life which rests upon science — has been celebrated as the way to happiness. Who believes in this? — aside from a few big children in university chairs or editorial offices. (Weber, 1946 [1917], p. 143)

Organization theory has traditionally espoused a systemic approach. To refer to something as 'systematic' is not to court disapproval. Systems thinking is orderly thinking; even a 'natural' way of thinking. At best, it prepares the way for predictability and certainty; at a lesser level, it rests on the probability of an event rather than on the possibility of it. Life should hold no surprises. What does not fit should be ironed out. Spontaneity has no place in systems thinking. All is normal, routine.

But this way of thinking has its limits. More recently, the systems approach to organization theory has attracted a critique which draws on the work of Derrida and Lyotard. Cooper (1987, p. 405) suggests that there are two ways of thinking about organizations: the first, a *systemic-functional* model; the second, an *agonistic* model. The systemic-functional model is rigid, rule-bound and rests on the performativity principle. This is modern organization theory *par excellence*: efficiency without ethics. But those who march under the banner of reason and progress can be a motley and murderous crew, for among them are both latter-day Fascists and those whose Great Leap Forward was accomplished by trampling all over the lives of millions of people. The agonistic model, informed by poststructuralist theory, is typified by contestations of meaning, of disruptions, of surprises. Gone is the notion of a fixed system: 'rules come *after* the event and not before' (*ibid.*). Thus, there can be no pre-formed meanings. Meaning is undecidable: it differs across space and is to be deferred over time. Nothing can be uniform.

The systemic-functional model informs not just the way of thinking at the site of production (the workplace) but also beyond it. In Cooper's telling phrase: '[. . .] what is really presented here is a *modus vivendi* as well as a *modus operandi*' (Cooper, 1987, p. 409). People are thereby regarded as a resource, to be managed, efficiently. (On this, note how personnel *officers* are currently being re-defined as human resource *managers*. They must therefore 'record' people as information which can be managed, as a resource.) All this is to say that the performativity, efficiency-seeking principle is thereby rendered almost as commonsense. The effect of this would be the 'suppression' of difference. Cooper's critique strikes at the very heart of organization theory and the management practices which it generates. Referring to Giddens, Cooper (1989, p. 493) underlines the view that *formal* organizational structures are in a written textual form. That is to say, the formal rules, timetables and procedures are written. And it is this very formality of definition which gives the appearance of the organization being organized! But:

> The 'theories' of bureaucracy theorists are essentially 'writings' and are therefore subject to the logic of divisions of difference that characterizes Derrida's conception of writing: they are motivated to hide their internal divisions in the interests of control and stable social order. (Cooper, 1989, p. 496)

It is these internal divisions which can be made explicit, continuously disorganizing that which purports to be organized, thereby opening up what has been hidden. In this process, what had hitherto been underprivileged in the hierarchy may itself eventually come to be dominant, but it too, once it becomes dominant, can never rest easily, for the deconstruction continues.

Consider a somewhat 'weaker' approach than Cooper's: the work of Kenneth Gergen. Viewed historically, he also argues that organization theory can be said to have embodied two dominant discourses: the nineteenth century *romanticist* discourse; and the *modernist* discourse of this century (Gergen, 1992, p. 208 *et seq.*). The romanticist discourse is in decline, to be seen and heard within the arts, literature and religion. But the affects — the deep emotions — tend to be expressed less and less in an unrestricted way. We are careful. This romanticist discourse has not, however, been without influence in organization theory. Human relations management theory is a case in point. Here was a soft bureaucratic management style in which workers' 'needs' were to be catered to so that they would be better motivated. Nevertheless, it became quite clear that the needs of the individual workers were to be very much framed by corporate needs. Bureaucracy was loosened, not replaced. Even so, implicit in the justificatory rhetoric of human relations management theory was something of an appeal to the romanticist notion of workers' happiness and feelings. This underlines the point that organization theory must accord with the 'cultural vernacular' (p. 210), to use Gergen's term. As for the modernist discourse in organization theory — referred to above — it too is beginning to lose its 'lived validity' (p. 212). Rehearsing the now-familiar postmodernist critique of the rational mode of understanding, Gergen puts it thus:

> The view of knowledge-making as a transcendent pursuit, removed from the trivial enthrallments of daily life, pristinely rational, and transparently virtuous, becomes so much puffery. (Gergen, 1992, p. 215)

If this post-positivist view holds, then the search for objective truth will be endless. If the purpose of theory is *only* to seek truth, then we might as well call it a day. But, Gergen suggests, there is a way forward, if we change our assumptions about the very function of theory. Logical positivism assumed that by analytical thought we could come to know the truth. Cultural hermeneutics argues that reality is a social construction — that we cannot be separated from what we define as knowledge. That is, if the function of theory rests not on truth-searching but on pragmatism, then this would provide a way out of the abyss into which postmodernist theory has pushed us. And in so doing, it would be informed by some of the deconstructionist insights offered by postmodernists.

Take an example: power in organizations. Within many organizations, units seek functional autonomy (to use a modernist term). They construct socially their ways of seeing, their definitions of reality, which become shared, and fixed, as time passes. Different departments in schools and universities construct sub-cultures. Outsiders can be distinguished from insiders, and this insulation produces isolation from the rest of the organization. At a broader level, the segmented organization can insulate itself from its surroundings. The end-result can be the disintegration and destruction of the organization. If no dissent or deconstruction is permitted, then the consensus within will probably stifle the system. To avoid this there must be an import and export of what Gergen calls 'alien realities' (p. 223); or, in Lyotardian terms, the production of a dissensus within the consensus. Gergen's approach, therefore, is a weaker version of the Derridean-inspired approach aired by Cooper.

Postmodernist theory poses a profound dilemma for so-called modernist organization theorists who have some sympathy for the profound epistemological insight which postmodernist theory provides — which is that there are no certainties about organization (Parker, 1995). On this, there is a strong view and a weak view: the strong view is uncompromising, and leads to a profound relativism, and a pessimism that Truth — objective, transcendent truth — is unattainable; the weak view is one that says that whilst Truth is unattainable, a kind of truth-for-the-moment (a provisional truth) is attainable, a truth which is the result of a consensus, however ephemeral. (In the earlier discussion of Giroux and the so-called critical postmodernist theorists of pedagogy, a similar line was taken.) This avoids the slide into nihilism. But where is this 'reasonable' ground between epistemological realism and Habermas's critical modernism? 'Is it that some bits are True, whilst other bits are only true (opinion)? Alternatively, is it all a bit True?' (Carter, 1995, p. 573) Furthermore, Parker leaves unexamined the question of who shall be party to the negotiated consensus? Which long-suppressed voice, if any, shall be admitted to the debate? These issues of inclusion and exclusion of 'voices' prompts a discussion of power, in its many forms.

Which brings us back to Foucault (1977). In his *Discipline and Punish* he contrasts the traditional mode of domination to the disciplinary mode. To illustrate the former, he compares the gruesome details of the execution of Damiens in 1757 with the mode of regulation inspired by Bentham's 'Panopticon', published shortly after in 1791. The latter is a disciplinary regulation which works on the 'soul', not against the body. Which is not to say that the body does not figure; it does, but in another way. Drawing metaphorical insight from factory machines, the new disciplinary power is 'exerted' through the close scrutiny of the body in all its aspects. Indeed, the body literally comes to be 'figured', in that it is examined, measured, classified and compared; and compared not only at one point in time, but longitudinally over time. In this statistically aided way the norm and deviant are defined, and they are defined by the 'judges' (Foucault, 1977, p. 304) — the teacher, the doctor, the social worker. The many organizational settings in which these 'judgments' occur underline the ubiquity of this disciplinary power. But it is more than this: the disciplines which inform management in education — that is, schools of thought within sociology, psychology, economics — are themselves the discourses of the Enlightenment. They constitute for us 'regimes of truth' — ways of thinking, of symbolizing ourselves; they 'manage' what we shall know and what we shall not know. Put this way, organizations are the settings in which 'subjects' are 'disciplined' by these discourses. For example, our earlier discussion of the work of Valerie Walkerdine attempted to show how Piagetian developmental theory *produced* the universal nature of the child which it purported to explain.

Foucault's work has consequences for research in the management of education (Ball, 1995). On one level, organizations should not be seen as well-oiled machines, with structure matching function, with goals and the technology for realizing them agreed; rather, they are complex, idiosyncratic and fragile, with different faces. And notwithstanding their seemingly different surface features, they are nevertheless disciplinary. How they discipline is itself important to 'know'. On the other hand, the answers to this 'how' question may allow for greater refinement of those very disciplinary procedures and discourses:

> But to talk about them [organizations], to develop discourses and classification schemes for their analysis actively contributes to the reproduction of this discipline. [. . .] *Only to the extent that we stop talking about types of organizations do we succeed in not reproducing the disciplinary society.* (Burrell, 1988, p. 233; my emphasis)

We have so far been considering the postmodernist critique of what has counted as modern organization theory. It is to all intents and purposes an *intellectually driven* position, with some tentative prescriptive suggestions from Gergen, who calls for the inclusion of outsiders who would challenge the hardened assumptions and practices of insulated organizations. But organizations are re-structured for other reasons: they may be inefficient; or, if commercial, not profitable. The bureaucratic behemoths of modernity are regarded now as unable to cope with fast-changing technologies, products and markets. Thus, for *commercial reasons*, a solution to the shortcomings of modern organization theory has been sought.

Japan is said to provide the way towards the so-called postmodern organization. The old bureaucratic notion of a fixed occupational role with clear specification is set aside. Roles are blurred, and are rotated. Loyalty is to the company, not to the role; internal competition among workers is weak in a company where seniority is an important determinant of pay, and where permanent employment (for core workers, mainly men) is assured. The constant audit of workers' competences generates a human resource data-base which can be exploited as the need arises. Just-in-time (JIT) management and self-managing groups produce commitment from both external suppliers and workers, respectively. Rewards are assigned to groups, not individuals. There are collective rituals which also serve to integrate. But there is another view. The peripheral workers (mainly female) are 'flexible' — they are poorly paid, work long hours, and have little job security. If this 'Nipponization' were to become typical of the postmodern organization, then the social divisions between the core and the periphery would be great: 'Postmodernity would be a series of privileged enclaves within the bleak vistas of modernity' (Clegg, 1992, p. 28).

In passing it is interesting to note the argument by Williams *et al.* (1992, p. 539) that the new Japanese manufacturing practices of the late 1970s were '(at least partly) independent rediscoveries of Highland Park practice'. (Highland Park was Henry Ford's car assembly in Detroit, and ironically it anticipated many of the so-called *post*-Fordist work practices.) They argue that '[...] there are uncanny similarities between Highland Park and the current practice of the Japanese' (p. 519), among which were: decentralized final assembly; a reduction of total labour hours per car between 1910 and 1916 which 'makes the late twentieth century Japanese look like sluggards' (p. 522); lean production methods whereby stocks were kept very low (p. 523); flexible workers — 'the Highland Park regime imposed two general requirements on the workforce: they had to be infinitely flexible about the definition of the task to be performed and, at the same time, had to acquiesce in progressive de-manning of most operations' (p. 532); and a flat, informal organizational structure in which there were few job titles (p. 542). All this was hardly a description of a so-called Taylorist-inspired 'Fordist' approach.

Post-Fordism is a rather elastic concept. In order to elaborate on this, I draw heavily on Watkins' (1994) useful conceptualization of post-Fordism. He defines a number of theoretical strands: the French Regulation School; the work of Piore and Sabel; the 'Japanese model'; the 'New Times' approach; and the managerialist/ flexible-firm position of Atkinson. Take the Regulationists (Boyer, 1990): far from seeing the demise of Fordism, they argue that multi-skilling and work-groups mean that greater productivity is 'extracted' — but not coercively — from workers. There is but an appearance of worker autonomy. This contrasts considerably with the ideas set out in *The Second Industrial Divide* (Piore and Sabel, 1984). Beyond the divide of mass-production lies flexible specialization. This is said to hold out the possibility for a liberating association of independent and skilled workers.

Consensus, collaboration and trust will typify their working relationships. In Watkins' third approach — the Japanese model — worker flexibility again looms large. But with it come personal pay packages which individualize the worker's relationship with management (thereby setting aside collective action). With it, too, come quality circles, weak task-demarcations and task-rotations, all of which maximize productivity whilst at the same time serve to legitimate the intensification of effort under a slogan system of participatory decision-making. Watkins' fourth category is the New Times thesis set out by Hall and Jacques (1989). This thesis sees an affinity between new work regimes in the economy and consumerism in the broader culture. By making this 'link' between economy and culture, Watkins suspects that New Times theorists come very close to a cultural determinist account of post-Fordism, and by so doing they appear to underwrite New Right economics.

Returning to flexibility, Watkins cites Atkinson's (1984) typology of the term. Three types are discerned: *functional flexibility* (which allows management to allocate workers quickly to different tasks); *numerical flexibility* (which sees management releasing or hiring non-core, temporary workers, as the need arises); and, linked to numerical and functional flexibility, is *financial flexibility* whereby management pay the rate for the job which the labour market at any given time and place will bear. Implicit in Atkinson's typology is a strong managerialist thread which is more overtly coercive in ensuring compliance. In this coercive approach, it is — at least explicitly — less consensual and subtle than, say, the 'Japanese model' or the optimistic assertions of Piore and Sabel. Central to Watkins' analysis is a concern to look beneath the surface rhetoric of these strands of post-Fordist approaches to the workplace, and in particular to consider that the discourse of post-Fordism can contain both appeals to consent and directives to comply. And what they share is a quest to have more done with less.

TQM and the Rise of the Qualitariat

'Doing more with less': at a period when the traditional capitalist societies are feeling the chill wind of competition from the East; and at a time when their welfare states are under a strain brought about by increasing demands on public services but decreasing tax revenues to support them — in these times, so the argument runs, the solution lies with management, a 'new' management. The 'old' management born of Taylorism is now said no longer to be effective, for these reasons: Taylorism separated thinking from doing, with the consequent diminution in the extent to which the worker took pride in work; Taylorism inspired short-term profit; Taylorism assumed that workers were not intrinsically motivated to work; it set much store by quality-control inspection of the final product; it sought the accomplishment of minimum requirements; it supported the disciplining of workers within a firm hierarchical structure; and it stressed numerical quotas (Schiff and Goldfield, 1994). Public institutions like health and education were assumed to be exemplars of overly bureaucratic structures. They were said to be insensitive to the clients' needs: you got what was on offer. Here was producer-capture writ large. Take it or leave it.

As business has become attracted to some of the practices of Japanese management styles — loosely called post-Fordist — the way forward for a cash-starved public sector has been deemed to be in the direction of Total Quality Management (TQM) or Continuous Quality Improvement (CQI), pioneered and developed in the 1950s in Japan by W. Edwards Deming (1900–93). Deming had been a statistician at the Western Electric Hawthorne Plant in Chicago during the early 1930s, and obviously would have been well versed in the Human Relations approach to management which had been developed there. For many, TQM has become something of a cult. Its very title implies a totalizing, all-encompassing message — QUALITY — which is to be managed, wherever and whenever, privileging the customer above all else.

The central purpose of TQM is quality: 'What is quality? The quality of a product or service is defined operationally as conformance with a pre-established standard' (Eriksen, 1995, p. 18). Let the customer decide wherein quality lies. Simplicity and standardization are crucial to TQM — variability is to be eliminated; there must be a system. A second key concept is that of ownership. That is, there should be a high level of self-management (often in teams). Workers should be encouraged not to suppress mistakes, but to admit them, quickly, so they can be put right. Collaboration, not competition, is said to ease anxiety levels and to drive out fear. Related to this, numerical quotas should be removed, as should individual appraisal related to merit pay. A third aspect is the notion of zero-defects. A faulty product should never be made. Mass inspection should not be undertaken after the product has been made, but continuously during the very production process itself. Fourth, improvement should be continuous.

Deming's 'fourteen points' (synthesized above) are complemented by his 'seven deadly diseases' which weaken management. These are: high medical costs; high litigation costs; lack of constancy of purpose; short-termism; individual performance-related pay based on appraisal; job-switching; management by the use of visible figures (Sallis, 1993, pp. 46–47). British higher education of late has done little to endear itself to Deming.

TQM is not without its contradictions. The elimination of variability — as if it were a virus infecting the system — raises many questions for education in a democracy. Eriksen (1995, p. 19), referring to the move towards a mass system of higher education in the United Kingdom, notes that, 'First and most importantly, a mass system of production can only be achieved with the development of *standardized* components [. . .].' Coincidentally, the Higher Education *Quality* Council (HEQC) in 1995 published its interim report: *Graduate Standards Programme*. There is not a little equivocation in its message:

> There is strong, and almost universal feeling, however, within higher education and beyond, that academic standards must not be inflexible, externally imposed yardsticks since these would impede creativity and curricular change. *Nevertheless*, the consultations reflect a widespread

acknowledgement in all quarters that shifts in the nature of higher education and its social and economic context have created an urgent need for
more explicitness in academic practice, as well as for a broader conception
of higher education curricula. (HEQC, 1995, p. 14; my emphasis)

Clearly, this is only an interim report, but its general tenor is replete with allusions
to standards, articulation, comparability and robustness — in sum, a modernist
edifice is under discussion. Running beneath the surface of the Report is an undeclared assumption that within a subject there is a body of knowledge which can
be rendered as standardizable, measurable and comparable. The purpose is performativity; it is efficiency, not epistemology, which is at issue. Dion takes this
further:

The term performativity refers to management modalities that regard
continuous refinement of maximal input/output flows as a terminal end in
itself. *Absent from performative analyses are critiques of whether a particular process or end is even desirable.* This fetishization of abstract technique,
divorced from social and political reality, is a common theme on the
LISTSERV TQM-L. (Dion, 1995, unpaginated, my emphasis)

This raises a second contradiction. Total quality management makes much of
worker empowerment — of giving workers 'ownership of the work process'. It
bears mentioning that Deming's philosophy was seen as an antidote to the strictures
of Taylorism. His own exposure to Human Relations management theory in Chicago may have attuned him to the importance of sustaining a progressive, 'needs'-
related rhetoric in his work. (Taylor, too, regarded his piece-rate pay as progressive,
for it was said to be more rational than the whims of managers (Schiff and Goldfield, 1994).) Deming's approach resonates with both humanism and consumerism.
But there are few businesses in which the workers literally have a stake. (The John
Lewis Partnership, a large retailing concern in Britain, is an example.) For much
of the nineteenth and early twentieth centuries, entrepreneurs fought to remove
control over the work process from the craft guilds. Are they now set on giving it
back? Will workers now decide upon products, profits, production and pay? (Schiff
and Goldfield, 1994, p. 663). It is unlikely.

In education, the consumerist phrase a 'sense of ownership' — sometimes
extended to the democratic notion of 'empowerment' — seems to suffuse much
discourse on education. Pupils must have a sense of ownership of their own learning, of their own assessment; teachers must have a sense of ownership of their own
staff appraisal; schools must locally manage themselves; and even teachers should
have a stake in the action research which they participate in. Much of this is what
would be called process control in manufacturing terms. But what of the product,
the strategy? Here government has been heavy-handed. There is a new-model
Taylorism. In an under-funded education system, the product is being clearly
specified. The inputs and the outputs are monitored and measured; the throughput
less so. One of the proponents of TQM in education, Myron Tribus (undated), in

an interpretation of Deming, argues that it is management who shall define what counts as quality:

> In translating the redefinition of management to education, we redefine the jobs of the administrators (i.e., the superintendents, the principals and department heads) as follows:
> The teachers work IN a system.
> The job of the Principal (Superintendent, Department Head) is to work ON the system, to improve it, continuously, with their help. (Tribus, undated)

There is a certain elasticity in the meaning of quality, and it is for management to define it for workers, thereby assuring constancy of purpose, the elimination of variability. This is achieved through constant monitoring and auditing through statistical process control — Deming's original specialism.

But what if a 'democratic audit' were to be conducted on TQM itself? Clearly, TQM seeks to maximize efficiency, and in this sense it disperses a technocratic consciousness, albeit with a democratic or empowering ring to it. If anything, the proponents of TQM would at best see it as morally neutral. But McIntyre would see it differently:

> Whether a given manager is effective or not is in the dominant view a quite different question from that of the morality of the ends which his effectiveness serves or fails to serve. [...] For the whole concept of effectiveness is inseparable from a mode of human existence in which the contrivance of means is in central part the manipulation of human beings into compliant patterns of behaviour; and it is by appeal to his own effectiveness in this respect that the manager claims authority within the manipulative mode. (McIntyre, 1981, p. 71)

TQM is about customer satisfaction, doing more with less, continuous improvement, productivity. It seeks vendors of quality raw material. Now, if it is argued that in a school the pupil is the raw material to be processed, then it follows logically that vendors (parents) of raw material (children) will need to be vetted: is their 'raw material' such that it can be treated easily and efficiently in this production process which seeks to minimize variance; or will that raw material require special (that is, variable and expensive) treatment (Capper and Jamison, 1993)? Either the variance in the raw material would need to be 'ironed out', or the school would refuse to accept that raw material. In the latter case, segregation and a separate production process would be required. The logical difficulty is that children fill a range of easily-blurred statuses in the cycle: they are raw material; they are co-producers of the product; and they are co-customers (with parents, for example) of the product which they co-produce. In a democracy, their education should not depend upon whether they are part of a good batch of raw material to be 'bought in', or not, by the school.

Given this, the appeals to ownership and empowerment have a hollow ring: TQM becomes a new technology of persuasion — in Foucauldian terms, a new regime of truth. It bears mentioning that TQM seeks a culture change in the organization, away from hierarchy, away from a tight fit between task and role-incumbent. It calls for inspirational, not to say even evangelical, leaders whose thoughts attract the status of visions for the future. And there is the important question: why TQM now (though it is perhaps already on the wane)? The 1980s witnessed examples of macho management, coercive and heavy-handed, standing down the trade unions. TQM seeks to consolidate the bridgehead, 'devolving' power to teams, empowering them (Tuckman, 1994). The geometry changes from pyramidical structure to the circle, a less confrontational configuration.

For Dion (1995), TQM portends anything but quality:

> If TQM is successful in its reinscriptions, it will shape the total range of possible and thinkable activities and identities. The richness, diversity and uniqueness of human experiences across space, time and place will be flattened into the binary categories of customer [...] and producer/ provider. This is an econometric ethnocentrism, par excellence. Once the transformation has occurred, once social reality has been 're-engineered,' the perceptual fields and behaviors of populations, now defined in the binarisms of TQM (customer/provider) can be shaped by a mix of propagandistic campaigns and low-level positivistic techniques. (Dion, 1995)

TQM adopts an almost cult-like following, with visions on the road to profitability, and mission stations on the way. It is being proselytized with almost messianistic zeal, with postmodern urgency, with prophecies of apocalypic doom for those (nations, corporations and public services) which do not take up the cause. Up and down the land, the consultants — the new high-priests — seek converts to quality. As it takes root in business, so must the schools prepare the way for it, by becoming businesses themselves, totally framing thought within the blessed binary of customer and provider. Just as Taylorism at the turn of the century showed the way forward, so now does TQM. But Total Quality Management has a long tradition: in a self-monitoring Benthamic structure of surveillance; in a Tayloristic quest to rationalize production and to eliminate waste; and in a Human Relations management discourse which sought to bring under rational control the annoying tendency of human workers to have irrational inclinations. TQM, lean production and empowerment 'are neomodernist attempts to package modernism into postmodern language, while keeping the game the same' (Boje, 1994, p. 450). Is it the Next Step in the management of consent?

Perhaps. Hard on the heels of TQM is Business Process Reengineering — here referred to as Reengineering, after Hammer and Champy's *Reengineering the Corporation*, published in 1993. Reengineering is a fundamental and radical re-designing of business processes so that only value-added processes are enhanced, these being cost, quality, service and speed. Process should flow, avoiding long transit times and coordination costs; it should not be intermittent. Multi-tasking, interdependent workers, aided by group-ware software, should replace highly differentiated fixed roles. This is a wider application of just-in-time manufacturing processes, enhanced by information technology. Simplicity and standardization *precede* the use of IT. Conti and Warner (1994) refer to reengineering as 'mediated Taylorism', but recognize that service industries have greater ambiguity and range of inputs — it is usually human — than in manufacturing. All the same, reengineering is about 'right-sizing' (a euphemism for 'down-sizing' and lay-offs), and requires assurances of job security. But the efficiency gain can itself generate greater output capacity than a market can bear, and this can itself lead to further lay-offs. And beneath the advocacy of bottom-line improvements is the capacity of highly sophisticated software systems surreptitiously to monitor employees, which, if realized, will undermine the very commitment of workers on which reengineering relies. The impetus will be to seek ever more sophisticated processes which will design job security away by simply replacing people.

In education, the application of TQM and reengineering is for the moment very limited. Both share a Taylorist heritage. Both set great store by using technology once the process design has been standardized. Taylorism was not exactly popular either with workers or with managers, for it de-skilled the former and minimized the discretion of the latter; and its implementation in Britain did not really start until the 1930s (Urry, 1995, p. 90 *et seq.*). Contract replaces trust; the rhetoric of empowerment is weaker than its reality; job security sits weakly alongside a management credo set on downsizing and on performativity; empowerment is framed by management's imperatives.

Educational discourse is currently suffused by managerial jargon. Information technology is waiting in the wings, ready to translate and to transmit standardized curricula in time-compressed, easily consumable, totally portable packages called modules. The insight of reengineering is that performativity lies in the direction of redesigned curricular content and structure which can be electronically accessed and monitored. Once the curricular fix is taken, then the technical fix is practically possible. Education may be disembodied and replaced by charismatic software. Of little concern will be the flux of postmodern culture, or the epistemological uncertainties set in train by the post-positivists. Choice will be a chimera, confined to the selection available in the multi-provider educational boutiques, franchised out by the state which may adopt near-total regulatory powers.

Making the Right Choice?

Since the 1980s, a number of countries informed by monetarist economic theory have sought to prune spending on the welfare state. In the 1980s, a period of high unemployment, demands on the welfare state increased, but tax revenues to pay for them decreased. In addition to rising social security expenditure, the demand for education and health care rose. That said, the allocation of government spending reflects the political priorities of a government. In Britain, for example, expenditure on defence and on law and order remained high, but expenditure on education and social housing declined. Nevertheless, despite the Conservative government's concern to roll back expenditure on the welfare state, the general effect has been for it to be increased slightly overall. Public expenditure in Britain remains higher than in, say, the United States, but lower than in the Scandinavian countries.

Education has come to be governed in a new way. Put simply, funding now follows performance rather than precedes it, as hitherto. For example, universities used to receive a block grant, up front; now, funding turns on various performance measures. The metaphor which guides these changes is that of a market. This is not a market in the sense of a completely free market, an unregulated market; rather, it is a quasi-market (Glennerster, 1991), which is steered by the government, which sets the rules of exchange. Advocates of the market principle have argued that the professionals in the welfare state — including government bureaucrats — had for too long acted in their own interests, rather than in the interests of the consumer. This was producer capture: inefficient, ineffective and self-serving; and increasingly expensive. Customers — clients, patients and parents — did not know what was on offer. They had little choice of provider.

In education, not only did government decide upon the rules of exchange, but it also came to decide the nature of the product. For example, the National Curriculum in England was actually legislated (in Scotland, which has a separate education system, there were Curricular Guidelines — a *de facto* national curriculum). Once that national curriculum was in place, then standardized assessment could follow, thereby providing attainment results which would allow (customers) parents to compare schools. The league tables of results followed. But before all this, Scotland (in 1981) had enacted school-choice legislation which permitted parents to choose a state school beyond the normal catchment area, with rights of appeal. In addition, the Assisted Places Scheme funded some children who would not otherwise have been able to afford a private education to attend an independent school. Parents did not, however, necessarily use school performance ratings as the main reason for selecting a school.

Other considerations applied. Ball *et al.* (1995) have studied the sociological aspects of choice-making. Basing their choices on the factual evidence of school-attainment levels was not necessarily the case for many parents. Two types of discourse emerged: the working class 'choice' discourse turned on the practical and the immediate; that of the middle class was structured by what was ideal and advantageous. In other words, the working class parents regarded schooling as having to fit in more with the constraints and routines of their household, whereas their middle class counterparts seemed willing to be more flexible, fitting home to the school. This is an interesting study, for it weaves modernist conceptions of class with the local narratives of consumers, generating sociological patterns which a postmodernist critique would eschew. The demise of class-based analyses in favour of status-based and other local-narrative research is itself a sign of the demise of modernist categorizations. This is not to say that pluralist studies lack an emancipatory and ethical purpose — it is to say that sociological research in education runs the risk of literally defining social class out of account.

Not all types of parental choice fit the British models. In the Netherlands, for example, all schools — state and private (that is, mainly denominational) — receive equal government funding, and private schools cannot charge tuition fees, though schools sometimes charge a very small amount for extra-curricular activities. Sweden in the early 1990s permitted parents to choose from both private schools and non-local schools. In some countries (England, for example) funding formulae are closely tied to levels of enrolment; in others (France, for example), not (OECD, 1994).

So much for parental choice from within state-sector schools. The next stage was to side-step local government bureaucracies and to fund the schools directly from central government, perhaps through some kind of voucher system. Chubb and Moe (1990) have argued that schools and local government are overly bureaucratic, protected from demand-side practices which could favour the consumer. Instead, they adhere to supply-side practices which leave the wishes of the parent out of account. In addition, a highly-unionized teaching profession, with its firm commitment to collective bargaining, is hardly likely to embrace locally struck flexible salary deals. In England, the 1988 Education Reform Act permitted schools to opt out from local government control, and thereby to become grant-maintained schools (GMS). At the same time, the Act required local authorities to devolve much of their expenditure to school governing bodies. This initiative — known as local management of schools (LMS) — was made to give governing bodies experience of financial devolution in the hope that they would thereafter seek to opt out completely from local government control. (The situation in Scotland differed: devolved school management [DSM], occurred *after* legislation permitting opting out to become a self-governing school [SGS].) Only two Scottish schools have opted out, and about 1100 out of 25,000 English schools have done so. In an apparent attempt to increase the numbers of GMS schools, the Department for Education and Employment in England and Wales (DFEE) published a White Paper (DFEE, 1996) entitled *Self Government for Schools*, which proposes to increase from 85 per cent to 95 per cent the proportion of that expenditure which local education authorities must delegate to schools, and which would allow grant-maintained schools to select by ability or by aptitude up to 50 per cent of their pupils.

The counterpart in the United States to grant-maintained schools are the charter schools. (For a state-by-state survey, see Mauhs-Pugh [1995]; and for a comparison between England and the USA, see Whitty and Halpin [1996].) New Zealand, too, has developed these schools (Codd and Gordon, 1991). The regulations which govern charter schools vary across the states. For example, the degree of parental and teacher support varies: Minnesota does not specify any level of parental support, but 90 per cent of teachers must support it; Georgia requires that 66 per cent of both teacher and parents lend their support. Accountability criteria also vary: in some states, pupil performance is subject to standardized, state-wide tests (as in Michigan and Massachusetts); in Colorado, this is not the case. In some states, the charter school is legally autonomous (as in Arizona and California, for example);

in others, again Colorado, the charter school is under the authority of the school board. Existing private or state schools may seek charter status (and the state funding which attaches to it, usually for a three- to five-year period).

The idea is not without controversy. Whilst the present charter legislation prohibits discrimination in entrance conditions on the basis of race, creed, ethnicity and disability, the schools are otherwise free to establish their selection criteria. The result could be that these schools cream off both bright students and good teachers. Related to this is that information about schools may not be equally accessible to all parents, particularly the poor, who might not be able to afford the transportation costs incurred by their children if the school were to be a long way from their home. Moreover, the charter schools do not have to agree to collective bargaining for teachers' pay. This would weaken the teacher unions. At a time of fiscal retrenchment, state schools object to much-needed funds being siphoned off to charter schools. A further concern is the prospect of a voucher scheme. Its proponents predict that it would engender competition, higher quality and diversity. Its detractors see it otherwise: division, despair (for the 'losers'), and privatization of a once-public education system.

Support for 'school choice' has come from an unlikely source: Herbert Gintis, co-author of *Schooling in Capitalist America* (Bowles and Gintis, 1976), an influential neo-Marxist account of schooling. Gintis (in Glass, 1994) advocates competition and 'markets' in the public services: that is to say markets which are established on a level playing field, thereby allowing for fair competition. The market would be regulated, by the state, to ensure progressive outcomes, so that, for example, the value of vouchers would vary according to the needs of the pupil. In part, Gintis lapses into a biological determinist position on competition: 'I would also argue that a competitive spirit is biologically wired into us as human beings [. . .] of course, competition must be 'managed' or it becomes personally or socially destructive'.

A useful conceptualization of self-managing schools has been provided by Caldwell and Spinks (1992, pp. 192–4). In their 'vision for the 1990s', they offer a four-fold typology:

- First, the *market model*, whereby funding turns on enrolment. Self-governing schools must accept a national curriculum and testing system;
- Second, the *charter model*, as in New Zealand and in some American states, whereby a formal agreement on resources and accountability is struck between government and the school board;
- Third, the *local support model*, whereby geographically contiguous schools obtain central services more efficiently than would be the case were they independent; and
- Fourth, the *recentralization model*, a re-structured, centrally-defined re-emergence of structures which had obtained before the mid-1980s.

Caldwell and Spinks see the market model as realizable by 2001 in Australia, the United Kingdom (but not Scotland), Canada, New Zealand and the Untied States.

But the evidence so far lends little support to the market model. In their extensive review of research, Whitty and Halpin (1996) conclude,

> Empirical research does not, indeed in principle could not, show that such reforms can never have beneficial effects. Yet, the studies reported here suggest that going further in the direction of marketisation would be un-likely to yield major overall improvements in the quality of education and would almost certainly have damaging equity effects. (Whitty and Halpin, 1996, p. 25)

The Way Forward Back to Basics?

The English National Curriculum and America's Goals 2000 are slogans with nationalistic and millennialistic messages. The lurch to the Right in the 1980s was marked by panic reactions: the English Education Reform Act of 1988; a *Nation at Risk* in America. The wagons had been rounded up in a large quality circle to plan the way forward. The way forward was to be back to basics, topped up with a suite of transferable skills. In the making is a bureaucratic structure of truly modernist proportions, specifying in detail the ends of education, both epistemo-logical and moral. And yet all of this new-found epistemological certainty within the school is to be marketed as choice and diversity. The paradox is that although the government has trumpeted the cause of the consumer, it has singularly avoided recognizing consumer culture — that is, the culture of postmodernism.

It is not that government has been unaware of the contradiction. As we have said, the slogan of 'ownership' runs through the official discourse, thereby render-ing it suitably 'consumerist', and therefore agreeable. Thus, what we have is not so much a choice of *curricula* (for there is only one), but the choice of a school which transmits it. It is not, therefore, a matter of consumer choice and product diversity, but of choice and *efficiency*. Once that distinction is drawn, then it is easy to explain both back to basics and back to bureaucracy. If the product — here is meant the curriculum and national tests — is standardized, then 'providers' (schools, usually) can be left alone to get on with producing it as best they can. Hence the sense of ownership, but only of tactics. Thereafter, the product is translated into statistical form. Social and mental processes suddenly become objectified in num-bers, through the appliance of scientific testing, and arranged in league-tables, or 'market-stalls', awaiting the gaze of the consumer, the parent, who will 'choose' a school. These 'hard' facts are re-worked aesthetically into the marketing icons of the glossy brochure or the designer Web site, tempting the customer. In sum, the appeal to choice and consumerism may be no more than a simulacrum which has been constructed to effect a quite different end: that of efficiency.

Other league-tables which might be helpful to the consumer are curiously lacking. Parents are not pointed towards tables which publish either the percentage of government spending on education in this and other countries, or the *per-capita* amounts at different levels of the education system. For example, the percentage of

Gross Domestic Product (GDP) spent on education in 1991 in the UK (5.3 per cent) was higher than Australia, Germany and Japan, but lower than Canada, Sweden, Denmark (all three of which spent over 6 per cent), The Netherlands, the USA, Belgium and France. To give an indication of the range of expenditure: Japan spent 3.7 per cent and Canada 6.7 per cent. As a percentage of central government expenditure in the UK, in 1992–93 education expenditure amounted to 5.2 per cent of GDP, a sum lower than the 5.5 per cent which was spent in 1980–81 (Central Statistical Office, 1995, p. 59). These data all exist, but lie buried in documentation which is not on most parents' reading list. But in a sense, these data are crucial for a choosing consumer to know about, for they affect not the *distribution* of how funds earmarked for education are, but what the overall amount for distribution actually is.

The new managerialism exudes a sense of certainty: the way forward. Not only are its narrow curricular prescriptions a misrepresentation of choice, but the epistemological certainties which they define fly in the face of the epistemological lack of certainty within academe, an uncertainty which has been prompted partly by the postmodernist critique. This specification of certainty in the schools may be sustainable politically (because the state controls the purse-strings), but if such curricular standardization were to be imposed on the universities (in the interests of efficiency), then a democratic deficit would loom large.

And now education itself is coming to be appropriated by the market. It seems set to become another cultural product. To date, there is a quasi-market, with very strong central prescription of curricular ends. This is the government's 'cultural fix', the counterpart to the 'technical fix', to which I referred in Chapter 6. But the two 'fixes' are quite complementary: the technical fix is more efficiently effected if curricular content can be fixed and standardized prior to software development. Moreover, the curriculum can be rendered more agreeable to the child if it can be transmitted through both image-laden *and* word-laden media. Having established its curricular and technical fixes, the government can then, logically, open up the market. This it could do by enfranchising approved providers — not necessarily schools — to transmit the curriculum. The government would retain monopoly rights over credentialization and curriculum development (though it could probably contract out these aspects, too). All that said, it is worth stressing that much of the empirical and theoretical discourse on markets and education derives particularly from the Thatcherite-driven reforms in England. In the main, this discourse has been widely reported, but its generalizability should not be assumed, since what count as market reforms in, say, Scotland or Australia are not of the same order as in England. Whilst it is entirely appropriate that educational research should study the effects of policy through the collection of empirical data, it would ill serve education if, as a result, researchers were to foresake the pursuit of theory and radical alternatives in favour of undertaking research which at the time met official-dom's priorities and which attracted its much-needed research funds.

Educational research itself is set within cultural, epistemological and eco-nomic configurations. I have already alluded to the crisis of validity and reliability which postmodernist epistemological critiques have made of positivistic research.

But the culture in which researchers work is itself suffused with postmodern uncertainty and risk. The career of a research fellow is increasingly attenuated. Contract researchers become the new itinerant nomads of academe, some of them juggling different research agendas at the same time in different places. The contract researcher — usually female — is subjected to a post-Fordist regime *par excellence*, multi-tasking, flexible, often engaged in the value-added research agendas of government, and measured by the performance-related criteria of (usually male) grant-holders. But even the grant-holders themselves are not immune from the cultural and economic pressures to produce glossy and glib research reports which stressed-out practitioners and policy-makers can easily 'dip into' and digest. Paradoxically, analyses of the management of educational research itself — that is, of how and why it is currently framed by cultural, political, epistemological and economic influences — are few. And the sociology of education research conferences — virtual and real — remains but a dream in the sociological imagination.

Particularly in Britain, the education policies of the post-1979 Conservative government have had the effect of undermining trust within the professions of the welfare state. The professions were not to be trusted; rather, they were to be subjected to contractual relationships. The high-trust, *professional* accountability of the 1960s and 1970s gave way in the 1980s to low-trust *public* accountability; and this public accountability has been set subsequently within an almost Darwinian *market* accountability. Where the writ of the New Right neo-liberals has not run, the erosion of trust has been less marked. There the political space for teachers is less circumscribed, and there have been some important suggestions for teachers in dealing with the complexities of the age. For example, consider Fullan's 'Eight Basic Lessons of the New Paradigm of Change' (Fullan, 1993, pp. 21–41). I quote them:

Lesson One: You Can't Mandate What Matters (The more complex the change the less you can force it)

Lesson Two: Change is a Journey not a Blueprint (Change is non-linear, loaded with uncertainty and excitement and sometimes perverse)

Lesson Three: Problems are Our Friends (Problems are inevitable and you can't learn without them)

Lesson Four: Vision and Strategic Planning Come Later (Premature visions and planning blind)

Lesson Five: Individualism and Collectivism Must have Equal Power (There are no one-sided solutions to isolation and groupthink)

Lesson Six: Neither Centralization Nor Decentralization Works (Both top-down and bottom-up strategies are necessary)

Lesson Seven: Connection with the Wider Environment is Critical for Success (The best organizations learn externally as well as internally)

Lesson Eight: Every Person is a Change Agent (Change is too important to leave to the experts, personal mind set and mastery is the ultimate protection). (Fullan, 1993, pp. 21–2)

Implicit within the eight lessons are strands of thought from postmodern culture, postmodernist theory and post-Fordist management approaches. There is, first, the integrating concept — the persistence of change, which admits the flux and flow of postmodern culture. And, for Fullan, 'every person is a change agent': this resonates well with Giddens' important consideration that in a post-traditional order: 'Information produced by specialists (including scientific knowledge) can no longer be wholly confined to specific groups, but becomes routinely interpreted and acted on by lay individuals in the course of their everyday actions' (Giddens, 1995, p. 7; brackets in original). In other words, whereas in a traditional society our lives were more or less mapped out for us — we were custom-bound, so to say — now we interpret the world, reflect, and act accordingly, with a sense of autonomy. Those who would give us mantras, mandates and visions hark back to the certainties of tradition. They ignore what Giddens calls this 'social reflexivity'.

'Problems are Our Friends', Fullan says. One of the maxims of TQM is that problems are to be admitted, explained and corrected, there and then, not swept under the carpet. Equally, 'problems' are disruptions of order. They demand attention, and today's solutions may be tomorrow's problems, and in this sense they constitute the 'journey' (not the 'blueprint') of Fullan's second lesson. There are, too, shades of Gergen's post-positivist assertion that the quest for rational truth is but 'puffery'. And Fullan (Lesson Seven) comes close to Gergen's pragmatic counter to what might have been post-positivist despair: that is, Fullan, like Gergen, sees the value of getting to grips with the 'outside' — with Gergen's 'alien realities' beyond the organization — so that it does not ossify. But there is a risk here of tokenism: that is, of management co-opting a few 'alien' realities in a contrived way, hoping to neutralize them, rather than to be genuinely open to the views they express, be they dissenting or not. Or, management may seek safe and agreeable aliens, allowing them even to take charge of some segment of the institution's endeavours, giving them functional (but separate) autonomy, an organization within an organization, seen but sidelined. Alternatively, here could be an effective way of having these 'aliens' declare their hand. On the other hand, any such contrivance would close off the insights which the outsiders could make, thereby possibly endangering the institution even further.

All the same, Fullan seems somewhat caught between modern and postmodern mind-sets. The modern is revealed by his penchant for bi-polar opposites, rather than with the complexity of the chaotic; the postmodern — in addition to the reasons I have just given — is revealed also by the very ambiguity in the title, *Change Forces*, of his book (a point he makes), and also in his own understandable unwillingness to utter the quick-fix solutions which will make life certain again. If anything, Fullan offers useful social-psychological insights which may enable teachers not only to avoid drowning, but also to turn the tide, though he wisely does not tell us in which direction it will flow. Even so, the days of bureaucracy are far from numbered. Where trust is wanting, contract will suffice. Scase (1994) makes the interesting point that Britain is somewhat class-ridden, bereft of trust. If so, the opportunity to implement some of the suggestions made by Fullan will be limited in England compared, say, to southern Ontario.

In sum, these are uncertain and ambivalent times: the millennium looms; faith in science wanes; nationhood and personhood are under strain. One could go on. But the uncertainty produces its own certainties: management teams sequester themselves away in the monastic splendour of rural retreats, spawning visions, missions and plans aplenty. The Next Step; the Way Forward. Their task is formidable. The pressing need is said to be economic. The education system needs to be a lean machine, with certainty of purpose and process. The quest for quality has to be managed, totally. For this to occur, there needs to be both a cultural and a technical fix. Take the cultural fix: governments generate national curricula, and include within them definitions of the moral and the personal. Unnerved by the fracturing of culture, governments now attempt, belatedly, to restore order. The product — the curriculum in this case — comes to be defined with no loss of bureaucratic elegance. In further education, for example, mountains of modules beset the student, but the pathways onwards and upwards are very clearly marked, with checkpoints. Deviation is difficult. Guidance counsellors point the way. National identity can thereby be fixed and asserted, and the wayward tendencies of postmodernist theory and consumerism may be contained. If that were to be done, then the groundwork for the technical fix would be complete. The elimination of variability — so dear to the qualitariat — could be taken a step further. With the implementation of information technology, learning could be 'distanced' from the classroom. But this technical fix is not imminent. For the moment, the curricular fix needs to be consolidated, whilst the emergent post-Fordist social relations of the classroom synchronize with those of the workplace.

The education system is being governed in a new way: a centrally set strategy, and local ownership of tactics. Empowerment and ownership are the new mantras of management. Choice is chanted at the consumers; charters protect their 'rights'. But the choices are mainly of structures — that is, of schools — not of curriculum and pedagogy, for the latter are under the guidance and gaze of officialdom. As the private consumer becomes more at ease with national curricula it may become easier for government to sell the idea of the need for more information technology to transmit it. In the meanwhile, governments must tread a wary path, for parents may assume that they really do have choices — about school-closure, or about their right to send their child to this or that school — and they may demand that money be made available to pay for them.

The 'consumer' politics of all this may turn out to be intense. Local political rifts will be defined by central government as none of its business — little local difficulties, matters for local producers and consumers. Whether or not these little local difficulties will spawn broader social movements is difficult to say, but it will be unlikely that government can rest easily. Waiting in the wings might be a further 'empowering' measure — the voucher — which could itself enable government seemingly to distance itself even further from the consequences of its policies. Raab (1994, p. 18) is surely correct to put the question, 'Thus, can the combination of strong state, market forces and fragile networks of consensus achieve government's own objectives in education, let alone cope with the unanticipated and unintended consequences of these instruments, without innovating new forms of interaction?' And to this can be added the suggestions of those like Fullan who argue that teachers create space for themselves in the face of overly *dirigiste* directions from central government (Fullan and Hargreaves, 1992; Fullan, 1993). Power has its limits. Those who lack authority do not lack power, and 'compliance' from those below can be stage-managed in a variety of ways, from open resistance to cynical acts of 'submission'.

Chapter 9

Education Transformed?

The French Revolution of 1789 saw the demise of a society based on tradition and privilege, and it heralded the dawn of a political and social system based on rationalization. This social and political revolution had its economic counterpart in the Industrial Revolution in England, which saw the emergence of factory-based and rationalized production systems. This 'Great Transformation' — as Coleman (1993) terms it — is still going on. Not only has it transformed the mode of production, it has also changed where we live; it has seen what he calls the transcendence of place (enabled by developments in communications and transportation); and it has seen the transition from what he calls the 'primordial social organization' (developed through family ties) towards 'purposively constructed social organizations', which include schools. What Coleman's analysis suggests is a continuity, a long transformation, rather than some kind of break from the modern to the post-modern. Indeed, the very term postmodern implies *an after something* (the modern) *but not A something* (to replace it). It is not, therefore, a particularly helpful term; rather, it can leave us bewildered, a state of mind which, in the view of some postmodernists, is no bad thing.

The nature of our predicament has been well put. Take Giddens (1995):

> On the one hand neoliberalism is hostile to tradition — and is indeed one of the main forces sweeping away tradition everywhere, as a result of the promotion of market forces and an aggressive individualism. On the other hand, it depends upon the persistence of tradition for its legitimacy and its attachment to conservatism — the areas of nation, religion, gender and the family. (Giddens, 1995, p. 9)

Or Mestrovic (1991):

> [. . .] postmodernism espouses deregulation and anti-bureaucratic sentiments at the same time that conservative ideology calls for more regulation and bureaucracy. [. . .] Postmodern philosophies purport to rebel against these narratives of constraint, but they fail to address the question of what will replace the constraints, and, of course, the problem of human nature is left hanging by postmodernist thinkers: do postmodern humans need constraint or not? (Mestrovic, 1991, p. 164)

Upheavals beset us at every turn. Postmodern thought has sought to overturn our modernist 'faith' in reason and science. The quest for truth is misplaced, for there are said to be only truths-for-the-moment which may take on the appearance of an essence. Postmodernism as culture is marked by a tendency to narcissism, to reflexivity, to ephemerality, to superficiality. The products of the world can now be found in many a shopping mall, for the reach of consumers is now global, allowing both cultural and material products from afar to be bought, now. And the moral code is barely holding; we no longer baulk at the bizarre. As families fracture, as parents wrestle with their own uncertainties, many a child is consigned to walk the street or to sit before the video. Coleman's 'primordial social organizations' rapidly vanish, but the new 'constructed social organizations' are not yet in a position to step into the breach. In the workplace of the new information society, new forms of post-Fordist social relations generate a two-tier workforce: the core worker, 'empowered'; the peripheral worker, bureaucratized. So much for the intellectual, cultural and economic realms.

In the political sphere, old alliances break up. For those whose material needs are met it is lifestyle issues which come to the fore, waxing and waning. Having been perhaps exposed to learner-centred pedagogy at school and to post-Fordist empowerment at work, the new lifestyle politicos are well placed to take the expert to task or to court. On the other hand, for Alain Minc's *exclus*, languishing beyond the realms of the 'contented', emancipation — having the means to 'buy into' the good life — is but a distant dream. But it would be wrong to deny the emancipatory tide which is running elsewhere. Apartheid has fallen, and the demise of communist dictatorships has seen some societies in Eastern Europe moving towards capitalism. All this is hardly a sign of postmodern cynicism (Alexander, 1995, p. 86).

We have been concerned throughout the book with how the education 'system' is being influenced by these epistemological, cultural, economic and political changes. I have suggested how recent policy on curriculum, pedagogy, assessment and management has tried to cope with the dilemmas and distortions which Giddens and Mestrovic have defined. What is evident today seems to be a meshing of codes, a kind of rhetorical bricolage, a hybrid. That is to say, we see an attempt to reconcile these dilemmas and paradoxes which postmodernist thought and culture, on the one hand, and economic globalization, on the other, have generated.

There has been no firm break with modernity; rather, there have been shifts in the form of capitalism, with adjustments to them emerging in the education system, so that, for example, schools are put out to tender in the marketplace, so as to make them efficient producers of future and flexible workers, empowered and eager to take their place in the world of work. But changes in education have not just been managerial and structural. Consumer culture allows for and encourages frequent choices and changes of identity (if we can afford them). The moral order fractures, but the power of the school to 're-civilize' the child through formal civic and moral education seems limited in the face of 'competition' from the media. Governments try to stitch things together with 'national' this and that, but even the concept of 'nation' can fall to deconstruction: after all, what is it to be American, or Scottish? The influences on education have not only been economic and cultural. New flexible configurations of time and space are emerging. Intellectually, too, there have been epistemological questions raised about rationalism and objectivism as the dominant mode of understanding, a mode which has for too long been male, and one long enshrined in the school.

We have been concerned with four dimensions to the educational changes afoot. The first relates to curriculum. Curricula are increasingly defined by government with the adjective 'national' as a descriptor. Thus far, economic globalization has not produced much of a call for curricular internationalization; quite the opposite. The form which these curricula take has been bureaucratic. There has been a birth of new curricular subjects, which I referred to as *subjects of the self*. They seem to be emerging for two reasons: first, they teach a repertoire of social skills which are functional for both post-Fordist work regimes and for the service sector. This constitutes what I have termed elsewhere as 'the instrumentalisation of the expressive order of the school' (Hartley, 1987b, p. 99). And second, they transmit values and attitudes which hard-pressed parents are increasingly unable to provide because they must spend less time with their children, either because they work, or because they live apart; or because, even within the confines of the home, activities — from eating to leisure — may be individualized. Distance-parenting is a telling indicator of the weakening of Coleman's primordial social organization, the family. These new subjects of the self teach reflexivity, the ability to interpret the world, to negotiate meanings, and to act as a consequence of these meanings. But unless they are set within limits there is the potential for an a-morality to emerge:

> Unlimited desires without moral checks spell a disastrous dose of anomie
> if one takes Durkheim seriously. (Mestrovic, 1994, p. 143)

As national governments seek both to shore up a crumbling sense of national identity and to re-assert a set of moral standards, the epistemological certainties set in train by the Enlightenment are called into question. In literature and the social sciences — less so in the natural sciences — the postmodernist critique has given the lie to the inevitability and desirability of clinging solely to the rational mode of understanding, and it calls for moral and aesthetic modes of understanding to have their place in a new emancipatory curriculum. On the part of government there has been something of a knee-jerk reaction. It has woken up to the threat to the moral and social order which the fragmentary tendencies of postmodernist epistemology and of postmodernist culture have occasioned. The reaction has been reactionary: it is back to basics, to certainty, to reason; but for the critical postmodernists it is the very disruption of these old certainties which can serve to enable a political awakening for groups who have been long consigned to the wilderness.

Second, pedagogy is changing. On the one hand, the old didacticism no longer holds sway. A new learner-centred pedagogy is being ushered in. Much is made of empowering the learner who can take responsibility for his or her own learning. Perhaps this marks a goodness of fit between the emerging post-Fordist social relations of the workplace and the social relations of the classroom: a new 'correspondence principle' (Bowles and Gintis, 1976). But the freedom which this progressive pedagogy confers on the pupil can also be regarded as a new form of

..mentality'. Commands no longer come only from outside; they also come
.n within. The affects are self-controlled, a 'civilizing process', to use Elias's
phrase. The new pedagogy enables us to make choices, to take decisions, within
'reason'. Self-regulation is a feature of its rationale: 'postmodernism is merely *an
extension of* the modern civilizing process' (Mestrovic, 1991, p. 26; my emphasis).
On the other hand, radical pedagogy can have the capacity to breach conservative
curriculum, even when governments make strenuous efforts to define its content.
So, whilst learner-centred pedagogy may indeed be functional for post-Fordist work
regimes, it nevertheless tacitly conveys to the learner a questioning and reflective
attitude, a potential empowerment of the learner, one which could lead to the
construction of counter-discourses.

But officialdom retains nagging doubts about how far to allow learner-centred
pedagogy to go. The OFSTED inspections in England and Wales contain an uneasi-
ness about any practice which goes beyond 'good class teaching'. And there are
reasons for this: OFSTED's concerns are with *standards*, and these are easier to
discern if the process and the product can be framed bureaucratically and apprehended empirically. Few teachers would run the risk of innovating in front of the
OFSTED inspectorate. And in the United States, the call for national standards (and
the standardized curriculum which it implies) also continues to be made (Ravitch,
1995). There is a further point: waiting in the wings is information technology.
Here is not face-to-face, whole-class teaching. The social and temporal arrangements for information technology are more distant and impersonal, even though
they may be more open, in terms of access. Its 'distance' may well exacerbate the
absence of a sense of the social among the young, rendering communication virtual,
not real. Paradoxically, information technology may lead to curricular closure even
though it has the capacity to allow greater access or openness to education. What
may occur is that in order to use IT efficiently, government (or business, regulated
by government) may wish to standardize the curricular product and the pedagogical
process within the software.

A third aspect of the emerging tensions in education is related to recent shifts
towards 'authentic' assessment. The emerging use of pupil profiles, diaries and
other forms of continuous assessment requires more of the pupil's personality to be
both confessed and expressed, to be assessed against 'effectiveness' criteria; and to
go on the record, digitally. The possibility of a pupil leaving a digital trail which
records electronically these accumulated assessments is a real one. The same concern can be expressed for the appraisal records of teachers. Although these new
modes of assessment are undoubtedly very valid (and less reliable than their norm-
referenced counterpart), they delve deep beneath the surface of the psyche of the
pupil. Logically, they are part of the reflective self-audit procedure which seems set
to emerge at each level of education, from pupil to organization.

Here again, governments seem uneasy at the loss of reliability, at the loss of
an assessment which is reducible to an easily compared number, or to a letter-
grade. Government wishes to ensure that the new informed, consumer-parent can
easily understand the 'value' of the school. National tests seek to standardize these
assessment procedures. Put another way, the move towards authentic assessment

resonates well with the culture of postmodernism, but it is decidedly at odds with government's quest to effect between-school competition and efficiency-gains within a quasi-marketplace for education. The *economic* arguments seem at odds with the emerging *culture* of postmodernism.

Fourthly, the very governance and management of education contain mixed messages. Strategic decisions about funding, curriculum and assessment are all being increasingly confined to government; the tactical implementation of these strategies falls to the 'empowered' pupil, teacher and school. Funding follows performance, a performance whose categories rest with officialdom to decide upon, after 'consultation'. It is little wonder that the professionals within the education system are experiencing stress: their pupils inhabit a complex cultural milieu; national directives limit their professional discretion; resources dwindle, organizations are down-sized, jobs are threatened and professional relationships can become overly individualistic and competitive; no longer is the school a safe haven from drugs and violence; contract replaces trust, fault replaces fate; parents and industry seek a stake; government-defined innovations weigh on the mind; in-service education provides few analyses of what is happening, preferring to provide ready-mixed, stop-gap solutions; and meanwhile the qualitariat hover above. The tensions seem to be irreconcilable. There is little space for manoeuvre, and it takes a lot of effort and risk to create it. The vocabulary of educational discourse does not ring true: how is empowerment possible when surveillance is so strong; how can cynicism be avoided?

I have suggested that the cultural code and the economic code are at odds. In a sense, this is a false distinction, for the two codes are mutually influenced. As western capitalism was required to generate both cultural and material products in order to fuel demand, potential consumers were lured by easy credit and sophisticated advertising. The work ethic of production was challenged by the new hedonistic ethic of consumption. This new individualism was functional for consumption. Individuality could be manifested by owning and revealing these products. Customization replaced standardization. The dawning of what some refer to as postmodern culture saw an unwillingness to accept moral absolutes. The certainties of technical rationality came into question. For some, all this was liberating; for others, a threat to tradition and nationhood. And at the same time as these moral uncertainties were emerging, so too were economic ones — Asia was awakening, and the 1980s recession had stemmed spending on the welfare state. The response to the cultural tide was to try to turn it back; or at least to throw up a curricular dyke and to wave the national flag from the top of it. The response to the economic recession was to set rigid funding formulae at the centre and to devolve more of the spending to the school. And all this had the elegant result of deflecting criticism to the school or university for spending cuts; government washed its hands of blame. But this continuing emphasis in education on consumption and production may have unforeseen consequences for education in a democracy, with consumption leading to an association between thought and advertising, and production reducing thought to performance (Wexler, 1995, p. 76). All of this was done in a hurry, on officialdom's terms, with hasty consultation and no negotiation. There was no real dialogue, despite references to empowerment and ownership. Only management and markets had the answer.

What is emerging in education policy is an attempt by the state to reconcile these cultural and economic codes. Thus there have been appeals to desire, to choice, to diversity, to ownership, to selfhood, to democracy. And at the same time, the litany of efficiency, effectiveness and technique runs on. These two discourses — the cultural and the economic — have been seamlessly woven together in policy documents. The resulting rhetoric is indeed a contra-*diction*, for it is the case that the very words — the diction — of these two codes are logically at odds with each other, but they are presented as if they are as one. It comes close to part of the definition of 'doublethink' in George Orwell's *Nineteen Eighty-Four*: It is defined as 'the power of holding two contradictory beliefs in one's mind simultaneously, and accepting both of them' (Orwell, 1989 [original 1949], p. 37). It has indeed been an eloquent attempt to return to old certainties in the face of what Touraine (1995) refers to as 'fragmented modernity':

> In the midst of these fragments of social life and conflicting values, a swarm of human ants pursue goals set by technical rationality. [. . .] It is impossible to run the film backwards and to rediscover the irremediably lost unit of the world of Enlightenment and Progress. (Touraine, 1995, p. 217)

This kind of reaction by government will not intend away cultural, political and economic changes. Reactionary forces are now gathering, faced as they are by the confusion of the times. In the main, they resort to 'what works', by which they mean what has worked in the past. New 'museums' to modernity are surely in the offing. Given the immediacy and immensity of the issues today, it is not surprising that government has shied away from what Giddens (1995, p. 117) calls 'dialogic democracy'. Democratic decision-making takes time, and time is money. Even so, Giddens refers to a series of democratizing tendencies in society. For example, the rigidities of life in the family are weakening; there is a 'plasticity' of role-definitions, an aversion to coercion. To take another: many self-help groups are being formed. In the organizational sphere, there is a move away from the ideal-typical Weberian bureaucracy:

> A post-bureaucratic organization can both harness social reflexivity and respond to situations of manufactured uncertainty much more effectively than a command system. Organizations structured in terms of active trust necessarily devolve responsibility and depend on an expanded dialogic space. (Giddens, 1995, p. 123)

In the schools, as elsewhere, trust and tolerance brought about by open dialogue — to which all can be party — is probably a better way to proceed than the pursuit of calculating self-interest within the confines of a market. Do we wish our children to privatize their passions, to individualize their success and failure, to personalize their identities with consumables, to engage others at a 'distance', to mistrust, to market themselves, to live for the moment; is all this what we call ownership and empowerment? Does it nourish the spirit as well as the market? In Britain, especially in England, less so in Scotland, bureaucratic structures of bewildering complexity are being constructed, structures which not only retain the precision of job specifications but which add to them even more detailed performance specifications. These performance specifications have two functions: first, to ensure that the consumer in the quasi-market shall be informed with meaningful and comparable output statistics; and second, they are said to constitute the indicators which shall be used as the basis for the funding of the institution and, by implication, the monitoring of the individual or organizational unit. The crucial point made by Giddens that the post-bureaucratic organization requires trust is missed in current reforms in Britain.

Touraine, however, has been critical of Giddens' emphasis on the notion of individual reflexivity which has been a hallmark of de-traditionalized societies: that is, societies in which stable, explicit and ritualized codes of behaviour are set aside in favour of individual constructions of identity. In sum, Touraine (1995) regards Giddens' notion of individual reflexivity as overly psychological and adaptive, not sufficiently critical structurally. Instead, Touraine stresses the 'Subject':

> The subject does not imply the care of the self, but the defence of the ability to be an actor, or in other words to modify one's social environment by resisting the norms and forms of social organization which the Self is constructed. [...] The shaping of the Subject is not a matter of the care of the self, but of defending freedom of power. (Touraine, 1995, pp. 263–64)

For Touraine, we should act as 'subjects', not as consumers. And we must learn to act as subjects particularly in the family and in education, for these two institutions 'must transform individuals in to (sic) subjects who are conscious of their freedoms and their responsibilities towards themselves. *Unless individuals become subjects, democracy has no solid foundations*' (Touraine, 1995, pp. 348–49; my emphasis).

To repeat: recent education policy has sought to merge the cultural and economic codes, incorporating the former to justify the latter in a discourse of duplicity. This is a managed merger, a play on words. It freeze-frames the flux and flow of postmodern culture into a set pattern. Government may indeed recognize the consumer but it seeks to suppress the diversity of postmodern consumer culture. Rather than admit this plurality, it seeks to standardize it, not only because it is cheaper, but also because it is wary of its chaotic tendencies. On the one hand, out of school our children are beset by media telling them to consume, to be different, to see the illusion as the real; and on the other hand, in school they face 'empowering' pedagogy which transmits the certainties of a national curriculum and core values.

Society is being re-schooled. An elaborate mode of regulation is being constructed. It engenders calculation not cooperation, despite the rhetoric to the contrary. It rewards self-interest; it sees education as a private interest, not a public good. It seeks to channel the cultural shifts in train onto a narrow track, under its own management. But there cannot easily be collaboration and commitment within a profession when it is continually caught in the middle of a myriad of competing interest groups, or when its discretion is undermined by overly bureaucratic direct-ives. This is not to say that quality-management does not matter, but the distinction needs to be drawn between the management of support functions and the manage-ment of pupils, students and teachers. Total quality management reduces variability and process hold-ups. In the management of administration and resource alloca-tions, this kind of managerial approach has benefits. But when TQM is applied to curriculum and to pedagogy — that is, when it seeks to eliminate variability in order to monitor efficiency and effectiveness — then it can lead to a narrow sys-tematization and to a lack of trust. It has to be stressed that the 'raw material' of education — our children — are not inert, well-understood matter. Equally, the technical processes of education — the pedagogy — are themselves poorly under-stood, and these processes are culturally grounded. And so it is with curriculum: a democracy is little served by a narrow and legislated national curriculum; and nor is it served in the long run by teachers and pupils who feel unable to take risks, to innovate, to see beyond what counts as convention.

All this raises the question of where lies the political space for manoeuvre in education. Governments have attempted to merge by fiat what appear to be contra-dictory codes: the economic and cultural. They have sought to appropriate the latter in order to justify financial cutbacks so that we 'own' the cuts. The politics of cost-reductions is somehow 'sold' to us, surely an appropriate tactic in a consumerist culture. Postmodern culture is difficult to fix, and long-silenced groups are stirring into action, seeking emancipation. The politics of left and right are now too simp-listic a categorization. Groups come and go with the issues of the hour. Life is becoming more politicized as reflective individuals become ever more 'choosey' about their causes and desires. There is always, of course, the option to go the way of the postmodern pessimists, which allows us to slide easily into the abyss, to lapse into relativism, quietly reflecting.

These uncertainties and ambivalences cannot be intended away by the likes of a legislated national curriculum, by appeals to Darwinist individual 'fitness', by back-to-basics moral pleas, or by get-tough punishment regimes. None of these addresses the origins of postmodernist culture. As a coping strategy, government purports to keep the lid on, lurching into a *dirigisme* which it knows it probably cannot sustain. And if not, the way will be open to the quick-fix extremists to stake their claim. The search for solutions which embraces a strong individualism or a strong collectivism is misplaced. Technical rationality has brought great benefits, but it has breached the moral and the aesthetic domains, so that we have become overly concerned with means, not ends; with 'how' questions, not 'why' questions. 'Are there no intermediary territories where thought, collective action and ethics can find a home?' (Touraine, 1995, p. 232). For the moment the contradictory economic and cultural codes have been forced together in a discourse of duplicity, at one and the same time claiming an accord between moral regulation and eco-nomic de-regulation. The 'stresses' which result from this are apparent throughout education. They are the result of a forced arrangement which already spawns some cynicism, if not despair. To be sure, the relationship between democracy and capitalism has never been easy, but the quasi-market in education now emerging has the feel of a choice which has been compelled, not one which has been democratically arrived at. This is a rigged market. The new managerialism, however, may soon reach the limits of its legitimacy, and it remains an open question whether or not the Thatcherite-inspired regulatory procedures in England turn out to be the new global paradigm for the public sector. Sooner or later, the limits of technical rationality and the marketization of morality in education will need to be set, preferably democratically; or dialogically, as Giddens would say. Touraine expresses well the shift which is needed:

> We therefore have to look for ways to reunite life and consumption, nation and company, and to relate them to the world of instrumental rationality. *If that reconstruction proves impossible, we would do better to stop talking about modernity.* (Touraine, 1995, p. 217, my emphasis)

State education is a monument to modernity. Although educational ideas have been open to debate, the form and content of education have proven to be very resistant to change. But there are important cultural and economic transformations now taking place, and schools and universities are necessarily caught up in them, and must react to them. Despite the great expectations made by those who desire a technical fix, it seems unlikely that society will be de-schooled, leaving us all enmeshed in Illichian webs and nets (Illich, 1973). It is more likely that society is, and will be, re-schooled, not de-schooled, and that this process will as usual be framed within the competing claims and complexities of democracy and capitalism. The re-schooling now in process does much to emphasize the cognitive, the managerial and the financial. Aside from tinkering about with a curriculum and calling it 'national', very little is being done to curb the centrifugal tendencies of postmodern culture and the socially divisive effects of 'choice' in a marketplace. On present trends, re-schooling is not about to *resocialize* us, but if it does not then democracy may indeed pay a high price.

References

ABBS, P. (1987) *Living Powers, The Arts and Education*, London, Falmer Press.

ALEXANDER, J.C. (1995) 'Modern, anti, post and neo', *New Left Review*, **210**, pp. 63–104.

ARCHER, M.S. (1993) 'Theory, culture and post-industrial society', in FEATHERSTONE, M. (Ed) *Global Culture: Nationalism, Globalization and Modernity*, London, Sage.

ARONOWITZ, S. (1988) 'Postmodernism and politics', in Ross, A. (Ed) *Universal Abandon: The Politics of Postmodernism*, Minneapolis, University of Minnesota Press.

ARONOWITZ, S. and DiFAZIO, W. (1994) *The Jobless Future: Sci-tech and the Dogma of Work*, Minneapolis, University of Minnesota Press.

ARONOWITZ, S. and GIROUX, H.A. (1991) *Postmodern Education: Politics, Culture and Social Criticism*, Minneapolis, University of Minnesota Press.

ATKINSON, J. (1984) 'Manpower strategies for flexible organisation', *Personnel Management*, August, pp. 27–31.

BAGLEY, W.C. (1905) *The Educative Process*, New York, Macmillan.

BAIN, A. (1879) *Education as a Science*, London, Kegan Paul.

BALL, S.J. (1995) 'Intellectuals or technicians: The urgent role of theory in educational studies', *British Journal of Educational Studies*, **43**, 3, pp. 255–71.

BALL, S.J., BOWE, R. and GEWIRTZ, S. (1995) 'Circuits of schooling: A sociological exploration of parental choice of school in social class contexts', *Sociological Review*, **43**, 1, pp. 52–77.

BARROW, R. (1995) 'The erosion of moral education', *International Review of Education*, **41**, 1–2, pp. 21–32.

BARROW, R. and WHITE, P. (1993) *Beyond Liberal Education: Essays in Honour of Paul Hirst*, London, Routledge.

BATESON, D. (1994) 'Psychometric and philosophic problems in "authentic" assessment: Performance tasks and portfolios', *Alberta Journal of Educational Research*, **40**, 2, pp. 233–45.

BAUDRILLARD, J. (1988) *America*, translated by Turner, C., London, Verso.

BAUMAN, Z. (1988) 'Sociology and postmodernity', *Sociological Review*, **36**, pp. 790–814.

BAUMAN, Z. (1991) *Modernity and Ambivalence*, Oxford, Polity Press.

BELL, A. (1807) 'Extract of a sermon on the education of the poor under an appropriate system', Preached at St Mary's , Lambeth, 28 June 1807, London, Cadell and Davies.

BELL, D. (1990a) 'Resolving the contradictions of modernity and modernism', 1, *Society*, **27**, pp. 43–50.

BELL, D. (1990b) 'Resolving the contradictions of modernity and modernism', 2, *Society*, **27**, pp. 66–75.

BENTHAM, J. (1962, original 1791) 'Panopticon; or, the Inspector's house', reprinted in *The Works of Jeremy Bentham*, Volume 4, New York, Russell and Russell.

BERGER, P. and LUCKMANN, T. (1967) *The Social Construction of Reality*, Harmondsworth, Penguin.

BERGER, P., BERGER, B. and KELLNER, H. (1973) *The Homeless Mind*, Harmondsworth, Penguin.

BERLAK, A. and BERLAK, H. (1981) *Dilemmas of Schooling: Teaching and Social Change*, London, Methuen.

BERMAN, M. (1983) *All That Is Solid Melts into Air*, London, Verso.

BERMAN, M. (1992) 'Why modernism still matters', in LASH, S. and FRIEDMAN, J. (Eds) *Modernity and Identity*, Oxford, Blackwell.

BERNSTEIN, B. (1977) 'Class and pedagogies: Visible and invisible', in BERNSTEIN, B. (Ed) *Class Codes and Control*, Volume III, London, Routledge and Kegan Paul.

BERNSTEIN, C. (1992) 'Idiot culture of the intellectual masses', *The Guardian*, 3 June, p. 19.

BERNSTEIN, R. (1991) *The New Constellation: The Ethical-political Horizons of Modernity/Postmodernity*, Cambridge, Polity.

BEST, S. and KELLNER, D. (1991) *Postmodern Theory: Critical Investigations*, Basingstoke, MacMillan.

BIESTA, G. (1995) 'Postmodernism and the repoliticization of education', *Interchange*, **26**, 2, pp. 161–83.

BIRKERTS, S. (1994) *The Gutenberg Elegies: The Fate of Reading in an Electronic Age*, Boston, Faber and Faber.

BLAKE, N. (1996) 'Between postmodernism and anti-modernism: The predicament of educational studies', *British Journal of Educational Studies*, **44**, 1, pp. 42–65.

BLOOM, A. (1987) *The Closing of the American Mind: How Higher Education Has Failed Democracy and Impoverished the Souls of Today's Students*, New York, Simon and Schuster.

BOJE, D.M. (1994) 'Organizational storytelling: The struggles of pre-modern, modern and postmodern organizational learning discourses', *Management Learning*, **25**, 3, pp. 433–61.

BOURDIEU, P. (1979) *Distinction: A Social Critique of the Judgement of Taste*, translated by NICE, R., London, Routledge and Kegan Paul.

BOWERS, C.A. (1991) 'Some questions about the anachronistic elements in the Giroux-McLaren theory of a critical pedagogy', *Curriculum Inquiry*, **21**, 2, pp. 239–52.

BOWLES, S. and GINTIS, H. (1976) *Schooling in Capitalist America*, London, Routledge and Kegan Paul.

BOYER, R. (1990) *The Regulation School: A Critical Introduction*, New York, Columbia University Press.

BOYNE, R. and RATTANSI, A. (1990) *Postmodernism and Society*, London, MacMillan.

BROUGHTON, J.M. (1984) 'The surrender of control: Computer literacy as political socialization of the child', in SLOAN, D. (Ed) *The Computer in Education: A Critical Perspective*, New York, Teachers College Press.

BROWN, S. and BLACK, H. (1988) 'Profiles and records of achievement', in BROWN, S. (Ed) *Assessment: A Changing Practice*, Edinburgh, Scottish Academic Press.

BURCH, B. and IMIG, D. (1996) 'Professionalization or deregulation: A case study of American Teacher Education', Paper presented to the meeting of Network Education Science Amsterdam (NESA), University of Stockholm, 13–16 June.

BURMAN, E. (1994) *Deconstructing Developmental Psychology*, London, Routledge.

BURRELL, G. (1988) 'Modernism, postmodernism and organisational analysis 3', *Organization Studies*, **9**, 2, pp. 221–35.

CALDWELL, B.J. and SPINKS, J.M. (1992) *Leading the Self-Managing School*, London, Falmer Press.

CALLAHAN, R.E. (1962) *Education and the Cult of Efficiency*, Chicago, Chicago University Press.

CAPPER, C.A. and JAMISON, M.T. (1993) 'Let the buyer beware: Total quality management and educational research and practice', *Educational Researcher*, **22**, 8, pp. 15–30.

CARLSON, D. (1995) 'Making progress: Progressive education in the postmodern', *Educational Theory*, **45**, 3, pp. 337–57.

CARTER, P. (1995) 'A response to Parker', *Organization Studies*, **16**, 4, 573–75.

CENTRAL STATISTICAL OFFICE (1995) *Social Trends 1995*, London, HMSO.

CHERRYHOLMES, C. (1988) *Power and Criticism: Poststructural Investigations in Education*, New York, Teachers College Record.

CHERUBINI, F. (1990) 'The peasant and agriculture', in LE GOFF, J. (Ed) *The Medieval World*, translated by COCHRANE, L.G., London, Collins and Brown.

CHUBB, J. and MOE, T. (1990) *Politics, Markets and America's Schools*, Washington, DC, The Brookings Institution.

CHUBB, J. and MOE, T. (1992) *A Lesson on School Reform from Great Britain*, Washington, DC, The Brookings Institution.

CLARE, J. (1996) 'Government lays down rules on how to teach the teachers', *Daily Telegraph*, 13 June.

CLARK, B. (1961) 'The cooling out function in higher education', in HALSEY, A.H., FLOUD, J. and ANDERSON, A.C. (Eds) *Education Economy and Society: A Reader in the Sociology of Education*, New York, The Free Press of Glencoe.

CLEGG, S. (1992) 'Modern and postmodern organisations', *Sociology Review*, 24–28, April.

CODD, J. and GORDON, L. (1991) 'School charters: The contractualist state and education policy', *New Zealand Journal of Educational Studies*, **26**, 1, pp. 21–34.

COLE, M. and HILL, D. (1995) 'Games of despair and rhetorics of resistance: Postmodernism, education and reaction', *British Journal of Sociology of Education*, **16**, 2, pp. 165–82.

COLEMAN, J. (1993) 'The rational reconstruction of society', *American Sociological Review*, **58**, 1, pp. 1–15.

COMMITTEE OF SCOTTISH UNIVERSITY PRINCIPALS (CSUP) (1992) *Teaching and Learning in an Expanding Higher Education System* (The MacFarlane Report), Edinburgh, CSUP.

CONTI, R.F. and WARNER, M. (1994) 'Taylorism, teams and technology in "reengineering" work-organization', *New Technology, Work and Employment*, **9**, 2, pp. 93–101.

COOPER, B. (1989) 'Modernism, postmodernism and organizational analysis 3: The contribution of Jacques Derrida', *Organization Studies*, **10**, 4, pp. 479–502.

COOPER, C. and KELLY, M. (1993) 'Occupational stress in head teachers: A national UK study', *British Journal of Educational Psychology*, **63**, pp. 130–43.

COOPER, R. (1987) 'Information, communication and organisation: A post-structural revision', *Journal of Mind and Behaviour*, **8**, 3, pp. 395–416.

CORNBLETH, C. (1995) 'Controlling curriculum knowledge: Multicultural politics and policymaking', *Journal of Curriculum Studies*, **27**, 2, pp. 165–85.

DAVIS, M. (1995) 'Fortress Los Angeles: The militarization of urban space', in KASINITZ, P. (Ed) *Metropolis: Centre and Symbol of Our Times*, Basingstoke, MacMillan Press.

DEPARTMENT OF EDUCATION AND SCIENCE (1984) *Records of Achievement: A Statement of Policy*, London, DES.

DEPARTMENT FOR EDUCATION (1995) *Superhighways for Education: Consultation Paper on Broadband Communication*, London, HMSO.

DEPARTMENT FOR EDUCATION AND EMPLOYMENT (1995) *The National Curriculum*, London, HMSO (The publication is also on the Internet: http://www.dfee.gov.uk/nc/, current at 3 October, 1996).

DEPARTMENT FOR EDUCATION AND EMPLOYMENT (1996) *Self Government for Schools*, Cmnd 3315, London, HMSO.

DION, D. (1993) 'License and commodification: The birth of an information oligarchy', *Humanity and Society*, **17**, 1, pp. 48–69.

DION, D. (1995) 'Brave new reductionism: TQM as ethnocentrism', *Education Policy Analysis Archives*, **3**, 9 (Internet WWW page at http://info.asu.edu/asu-cwis/epaa/v3n9.html, current at 19 August, 1996).

DOLL, W.E. JR. (1989) 'Foundations of a post-modern curriculum', *Journal of Curriculum Studies*, **21**, 3, pp. 243–53.

DOLL, W.E. JR. (1993) *A Post-modern Perspective on Curriculum*, New York, Teachers College Press.

DUNN, K. (1996) 'Talk radio extremism', *Once a Year Magazine* (Internet WWW page at http://www.tefnet.org/oay/dunn.html).

DURKHEIM, E. (1977) 'On education and society', in KARABEL, J. and HALSEY, A.H. (Eds) *Power and Ideology in Education*, New York, Oxford University Press.

ECO, U. (1985) 'Towards a new Middle Ages', in BLONSKY, M. (Ed) *On Signs*, Oxford, Blackwell.

References

ELIAS, N. (1978) *The Civilizing Process: Volume I, The History of Manners*, translated by JEFFCOTT, E., Oxford, Basil Blackwell (Originally published in 1939 by Haus zum Falken, Basel).

ELLSWORTH, E. (1989) 'Why doesn't this feel empowering?: Working through the repressive myths of critical pedagogy', *Harvard Educational Review*, **50**, 3, pp. 297–324.

ERASMUS, D. (1560) *De Civilitate Morum Puerilium*, Antwerpiae, J. Latius.

ERIKSEN, S.D. (1995) 'TQM and the transformation from an elite to a mass system of higher education in the UK', *Quality Assurance in Education*, **3**, 1, pp. 14–29.

ETZIONI, A. (1975) *A Comparative Analysis of Complex Organisations*, New York, The Free Press.

FEATHERSTONE, M. (1991) *Consumer Culture and Postmodernism*, London, Sage.

FISCHER, C.F. and KING, R.M. (1995) *Authentic Assessment: A Guide to Implementation*, Thousand Oaks, CA, Corwin Press.

FLAX, J. (1990) 'Postmodernism and gender relations in feminist theory', in NICHOLSON, L.J. (Ed) *Feminism/Postmodernism*, London, Routledge.

FOUCAULT, M. (1977) *Discipline and Punish: The Birth of the Prison*, translated by Sheridan, A., New York, Pantheon Books.

FRANKLIN, B.M. (1988) 'Education for an urban America: Ralph Tyler and the curriculum field', in GOODSON, I. (Ed) *International Perspectives in Curriculum History*, London, Routledge.

FRASER, N. and NICHOLSON, L. (1988) 'Social criticism without philosophy: An encounter between feminism and postmodernism', in ROSS, A. (Ed) *Universal Abandon: The Politics of Postmodernism*, Minneapolis, University of Minnesota Press.

FRIEDMAN, J. (1992) 'Narcissism, roots and postmodernity: The constitution of selfhood in the global crisis', in LASH, S. and FRIEDMAN, J. (Eds) *Modernity and Identity*, Oxford, Basil Blackwell.

FULLAN, M. (1993) *Change Forces: Probing the Depths of Educational Reform*, London, Falmer Press.

FULLAN, M. and HARGREAVES, A. (1992) *What's Worth Fighting for in Your School?*, Buckingham, Open University Press in association with the Ontario Public School Teachers' Federation.

GALBRAITH, J.K. (1992) *The Culture of Contentment*, London, Sinclair-Stevenson.

GALTON, F. (1869) *Hereditary Genius: An Inquiry into Its Laws and Consequences*, London, MacMillan and Co.

GARDINER, M.F., FOX, A., KNOWLES, F. and JEFFREY, D. (1996) 'Learning improved by arts training', *Nature*, **381**, 23 May, p. 284.

GARFINKEL, H. (1967) *Studies in Ethnomethodology*, Englewood Cliffs, Prentice-Hall.

GATES, H.L. JR. (1992) *Loose Canons: Notes on the Culture Wars*, New York, Oxford University Press.

GELLNER, E. (1992) *Postmodernism, Reason and Religion*, London, Routledge.

GERGEN, K. (1992) 'Organization theory in the postmodern era', in REED, M. and

HUGHES, M. (Eds) *Rethinking Organization: New Directions in Organization Theory and Analysis*, London, Sage.

GIBSON, R. (1984) *Structuralism and Education*, London, Hodder and Stoughton.

GIDDENS, A. (1991) *Modernity and Self Identity: Self and Society in the Late Modern Age*, Cambridge, Polity Press.

GIDDENS, A. (1995) *Beyond Left and Right: The Future of Radical Politics*, Cambridge, Polity Press.

GIROUX, H. (1993) *Living Dangerously: Multiculturalism and the Politics of Difference*, New York, Peter Lang.

GIROUX, H.A. (1995) 'Right wing pedagogy', *Cultural Studies Times*, Fall (Internet electronic journal at http://zelda.thomson.com/routledge/cst/giroux.html current at 21 August 1996).

GIROUX, H. and McLAREN, P. (1991) 'Radical pedagogy as cultural politics: Beyond the discourse of critique and anti-Utopianism', in MORTON, D. and ZAVARZADEH, M. (Eds) *Theory/Pedagogy/Politics: Texts for Change*, Urbana, University of Illinois Press.

GIROUX, H. and McLAREN, P. (1994) 'Multiculturalism and the postmodern critique: Toward a pedagogy of resistance and transformation', in GIROUX, H. and McLAREN, P. *Between Borders: Pedagogy and the Politics of Cultural Studies*, London, Routledge.

GLASER, B. and STRAUSS, A. (1968) *The Discovery of Grounded Theory*, London, Weidenfeld and Nicolson.

GLASS, G. (1994) 'School choice: A discussion with Herbert Gintis', *Education Policy Analysis Archives*, **2**, 6 (Internet electronic journal at http://sea-monkey.ed.asu.edu/epaa/v2n6.html, current at 19 August 1996).

GLENNERSTER, H. (1991) 'Quasi-markets for education', *The Economic Journal*, 101, pp. 1268–76.

GOODMAN, J. (1995) 'Change without difference: School restructuring in historical perspective', *Harvard Educational Review*, **65**, 1, pp. 1–29.

GOODSON, I. (1994) *Studying Curriculum*, Buckingham, Open University Press.

GRAFF, G. (1990) 'Other voices, other rooms: Organizing and teaching the humanities conflict', *New Literary History*, **21**, 4, pp. 817–39.

GRAFF, G. (1992) *Beyond the Culture Wars: How Teaching the Conflicts Can Revitalize American Education*, New York, Norton.

GRAHAM-CUMMING, J. (1996) 'We know all about you', *The Guardian* (On-Line supplement), 26 September, p. 9.

GUREVITCH, A. (1988) *Medieval Popular Culture: Problems of Belief and Perception*, translated by BAK, J.M. and HOLLINGSWORTH, A., Cambridge, Cambridge University Press.

HABERMAS, J. (1971) *Towards a Rational Society*, London, Heinemann.

HABERMAS, J. (1990) *Moral Consciousness and Communicative Action*, translated by LENHARDT, C. and NICHOLSEN, S.W., Cambridge, Polity Press.

HALL, S. and JACQUES, M. (1989) *New Times: The Changing Face of Politics in the 1990s*, London, Lawrence and Wishart.

HAMILTON, D. (1986) 'Adam Smith and the moral economy of the classroom system', in TAYLOR, P.H. (Ed) *Recent Developments in Curriculum Studies*, Windsor, NFER-Nelson.

HAMMER, M. and CHAMPY, J. (1993) *Reengineering the Corporation*, New York, Collins.

HARDING, S. (1990) 'Feminism, science and the anti-Enlightenment critiques', in NICHOLSON, L.J. (Ed) *Feminism/Postmodernism*, London, Routledge.

HARGREAVES, A. (1986) 'Record breakers?', in BROADFOOT, P. (Ed) *Profiles and Records of Achievement: A Review of Issues and Practice*, London, Holt, Rinehart and Winston.

HARGREAVES, A. (1994a) *Changing Teachers, Changing Times: Teachers' Work and Culture in the Postmodern Age*, New York, Teachers College Press.

HARGREAVES, A. (1994b) 'Dissonant voices: Teachers and the multiple realities of restructuring', Paper presented to the Annual Meeting of the American Educational Research Association, New Orleans, April.

HARGREAVES, A. (1995a) 'Renewal in the age of paradox', *Educational Leadership*, **52**, 7, pp. 14–19.

HARGREAVES, A. (1995b) 'Towards a social geography of teacher education', in SHIMAHARA, N.K. and HOLOWINSKY, I.Z. (Eds) *Teacher Education in Industrialized Nations*, New York, Garland.

HARTLEY, D. (1985) 'Social education in Scotland — Some sociological considerations', *Scottish Educational Review*, **17**, 2, pp. 92–8.

HARTLEY, D. (1987a) 'The convergence of learner-centred pedagogy in primary and further education in Scotland: 1965–85', *British Journal of Educational Studies*, **35**, 2, pp. 115–28.

HARTLEY, D. (1987b) 'Re-schooling society', *Scottish Educational Review*, **19**, 2, pp. 98–107.

HARTLEY, D. (1993a) *Understanding the Nursery School: A Sociological Analysis*, London, Cassell.

HARTLEY, D. (1993b) 'Confusion in teacher education: A postmodern condition?', in GILROY, P. and SMITH, M. (Eds) *International Analyses of Teacher Education*, Abingdon, Carfax (A special issue of the *Journal of Education for Teaching*).

HARTLEY, D. (1994) 'Mixed messages in education policy: sign of the times?', *British Journal of Educational Studies*, **42**, 3, pp. 230–44.

HARVEY, D. (1989) *The Condition of Postmodernity: An Enquiry into the Origins of Cultural Change*, Cambridge, Basil Blackwell.

HARWOOD, J. (1979) 'Nature, nurture and politics: A critique of the conventional wisdom', in SMITH, J.V. and HAMILTON, D. (Eds) *The Meritocratic Intellect*, Aberdeen, Aberdeen University Press.

HAWKES, N. (1996) 'Power of music extends across curriculum', *The Times*, 25 May, p. 9.

HIGHER EDUCATION QUALITY COUNCIL (HEQC) (1995) *Graduate Standards Programme — Interim Report*, London, HEQC.

HILL, P.J. (1994) 'Conflict, curriculum and reform', in CAIN, W.E. (Ed) *Teaching the Conflicts: Gerald Graff, Curricular Reform and the Culture Wars*, New York, Garland.

HIMMELFARB, G. (1995) *The De-moralization of Society: From Victorian Virtues to Modern Values*, London, IEA Health and Welfare Unit.

HIRST, P.H. (1974) *Knowledge and the Curriculum*, London, Routledge and Kegan Paul.

HIRST, P.H. (1993) 'Education, knowledge and practices', in BARROW, R. and WHITE, P. (Eds) *Beyond Liberal Education: Essays in Honour of Paul Hirst*, London, Routledge.

HIRST, P. and ZEITLIN, J. (1991) 'Flexible specialization versus post-Fordism: Theory, evidence and policy implications', *Economy and Society*, **20**, 1, pp. 1–56.

HLEBOWITSH, P.S. (1995) 'Interpretation of the Tyler *Rationale*: A reply to Kliebard', *Journal of Curriculum Studies*, **27**, 1, pp. 89–94.

HODGSON, V.E. (1993) 'Educational computing — Mirrors of educational values', *Educational and Training Technology International*, **30**, 1, pp. 32–8.

HOGGETT, P. (1996) 'New modes of control in the public service', *Public Administration*, **74**, Spring, pp. 9–32.

HOLMES GROUP (1986) *Tomorrow's Teachers*, East Lansing, Michigan, The Holmes Group.

HOLMES GROUP (1990) *Tomorrow's Schools*, East Lansing, Michigan, The Holmes Group.

HOLMES GROUP (1995) *Tomorrow's Schools of Education*, East Lansing, Michigan, The Holmes Group.

HOSKIN, K. (1979) 'The examination, disciplinary power and rational schooling', *History of Education*, **8**, 2, pp. 135–46.

HOWLEY, A. and HARTNETT, R. (1992) 'Pastoral power and the contemporary university: A Foucauldian analysis', *Educational Theory*, **42**, 3, pp. 271–83.

ILLICH, I. (1973) *Deschooling Society*, Harmondsworth, Penguin.

JAMESON, I. (1984) 'The cultural logic of late capitalism', *New Left Review*, **146**, pp. 53–92.

JENCKS, C. (1986) *What Is Postmodernism?*, London, Academy Editions.

JENCKS, C. (1992) *The Post-modern Reader*, London, Academy Editions.

JESSUP, G. (1991) *Outcomes: NVQs and the Emerging Model of Education and Training*, London, Falmer Press.

JIMACK, P.D. (1989) 'Editional introduction', in ROUSSEAU, J.-J. *Emile*, (translated by Foxley, B.), London, J.M. Dent.

JONATHAN, R. (1995) 'Liberal philosophy of education: A paradigm under strain', *Journal of Philosophy of Education*, **29**, 1, pp. 93–107.

JONES, P. (1996) 'Academic jargon: How to publish it', *The Times*, 25 May, p. 18.

KAMIN, L. (1977) *The Science and Politics of IQ*, Harmondsworth, Penguin.

KANPOL, B. (1992) 'Postmodernism in education revisited: Similarities within differences and the democratic imaginary', *Educational Theory*, **42**, 22, pp. 217–29.

KANT, I. (1784/1991) 'An answer to the question, What is Enlightenment?', in REISS, H. (Ed) *Kant: Political Writings*, translated by NISBET, H.B., Cambridge, Cambridge University Press.

KEARNEY, R. (1984) *Dialogues with Contemporary Continental Thinkers*, Manchester, Manchester University Press.

KENWAY, J. (1995) 'Having a postmodernist turn or postmodernist *Angst*: A disordered experienced by an author who is not yet dead or even close to it', in SMITH, R. and WEXLER, P. (Eds) *After Post-modernism*, London, Falmer Press.

KENWAY, J., BIGUM, C., FITZCLARENCE, L. and COLLIER, J. (forthcoming) 'Pulp fictions?: Education, markets and the information superhighway', in CARLSON, D. and APPLE, M. (Eds) *Critical Education Theory in Upsetting Times*, New York, Teachers College Press.

KENWAY, J., BIGUM, C., FITZCLARENCE, L., COLLIER, J. and TREGENZA, K. (1994) 'New education in new times', *Journal of Education Policy*, **9**, 4, pp. 317–33.

KINCHELOE, J.L. (1993) *Towards a Critical Politics of Teacher Thinking: Mapping the Postmodern*, Westport, Connecticut, Bergin and Garvey.

KING, R. (1978) *All Things Bright and Beautiful?*, Chichester, Wiley.

KIZILTAN, M.U., BAIN, W.J. and CANIZARES M. (1990) 'A postmodern condition: Rethinking public education', *Educational Theory*, **40**, 3, pp. 351–69.

KLIEBARD, H.M. (1992) *Forging the American Curriculum*, London, Routledge.

KLIEBARD, H.M. (1995) 'The Tyler *Rationale* revisited', *Journal of Curriculum Studies*, **27**, 1, pp. 81–8.

LABAREE, D.F. (1992) 'Power, knowledge and the rationalization of teaching: A genealogy of the movement to professionalize teaching', *Harvard Educational Review*, **62**, 2, pp. 123–53.

LABAREE, D.F. (1995) 'Reforming the preparation of teachers: The Holmes Group proposals in *Tomorrow's Schools of Education*', Paper presented to the PACT Conference on Teachers' Experiences of Educational Reform, 2–4 April.

LACLAU, E. (1988) 'Politics and the limits of modernity', in ROSS, A. (Ed) *Universal Abandon: The Politics of Postmodernism*, Minneapolis, University of Minnesota Press.

LANGMAN, L. (1991) 'From pathos to panic: American character meets the future', in WEXLER, P. (Ed) *Critical Theory Now*, Lewes, Falmer Press.

LASH, S. and URRY, J. (1987) *The End of Organized Capitalism*, Cambridge, Polity Press.

LASH, S. and URRY, J. (1994) *Economics of Signs and Space*, London, Sage.

LATHER, P. (1991) *Feminist Research and Pedagogy with/in the Postmodern*, London, Routledge.

LATHER, P. (1993) 'Fertile obsession: Validity after poststructuralism', *Sociological Quarterly*, **34**, 4, pp. 673–93.

LE GOFF, J. (1990) *The Medieval World*, translated by COCHRANE, L.G., London, Collins and Brown.

LLOYD, G. (1984) *The Man of Reason: 'Male' and 'Female' in Wester Philosophy*, London, Methuen.

LUCHAIRE, A. (1912) *Social Justice at the Time of Philip Augustus*, New York, Holt.

LUNN, E. (1985) *Marxism and Modernism*, London, Verso.

LYOTARD, J.-F. (1984) *The Postmodern Condition*, translated by BENNINGTON, G. and MASSUMI, B., Manchester, Manchester University Press.

MANN, H. (1857) *Report of an Educational Tour in Germany, France, Holland,*

and Parts of Great Britain and Ireland (4th edition), London, Simpkin, Marshall and Company.

MAUHS-PUGH, T. (1995) 'Charter schools: A survey and analysis', *Education Policy Analysis Archives*, **3**, 13 (Internet page at http://seamonkey.ed.asu.edu/~gene/epaa/charter/home.html, current at 19 August 1996).

McCORMICK, K. (1994) 'Determination/agency, critique/legitimation: Difference and dialogue in classroom practice or what's left when the lefter-than-thou-speak stops?', *College Literature*, **21**, 3, pp. 67–76.

McHUGH, P. (1968) *Defining the Situation*, Indianapolis, Bobbs Merrill.

McINTYRE, A. (1981) *After Virtue: A Study in Moral Theory*, London, Duckworth.

McLAREN, P. (1989) *Life in Schools: An Introduction to a Critical Pedagogy in the Foundations of Education*, New York, Longman.

McLAREN, P. (1994) *Critical Theory and Predatory Culture*, London, Routledge.

McLELLAN, D. (Ed) (1977) *Karl Marx: Selected Writings*, Oxford, Oxford University Press.

McMURRY, A. (1996) 'The slow apocalypse: A gradualistic theory of the world's demise', *Postmodern Culture*, **6**, 3 (Internet page at http://jefferson.village.virginia.edu/pmc/issue.596/contents.596.html, current at 19 August 1996).

McWILLIAM, E. (1995) '(S)education: A risky enquiry into pleasurable teaching', *Education and Society*, **13**, 1, pp. 15–24.

McWILLIAM, E. (1996) 'Seduction or schoolmarm: On the improbability of the Great Female Teacher', *Interchange*, **27**, 1, pp. 1–11.

MELUCCI, A. (1989) *Nomads of the Present*, London, Hutchinson.

MESTROVIC, S. (1991) *The Coming Fin de Siècle: An Application of Durkheim's Sociology to Modernity and Postmodernism*, London, Routledge.

MESTROVIC, S.G. (1993) *The Barbarian Temperament: Towards a Postmodern Critical Theory*, London, Routledge.

MESTROVIC, S.G. (1994) *The Balkanization of the West: The Confluence of Postmodernism and Postcommunism*, London, Routledge.

MILL, J.S. (1930) *A System of Logic, Ratiocinative and Inductive, Being a Connected View of the Principles of Evidence and the Methods of Scientific Investigation*, London, Longmans Green.

MINC, A. (1993) *Le Nouveau Moyen Age*, Paris, Gallimard.

MISGELD, D. (1992) 'Pedagogy and politics: Some critial reflections on the postmodern turn in critical pedagogy', *Phenomenology and Pedagogy*, **10**, pp. 125–42.

MORTON, D. and ZAVARZADEH, M. (1991) *Theory/Pedagogy/Politics: Texts for Change*, Urbana, University of Illinois Press.

MURRAY, R. (1992) 'Fordism and Post-Fordism', in JENCKS, C. (Ed) *The Postmodern Reader*, London, Academy Editions.

NASAW, D. (1979) *Schooled to Order: A Social History of Public Schooling in the United States*, New York, Oxford University Press.

NEIMEYER, R.A., NEIMEYER, G.J., LYDDON, W.J. and TSOI HOSHMAND, L. (1994) 'The reality of social construction', *Contemporary Psychology*, **39**, 5, pp. 459–63.

NEWSOM REPORT (1963) *Half Our Future*, London, HMSO.

NICHOLSON, L.J. (1990) *Feminism/Postmodernism*, London, Routledge.

OECD (1994) *School: A Matter of Choice*, Paris, OECD.

OLIVER, D. and GERSHMAN, K. (1989) *Education, Modernity and Fractured Meaning*, Albany, NY, State University of New York Press.

OLSON, J. (1989) 'Surviving innovation: Reflection on the pitfalls of practice', *Journal of Curriculum Studies*, **21**, 6, pp. 503–08.

O'NEILL, J. (1988) 'Religion and postmodernism: The Durkheimian bond in Bell and Jameson', *Theory Culture and Society*, **5**, 2–3, pp. 493–500.

ORME, N. (1973) *English Schools in the Middle Ages*, London, Methuen.

ORWELL, G. (1989, original 1949) *Nineteen Eighty-Four*, Harmondsworth, Penguin.

PACKARD, V. (1981) *The Hidden Persuaders*, Harmondsworth, Penguin.

PAPERT, S. (1984) 'New theories for new learning', *School Psychology Review*, **13**, 4, pp. 422–8.

PARKER, M. (1995) 'Critique in the name of what? Postmodernism and critical approaches to organisation', *Organization Studies*, **16**, 4, pp. 553–64.

PARKER, M. and JARY, D. (1995) 'The McUniversity: Organisation, management and academic subjectivity', *Organisation*, **2**, 2, pp. 319–38.

PATERSON, F.M.S. (1988) 'Measures of schooling: Registers, standards and the construction of the subject', *Journal of Historical Sociology*, **1**, 3, pp. 278–300.

PETERS, M. and LANKSHEAR, C. (1996) 'Critical literacy and digital texts', *Educational Theory*, **46**, 1, pp. 51–70.

PIAGET, J. (1970) *Genetic epistemology*, New York, W.W. Norton and Company.

PICKERING, J. (1995) 'Teaching on the Internet is learning', *Active Learning*, **2**, July, pp. 9–12.

PINAR, W.F. and REYNOLDS, W.M. (1992) *Curriculum as Text Understanding Curriculum as Phenomenological and Deconstructed Text*, New York, Teachers College Press.

PIORE, M. and SABEL, C. (1984) *The Second Industrial Divide: Possibilities for Prosperity*, New York, Basic Books.

PLOWDEN REPORT (1967) *Children and Their Primary Schools*, London, HMSO.

PRING, R. (1975) 'Knowledge out of Control', in GOLBY, M., GREENWALD, J. and WEST, R. (Eds) *Curriculum Design*, London, Croom Helm in association with the Open University Press.

PRING, R. (1993) 'Liberal education and vocational preparation', in BARROW, R. and WHITE, P. (Eds) *Beyond Liberal Education, Essays in Honour of Paul Hirst*, London, Routledge.

RAAB, C. (1994) 'Theorising the governance of education', *British Journal of Educational Studies*, **42**, 1, pp. 6–22.

RABINOW, P. (1991) *The Foucault Reader*, Harmondsworth, Penguin Books.

RAVITCH, D. (1995) *Debating the Future of American Education: Do We Need National Standards and Assessments?*, Washington DC, The Brookings Institution.

REID, T.A. (1994) 'Perspectives on computers in education: The promise, the pain, the prospect', *Active Learning*, **1**, December, pp. 4–10.

REID, W.A. (1993) 'Does Schwab improve on Tyler: A response to Jackson', *Journal of Curriculum Studies*, **25**, 6, pp. 499–510.

REIMER, E. (1971) *School is Dead: An Essay on Alternatives in Education*, Harmondsworth, Penguin.

RHEINGOLD, H. (1994) *The Virtual Community — Finding Connection in a Computerised World*, London, Secker and Warburg.

RIESMAN, D., GLAZER, N. and DENNY, R. (1950) *The Lonely Crowd: A Study of the Changing American Character*, New Haven, Yale University Press.

RITZER, G. (1993) *The McDonaldization of Society*, London, Pine Forge Press.

ROBINS, K. and WEBSTER, F. (1989) *The Technical Fix: Education, Computers and Industry*, Basingstoke, MacMillan.

ROSE, N. (1989) *Governing the Soul: The Shaping of the Private Self*, London, Routledge.

ROSENAU, P.M. (1992) *Post-Modernism and the Social Sciences*, Princeton, Princeton University Press.

ROSENTHAL, R. and JACOBSON, L. (1968) *Pygmalion in the Classroom*, New York, Holt, Rinehart and Winston.

ROSS, A. (1988) *Universal Abandon: The Politics of Postmodernism*, Minneapolis, University of Minnesota Press.

ROSSIAUD, J. (1990) 'The city-dweller and life in cities and towns', in LE GOFF, J. (Ed) (1990) *The Medieval World*, translated by COCHRANE, L.G., London, Collins and Brown.

ROUSSEAU, J.-J. (1989, original 1762) *Emile*, translated by FOXLEY, B., with an introduction by JIMACK, P.D., London, J.M. Dent.

RUBIN, L. (1991) 'Educational evaluation: Classic works of Ralph W. Tyler', *Journal of Curriculum Studies*, **23**, 2, pp. 193–97.

SALLIS, E. (1993) *Total Quality Management in Education*, London, Kogan Page.

SCASE, R. (1994) 'Organizational restructuring, corporate needs for changing managerial skills, and the role of higher education', in BROWN, P. and LAUDER, H. (Eds) *Education for Economic Survival: From Fordism to Post-Fordism?* London, Routledge.

SCHIFF, G.D. and GOLDFIELD, N.I. (1994) 'Deming meets Braverman: Toward a progressive analysis of the continuous quality improvement paradigm, *International Journal of Health Services*, **2**, 4, pp. 655–673.

SCHUTZ, A. (1972) *The Phenomenology of the Social World*, London, Heinemann Educational.

SCOTTISH OFFICE (1992) *Staying on Course: Student Guidance in Scottish Further Education Colleges*, Edinburgh, Scottish Office.

SCOTTISH OFFICE EDUCATION DEPARTMENT (1965) *Primary Education in Scotland (The Primary Memorandum)*, Edinburgh, HMSO.

SELIGMAN, A.B. (1990) 'Towards a reinterpretation of modernity in an age of postmodernity', in TURNER, B.S. (Ed) *Theories of Modernity and Postmodernity*, London, Sage.

SHAPIN, S. and BARNES, B. (1976) 'Head and hand: Rhetorical resources in British pedagogical writing, 1770–1850', *Oxford Review of Education*, **2**, 3, pp. 231–54.

SHARP, R. and GREEN, R. (1975) *Education and Social Control*, London, Routledge and Kegan Paul.

SHOR, I. (1986) *Culture Wars School and Society in the Conservative Restoration*, London, Routledge and Kegan Paul.

SHULMAN, L. (1987) 'Knowledge and teaching: Foundations of the new reform', *Harvard Educational Review*, **57**, 1, pp. 1–22.

SIANN, G. and UGWUEGBU, D.C.E. (1989) *Educational Psychology in a Changing World*, London, English Language Book Society/Unwin Hyman.

SIEGEL, H. (1995) ' "Radical" pedagogy requires "conservative" epistemology', *Journal of Philosophy of Education*, **29**, 1, pp. 33–46.

SILVERMAN, D. (1971) *The Theory of Organisations*, London, Heinemann.

SLATTERY, P. (1995) 'A postmodern vision of time and learning: A response to the National Education Commission Report Prisoners of Time', *Harvard Educational Review*, **65**, 4, pp. 612–33.

SLAUGHTER, R.A. (1989) 'Cultural reconstruction in the post-modern world', *Journal of Curriculum Studies*, **21**, 3, pp. 255–70.

SLOAN, A. (1964) *My Years with General Motors*, New York, Doubleday.

SMART, B. (1990) 'Modernity, postmodernity and the present', in TURNER, B.S. (Ed) *Theories of Modernity and Postmodernity*, London, Sage.

SMITH, D. (1992) 'Review article: Modernity, postmodernity and the new Middle Ages', *Sociological Review*, **40**, 4, pp. 755–71.

SMITH, J.V. and HAMILTON, D. (1980) *The Meritocratic Intellect: Studies in the History of Educational Research*, Aberdeen, Aberdeen University Press.

SMITH, R. and WEXLER, P. (Eds) (1995) *After Post-modernism*, London, Falmer Press.

SNOOK, I. (1993) 'The curriculum: The timeless and the time-bound', in BARROW, R. and WHITE, P. (Eds) *Beyond Liberal Education: Essays in Honour of Paul Hirst*, London, Routledge.

SOKAL, A. (1996a) 'Transgressing the boundaries: Towards a transformative hermeneutics of quantum gravity', *Social Text*, 46–47, pp. 217–52.

SOKAL, A. (1996b) 'A physicist experiments with cultural studies', *Lingua Franca*, May–June, pp. 62–4.

SOKAL AFFAIR (1996) Parts of the debate on the Internet are at http:/// www.nyu.edu/gsas/dept/physics/faculty/sokal/index.html#papers, current at 20 August 1996.

SPIECKER, B. (1984) 'The pedagogical relationship', *Oxford Review of Education*, **10**, 2, pp. 203–9.

STEUERMAN, E. (1992) 'Habermas vs Lyotard: Modernity vs postmodernity?', in BENJAMIN, A. (Ed) *Judging Lyotard*, London, Routledge.

TAYLOR, F.W. (1947) *Scientific Management*, NY, Harper.

TINNING, R. and FITZCLARENCE, L. (1992) 'Postmodern youth culture and the crisis in Australian secondary school physical education', *Quest*, **44**, pp. 287–303.

TORRANCE, H. (1995) *Evaluating Authentic Assessment*, Buckingham, Open University Press.

TOURAINE, A. (1995) *Critique of Modernity*, translated by MACEY, D., Oxford, Basil Blackwell.

TRIBUS, M. (undated) *Quality Management in Education*, Hayward, CA, Exergy, (Internet page at gopher://deming.eng.clemson.edu/00/pub/tqmbbs/education/ qualed.txt, current at 19 August 1996).

TUCKMAN, A. (1994) 'The yellow brick road: Total quality management and the restructuring of organizational culture', *Organization Studies*, **15**, 5, pp. 727–51.

TYACK, D. and TOBIN, W. (1994) 'The "grammar" of schooling, why has it been so hard to change?', *American Educational Research Journal*, **31**, 3, pp. 453–79.

UNITED NATIONS INDUSTRIAL DEVELOPMENT ORGANISATION (1992) *Handbook of Industrial Statistics*, Aldershot, Edward Elgar Publishers.

URRY, J. (1995) *Consuming Places*, London, Routledge.

USHER, R. and EDWARDS, R. (1994) *Postmodernism and Education*, London, Routledge.

VALLANCE, E. (1973) 'Hiding the hidden curriculum', *Curriculum Inquiry*, **38**, pp. 5–21.

VEBLEN, T. (1970, original 1899) *The Theory of the Leisure Class*, London, Allen and Unwin.

VILLA, D.R. (1992) 'Postmodernism and the public sphere', *American Political Science Review*, **86**, 3, pp. 712–21.

WALKERDINE, V. (1984) 'Developmental psychology and the child-centred pedagogy: The insertion of Piaget into early education', in HENRIQUES, J. HOLLOWAY, W., URWIN, C., VENN, C. and WALKERDINE, V. (Eds) *Changing the Subject: Psychology, Social Regulation and Subjectity*, London, Methuen.

WALKERDINE, V. (1993) 'Beyond Developmentalism?', *Theory and Psychology*, **3**, 4, pp. 451–69.

WALKERDINE, V. (1994) 'Reasoning in a post-modern age', in ERNEST, P. (Ed) *Mathematics, Education and Philosophy*, London, Falmer, Press.

WALLER, W. (1932) *Sociology of Teaching*, New York, Wiley.

WARDLE, D. (1974) *The Rise of the Schooled Society*, London, Routledge and Kegan Paul.

WATKINS, P. (1994) 'The Fordist/post-Fordist debate: The educational implications', in KENWAY, J. (Ed) *Economising Education: The Post-Fordist Directions*, Geelong, Deakin University Press.

WATKINS, P. (1996) 'Decentralising education to the point of production: Sloanism, the market and schools of the future', *Discourse: Studies in the Cultural Politics of Education*, **17**, 1, pp. 85–99.

WEBER, E. (1993) 'Review of *Postmodern Education: Politics , Culture and Social Criticism*' ARONOWITZ, S. and GIROUX, H. *Journal of Curriculum Studies*, **25**, 3, pp. 297–99.

WEBER, M. (1946, original 1917) 'Science as a vocation', in GERTH, H. and MILLS, C.W. (Eds) *From Max Weber*, Oxford, Oxford University Press.

WEBER, M. (1978, original 1922) 'Classes, status groups and parties', in RUNCIMAN, W.G. (Ed) *Weber: Selections in Translation*, Cambridge, Cambridge University Press.

WEXLER, P. (1992) *Becoming Somebody: Toward a Social Psychology of School*, London, Falmer Press.

WEXLER, P. (1995) 'After postmodernism: A new age social theory', in SMITH, R. and WEXLER, R. (Eds) *After Post-modernism*, London, Falmer Press.

WHITTY, G. (1989) 'The New Right and the national curriculum: State control of market forces?', *Journal of Education Policy*, **4**, 4, pp. 329–41.

WHITTY, G. and HALPIN, D. (1996) 'Quasi-markets in England and America: A review of recent research on parental choice and school autonomy', Paper presented at the annual meeting of the British Educational Research Association, University of Lancaster, 12–15 September.

WILLIAMS, K., HASLAM, C. and WILLIAMS, J. (1992) 'Ford versus "Fordism": The beginning of mass production?', *Work, Employment and Society*, **6**, 4, pp. 517–55.

WINTER, R. (1991) 'Postmodern sociology as democratic educational practice — Some suggestions', *British Journal of Sociology of Education*, **12**, 4, pp. 467–81.

WRIGHT, H.K. (1995) '(Re)conceptualising pedagogy as cultural praxis', *Education and Society*, **13**, 1, pp. 67–81.

YOUNG, M.F.D. (1971) *Knowledge and Control*, London, Collier MacMillan.

ZAVARZADEH, M. (1994) 'The stupidity that consumption is just as productive as production: The shopping mall of the post-al Left', *College Literature*, **21**, 3, pp. 92–114.

ZAVARZADEH, M. and MORTON, D. (1986) 'Theory, pedagogy and politics: The crisis of the "subject" in the humanities', *Boundary Two — A Journal of Postmodern Literature and Culture*, **15**, 1–2, pp. 1–22.

ZAVARZADEH, M. and MORTON, D. (1990) '(Post)modern critical theory and the articulations of critical pedagogies', *College Literature*, **17**, 2–3, pp. 51–63.

ZAVARZADEH, M. and MORTON, D. (1994) *Theory as Resistance*, New York, Guilford Press.

Index